The Eternal Ethers

A Theory of
Everything

The Eternal Ethers

A Theory of Everything

DOUGLAS GABRIEL

Our Spirit, LLC
2017

2017
OUR SPIRIT, LLC

P. O. Box 355
Northville, MI 48167

www.eternalcurriculum.com
www.ourspirit.com
www.gospelofsophia.com
www.neoanthroposophy.com

Library of Congress Control Number: 2017914214

ISBN: 978-0-9906455-9-7 (paperback)
ISBN: 978-0-9906455-8-0 (eBook)

Contents

Introduction. . . . . *xi*

Eternal Curriculum 1

   Theory of Everything 3

   Spiritual Beings in Nature. 7

   Beings of Greek Creation. 12

   Septenary Forces Pervade Nature 14

Magic of Seven. 17

   Going Beyond the Third Dimension 21

   The Three Great Axioms 26

   Theosophical Cosmology of Seven. 28

   Music and the Planets 36

   Seven Hierarchical Virtues and the Planets 39

   Seven in Relationship to Planetary Formation 41

An Eternal Curriculum for the Etheric Body 43

   Ancient Wisdom from Clairvoyants 44

   Intent of Evolution 53

   Curriculum for the Etheric Body 57

   Waldorf Curriculum and the Education of the Etheric Body. . 58

The Ever-Changing Understanding of the Ethers 61

   Classical View of the Aethers 64

   Modern Scientific Theories of the Aethers 66

   Aether Theorists throughout History 69

Helena Blavatsky on the Ethers 81

   Tattvic Correlations with the Aethers 86

   Blavatsky's Concept of Fohat 90

   Theosophical View of Fohat 99

   Alice A. Bailey on Fohat 101

   Hindu Tattvas 103

Rama Prasad's View of the Ethers (Tattvas) 109

   Svara 110

   Action of the Etheric 111

   Types of Tattvas 112

   Nature of Prana 114

   Origin of the Universe 115

The Etheric Land of Shamballa 119

   Tibetan View of Shamballa 120

   The Theosophical View of Shamballa 122

   What is Shamballa? 123

The Ethers According to Rudolf Steiner 127

   Human Spiritual Evolution 132

   Essential Nature of the Etheric Body 137

   Etheric Body During Initiation 140

   Etheric Birth of the First Teeth 144

   Human Heart and the Ethers 146

Christ and The Etheric Realm 153

How the Etheric Body Effects Health 155

Nature of the Etheric Body and the Music of the Spheres . 158

Etheric Radiance While Falling Asleep. 158

Etheric Donations of the Hierarchy. 158

Etheric Currents in the Human Body 163

Etheric Body After Death 163

Imaginative Pictures of the Etheric Realms. 166

Appearance of Christ in the Etheric Realm 171

Ethers and the Dimensions of Space 172

Elemental Beings and the Ethers. 174

Rudolf Steiner Concerning the Etheric Christ 177

Etheric Formative Forces of Guenther Wachsmuth 181

Types of Ether 186

Etheric Rhythms 191

Gravity and Magnetism 192

Atmospheric Ether 194

Etheric Metamorphoses. 197

Ethers in the Earth Organism. 201

Ethers in Science, Art and Religion 202

Further Anthroposophical Ideas on the Ethers 211

Dr. Ehrenfried Pfeiffer 211

Dr. Karl Koenig 212

Dr. Ernst Lehrs 213

Ernst Marti 215

Olive Wicher 218

Dennis Milner and Edward Smart 219

Sylvia Francke 221

The Language of Nutrition 223

The Four Primal Substances 227

Protein in Nutrition 238

The Twelve Substances 246

The Seven Metals 248

Amino Acids as the Building Blocks of Enzymes 250

Miracle of Enzymes 252

DNA Enzymes 255

Reading the Language of Nutrition 256

A Theory of Everything: The Etheric Formative Forces 259

Appendix 265

New Theories Concerning the Ethers 265

Charts and Diagrams 271

Bibliographical References and Literature 275

Create

Introduction

Do scientists ever consider that the "winding down clock" of the big bang might have first needed to be wound up?

Do they have a theory that adequately encompasses the growing, life-giving properties of the human body, or do they only see the body in entropy, nothing more than forces that are winding down and dying?

How would science be different today if, instead of asking, "Why did the apple fall from the tree," Newton asked, "How did it get up there to begin with?"

How are our bodies renewed each night when we are asleep? Why is it that we need to sleep for physical and psychological health? What is happening when we sleep?

What makes a plant grow and organize in a fashion that goes on indefinitely from seed to plant to seed again?

How does a tiny acorn, which fits in the crevice of your palm, become a mighty oak simply by being planted in the earth and receiving sunlight and water?

What forces are at work to help a child stand upright, speak, or think?

Where do these forces come from? What are these forces?

The spiritual scientist knows what scientists of the material world do not; the physical body is interpenetrated by currents of energy that bring it life and rejuvenation each day. This body of energy is not completely physical and is, in general, composed of forces that are invisible to the five common senses of sight, sound, touch, taste, and smell.

These forces come from the "life body" or "etheric body" of the human that holds the answers to these questions, and perhaps may be the very *Book of Seven Seals* that is referred to in the book of Revelation. This body of formative forces is showing its face in many new scientific discoveries, but because there is no theory of levity or the etheric, these discoveries are not placed into a workable cosmology of forces and beings that make sense.

The major reason for this scientific failing is because levity, like gravity, is invisible and can only be seen through its *effects*, and not its physical, visible manifestation. This is true for light, air, water, gravity, and many other substances and forces in nature. We can see the effects they produce, but we cannot directly see their workings.

Science is limited in what is perceived because it only uses the five senses that provide quantitative, measurable data. The challenge with quantum physics is that it defies the five senses and coaxes the materialistic scientist into a realm closer to religion and magic than science. Imagine a scientist studying light. Can he really learn all there is to know about light with his physical instrumentation? How much more would he know if he could examine light with senses and tools not bound by the limitations of physical science?

Eternal Wisdom

When is a life force fully realized so that one can say, "This being is now complete?"

The Gospel of Sophia trilogy reveals that to understand the invisible nature of the workings of spirit on Earth, we first must become lovers of wisdom. It is wisdom that takes us beyond the limited range of facts and information derived from the five senses and into a realm behind the visible. Wisdom draws forth those who love Sophia until they begin to see Her everywhere as a living being who ensouls the physical world.

Wisdom is far beyond the quickly changing scientific theories that seldom remain true and valid for very long.

Wisdom comes from experience that is found beyond sense-bound human thinking.

Wisdom leads beyond thinking to living forces and beings that surround and interpenetrate us.

Communication with these beings leads to other, higher beings, until a whole world of hierarchical and elemental beings is found to be active in and around us. These beings bring life and ectropy, the overall increase in the organization of a system, throughout the world and in the human being. These forces work through the etheric (life) body in the world and the human being.

The etheric body of formative forces brings the alternating pulse of life and death to the world. It is a seemingly everlasting or eternal set of forces that are continually renewing the etheric body of the earth and the etheric body of the human like a fountain of life. If this concept seems odd to you, then pause and think about the acorn and the oak tree. When is a life force fully realized so that one can say, "This being is now complete"? Life breeds more life.

For example, in the DNA of your cells, you have the entire history of your ancestors back to the first human. This is no theory; DNA has the past inscribed into it. It doesn't take much to imagine that something like DNA has the intent of the species encoded into it, much like the acorn has the imprint of the mighty oak. DNA, like the acorn, inherently knows its future nature.

Humans think we know all that we will become, but perhaps we are still in the stage of *becoming* and haven't even reached the stage of a sapling. From acorns to human beings, the etheric body is the mysterious, magical realm of all living things that shows us who we have been, who we are, and who we will become.

In a sense, the author is *preaching the everlasting gospel* to those who have chosen to listen to a new song. This gospel shows how the human being is created in the image of the divine and can become worthy enough to unlock the secrets of the future that are embedded in the etheric body, the source of levity and ectropy.

Each person who delves deeply into his own nature will find this *eternal curriculum* inscribed in his own etheric body. What the human being was, is, and will be is already inscribed within its original seed form. Throughout the passing of time and many incarnations, the etheric body becomes its potential through unfolding.

We must know what humanity is, where we came from, and where we are going.

These eternal secrets can be sung out loud, but only the chosen will be able to hear and join in the new song. It takes effort to seek and find Wisdom, and even more to love and defend Her. Those who know Her ways are called *wisdom children*. Her ways are sought after by few, and even fewer learn to hear Her song and dance in harmony with Her music. This new song is the harmony of the spheres that sounds in the human etheric body, specifically through the workings of the sound ether.

Just as song is punctuated through timing, so the etheric body is composed of the forces that help create time, space, and consciousness. These forces evolve along with the developing individual over time, while the future of human development already exists in latent form in the potentiality inside each human being. These forces of timing create the illusion of time and space, a place where our unfolding consciousness awakens, grows, and develops.

The etheric body is a living Temple of Wisdom that reveals the eternal curriculum for the initiated, the children of wisdom.

The wisdom child inherently knows this to be true and seeks a curriculum of life that is everlasting, eternal. Wisdom children already know about ectropy without having it explained because they have a new capacity of using all twelve senses instead of just the earthbound five senses. Wisdom children may even be born with the ability to see the etheric forces at work, even though they are invisible to others. They may already have etheric vision or intuitive clairvoyance necessary to perceive these forces with new supersensible organs of perception.

Even if you do not believe you are a wisdom child because you were born decades ago or you just have

*E*ach individual recapitulates the development of humanity from ancient times to modern.

an instinct that you are not, you can still develop these capacities with the slightest effort. Anyone with a pure heart and openness to look beyond the veils of the physical, material world can learn to read with etheric vision and develop organs of perception that penetrate the workings of the spiritual world.

This book is dedicated to wisdom children in the hopes that their parents, teachers, and they themselves have the appropriate curriculum to provide the soul with the content from world literature that is needed to nourish spiritual development.

Each individual person recapitulates the development of humanity from ancient times to modern. The child in utero goes through characteristic stages of development that need the mother's special attention and help at those different stages. Once the child is born, the *mother school* is responsible for teaching the most difficult things a child ever learns: standing upright, speaking, and thinking. Every home teaches a child the most important lessons through imitation in their earliest years. When the new developmental stage arrives, the child is ready to imitate, and she miraculously begins to mature into an adult.

If the child is presented with the wisdom of the world at the right stage of development of the etheric body, where memory resides, then an important spiritual need for evolution is met with the right soul content that provides nourishment. This nourishment is the eternal curriculum: teaching wisdom to the etheric body when the etheric body is in its most receptive stage of development, between the ages seven to fourteen.

The soul content needed to properly integrate each component of the human being is fed by reliving the stages of the past that are the foundation for collective human consciousness. Each wisdom child needs a curriculum that is imbued with all the past developments of humanity that have contributed to the evolving human intellect and spirit.

The Eternal Ethers: A Theory of Everything is not only an aid to developing cognition of human evolution in the past; it also helps prepare for the future. To be an "eternal" curriculum, it would have to incorporate the past development of humanity and have a very clear idea of future human evolution. This is where a cosmology is necessary for the developing human intellect. In our hearts, we must know where we came from, where we are, and where we are going.

The "seven Spirits of God" and the "seven horns and seven eyes" referenced in *Revelation* are key to understanding the past, present, and future. One way to look at these seven is as the seven components of the etheric body, called the seven ethers. Each component has a space, time, and consciousness component. In other words, there are seven parts of the etheric body, and each one rules a specific "time period" or stage in human evolution. Careful study of the etheric body reveals these ethers, as well as many other secrets.

There have been numerous attempts to create a comprehensive curriculum that meets the higher spiritual needs of wisdom children. Sri Aurobindo, a well-known Hindu guru and poet, developed an International Center of Education as an example of a school developed by a spiritual leader who realized that a new curriculum was necessary in our time. William Irwin Thompson's *Transforming History: A Curriculum for Cultural Evolution* is another example of an attempt to create a new approach of what to teach and when to teach it. Thompson is a proponent of Jean Gebser's idea that human consciousness is in transition and that "jumps" in consciousness involve structural changes in both mind and body. Gebser, the well-known philosopher, linguist, and poet, distinguished five structures: archaic, magic, mythical, mental, and integral. These structures evolve but continue to operate parallel to the new, emergent structure. A new curriculum was necessary to acknowledge and understand stages of development that each child would naturally evolve through during youth.

Maria Montessori lived her last years in Adyar, India, at the World Headquarters of the Theosophical Society with her good friend Annie Besant, who was the President of the Society. Though Montessori only became a theosophist in her later life, she added to her existing Montessori curriculum an addition of upper grades and the content of those grades to her existing Montessori curriculum. This curriculum is highly advanced, speculative, and inherently spiritual. Some of the ideas of theosophy ended up in this add-on cosmic curriculum that shows that Montessori also had the idea that spiritual content should be part of a healthy curriculum.

Many other thinkers, philosophers, and spiritual teachers have had a special mission to develop curricula for children, adults, and spiritual aspirants. These curricula reflect the wisdom that the spiritual teacher gleaned from life. The belief that education is an important concern for the future is long-standing. What children are taught has everything to do with what will unfold in the future. By equipping children with new capacities that go beyond traditional, state-sanctioned educational curricula, we are preparing children to go beyond the capacities of their parents and grandparents. As Einstein said, "We can't solve problems by using the same kind of thinking we used when we created them."

Children adapt to their environment quickly and learn rapidly by imitation, and then have the capacity to go beyond any prior human accomplishment. Because we have the shoulders of our ancestors to stand upon, which is the collective wisdom of the developing human intellect, each generation, if properly

xviii   *The Eternal Ethers*

nourished with an eternal curriculum, can have more advanced capacities than the generations that came before them. Children bring new genius and new capacities from the pre-birth world. These new additions to the collective experience and wisdom of humanity create our future state of being.

Science now knows that DNA is a type of memory device that informs current cell growth and division about lessons of the past as well as carries information that creates the organism's future. These discoveries are available for all to study, but few have begun to understand the profound implication that DNA also points us toward our future.

Nature changes DNA as part of the survival tendency of any living organism to adapt and reproduce for the survival of the species. Fifty years ago, a scientist might have considered the current working knowledge of DNA to be a ridiculous theory that would never be proven true. But here we are, working with the building blocks of creation without a philosophical discussion about whether such research should even be allowed to continue. Stem cell research is an example of science tinkering with the future of what a human might become.

The idea of the past being written into DNA was preposterous just a few years ago, but now it is an accepted concept. What will happen to our cosmological framework when science discovers that the future is also written into DNA? Before scientists alter the DNA structure of any organism—whether a kernel of corn or a human being—shouldn't they explore a more profound question of whether their interference will irrevocably change the unfolding wisdom that has already been written in DNA code?

Wisdom children of all ages know the future destiny of their soul is to become an angel.

The footprint of the mechanism for understanding this DNA language is found in studying the etheric formative forces and their connection to the movement of the sun and the planets in our solar system. A system of seven ethers works both in the human etheric body and the solar system. An exposition of these ethers becomes a passage through time, space, and consciousness. A description of the etheric body of the human being will show the entire evolution of humanity from beginning to end. This is the nature of the everlasting gospel, the good news of the eternal life of the etheric body and its connection to cosmic forces and beings. This is what a timeless curriculum for wisdom children would need to address.

The evolution of humanity is imprinted into the etheric body, and between ages seven and fourteen, the etheric body grows and develops most robustly. Whatever is in the environment of a child during these ages will go directly into helping create the composition and working of the seven organs. With a developmentally appropriate curriculum, the needs of the growing etheric body can be given the physical, soul, and spiritual nourishment that match the needs of the child at each stage of growth.

From birth to age seven, the physical body is nourished particularly by the *mother school*: the home of the child. When a seven-year-old child goes to school for the first grade, the curriculum should match the seven stages of growth and development found in the etheric body as its inherent pattern of growth. Grade by grade, from first through seventh, the stages of human development that are already written into the etheric body of the child are revealed. A child taught in this way experiences in his school environment (on the outside) that which is he is experiencing on the inside at any given moment.

Generally, in western countries, children go to first grade at age six instead of seven. Unfortunately, this push to hurry development is not healthy for young children, unless they choose to advance quickly out of their own freedom.

Some wisdom children are born with pure etheric bodies that already resonate with wisdom in their environment. Even if they are not given a spiritually beneficial curriculum, wisdom children will often create their own curriculum to educate themselves appropriately. Imagine the benefit if wisdom children were provided an "eternal curriculum" from the first time they entered school that embodied the spiritual evolution of humanity from early humans to future angels. Every wisdom child, no matter what age, knows the future destiny of her soul to become an angel. This *becoming an angel* usually entails having her name written into a *book of life,* which is found in the human etheric body. This is the basis of the everlasting gospel.

Any exposition on the etheric formative forces is bound to be controversial, because there are many opinions on the ethers from East to West. The most ancient Eastern texts refer to the ethers as *tattvas* and point at their primal importance in creation and the working of the hierarchy. Great mysteries surround the descriptions of the genesis of the ethers, which tend to reveal the genesis of all matter. In some texts, the ethers are considered divine beings. The highest praise is given to their place in the creation, death, and sustenance of the material world. They are envisioned to be emanations of divine beings who live on the sun.

In the West, so much confusion and misinformation abounds concerning the etheric formative forces that they are generally ignored. In the deepest parts of Theosophy, Anthroposophy, Rosicrucianism, Esoteric Masonry, and the Magical Revival, we find the ethers and tattvas are the subjects of the highest teachings and rituals. It is through the ethers that the practitioner may have direct contact with the spiritual world and elementals. The ethers are the currents of life that bring movement and organization to the elements. Alchemists worked with these forces and often referred to them as beings. They appear as planetary signatures, metals, notes, sigils, and many other manifestations of spirit in matter. Often, the task is to set the elemental forces free so that beings can be witnessed in the process.

This is also an objective of the Eternal Curriculum—to merge the microcosm of the human with the macrocosm of the divine human, which is written into the etheric body of each individual.

Part of this process is to introduce the developing human being to his ancestors from history and to his descendants of the future.

The child in first grade begins with the ancient consciousness of what Gebser calls the "archaic structure," where the student and teacher are still one, without any subjectivity. This stage moves on through the stages of magic (grade two), mythical (grade three), mental (grade four), and integral (grade five). Humanity, as a whole, is currently in the stage called "integral structure."

In the Eternal Curriculum, each student is presented with the mood that accompanies a particular stage of historical development through literature, architecture, music, and dance. Each of these cultures is associated with one of the seven archetypal aspects of the etheric body. Each stage of development nourishes an aspect of the etheric body.

Gebser's stages of structural growth in history and culture are similar to numerous other theories of history that highlight the natural development of the human intellect or consciousness. Gebser does not give us the future stages that might complete the seven, but does insinuate that further growth and development will come as new structures are birthed.

Oswald Spengler, the German historian and philosopher, believed that culture is birthed, goes through stages, and then dies. According to Spengler, humanity as a whole has gone through the following historic stages or periods: the pre-cultural, early culture, culture, late culture, and civilization. Again, like Gebser, five periods developed into our own time, which Spengler predicted was on its decline. He also grouped cultural development into the Indian, Egyptian, Classical (Greek), Arabian (Persian), and Western (Anglo-Germanic) as subsets of the historic stages. This insight has been the foundation of many other theories concerning historical stages and cultural groupings comprising the collective historical advancement of the human intellect.

Theosophists have a grand scheme of seven that shows that the human being is currently sharing space with other beings who have donated the mineral, plant, and animal kingdoms for the use of the human kingdom, whose stage of development is now at the fore of evolution. These great periods of seven are the septenary stages of the development of our solar system and the planets. This grand scheme follows the same one found in the human etheric body of formative forces working through the seven ethers, the seven organs, and numerous other systems of seven found in the human constitution.

The microcosm and the macrocosm mirror one another in a holographic resonance that has now been discovered by science. The most mysterious and primal of the ethers, the "Akasha Ether," has been discovered, and numerous theories have been presented to illuminate this ether. Ervin Laszlo, one the greatest thinkers alive, has demonstrated the working of an A-Field, or Akashic Field. It is similar to what is now called "zero-point physics." In his book, *Science and the Akashic Field, An Integral Theory of Everything,* Laszlo has begun a new age of scientific discovery of the ethers.

New discoveries about the ethers are exciting, as they validate and prove the work of the great spiritual scientist Rudolf Steiner, who is the definitive voice on the etheric. He is the modern prophet of etheric vision and has given us immense wisdom and insight into human nature and its connection to the etheric formative forces. Steiner's Waldorf curriculum is, by far, the best example of a comprehensive curriculum that educates the etheric body and is a model for an Eternal Curriculum that feeds and nourishes wisdom children.

The Eternal Curriculum, as it is appropriately named in *The Eternal Ethers: A Theory of Everything,* will reveal a full exposition of the nature of the etheric body through its history, workings, and future development utilizing ancient beliefs, modern discoveries, and the indications of Steiner's spiritual science. It provides a *cosmology of the ethers* wherein the individual, no matter what age or grade, can take control of the education of his or her own etheric body and bring it new life, creating the nourishment needed for spiritual evolution.

The Gift

Rudolf Steiner wrought this Cosmic Deed
For culture and social reform—a Wisdom Seed
That has grown into a movement, so humble at first,
To feed children's spirits, to nourish their thirst
For Oneness, the interconnected Wisdom of the Ages,
Revealed to the open heart, through childhood stages
That relive history in a new and higher form,
Showing us our world and its spiritual home.

Twelve teachers, plus one special friend
Gathered round Steiner their attention to lend
To hear deep wisdom, the "secret of teaching"
The reasons behind, the nature of reaching
Into spiritual realms where archetypes abound,
Into those worlds where learning resounds,
Like a bell, or a new-born clarion call—
To dance holy rounds in Natura's Hall,
The spirit of birth, life, and old age,
The path of fate, the grace of each stage.

Polarity

Inhale, exhale—expansion and contraction seem
Like rhythmic exchange between extremes
From worlds of light before our birth,
To new life here on Mother Earth;
From waking consciousness, alert and bright,
To dreamy sleep cradled in the long dark night.
These poles are balanced in the human heart,
This is where they end, this is where they start;
From Worlds on high our spirit descends,
To those realms each night where we all ascend,
Finding the balance between out and in,
Flying on high, to our home again.

Eternal Curriculum

An eternal curriculum can provide children now, and in the future, with a cosmology or theory of everything that can explain the human progression through time and space—not just where we have been, but where we are going, as our ultimate purpose. It is a curriculum that educates more than the intellect. It nourishes the human soul and spirit with Imagination, Inspiration, and Intuition so that a child can become all that she is spiritually intended to be, not just a good citizen of the state or skilled worker for commercial enterprises.

As legend and lore inform us, humans were created in the Garden of Eden around 4000 B.C. and will culminate with an apocalypse of some kind, when rapture, the second coming, or a divine occurrence change what is known as the general course of history. This worldview, or cosmology, involves a divine presence directing us through our evolution. Often this deity-centered cosmology might use "a book" that is followed literally as the source of authentication and proof of cosmological details.

Conversely, materialistic science purports that we evolved randomly from lower forms of life and live one life, beginning with birth and ending at death, on an insignificant planet in a universe that originated from a ball of matter that could fit into the palm of your hand and that exploded into the ordered universe we experience today. This view lacks a vision of the spiritual nature of our creation, and in doing so, can only speculate where we have physically come from and doesn't take into account the history of the developing

*B*oth science and religion require beliefs: science in theories, and religion in invisible beings.

intellect which, when added to all that we collectively understand as a species, can help us imagine what humanity is and will become. By adding a spiritual component to our view of life, we need to consider and elucidate a worldview that encompasses both religion and science.

The modern person may not agree with church or science on the sources of humanity, where we have evolved from, or if we have evolved at all. One way or another—big bang or big birth— neither cosmology, by itself, empowers humanity to know who we are, were we came from, and where we are going. Perhaps we should look to nature as an example of how creation emerges: the process of the male-female union, metamorphosis, and living cycles that sustain life in its multiplicity and abundance. Imaginably, the "intelligent design" that birthed the cosmos and humanity used the same elements, processes, and consciousness in the macrocosm as in the microcosm.

Both science and religion require beliefs: science in theories, and religion in invisible beings. Surely, there must be another way to find in ourselves and the cosmos the very beings, forces, and consciousness that are described in science and experienced in religion. This task is now one of the main focuses of science: to find a theory of everything.

Theory of Everything

Einstein used the speed of light as his standard of the universe and believed—not theorized—that there was a substructure of *ether* that had to exist for light to be able to propagate. He merged science and belief (religion) to attempt his theory of everything. Stephen Hawkins has labored most of his life to find a workable equation for a theory of everything. Ervin Laszlo has created a theory of everything that uses ancient religious beliefs (Vedic) and science (zero point and vortex vacuums) to put forth a wonderful idea called the Akashic Field Theory. Many other theories, found throughout this book and in the appendices, combine ancient ideas derived from sacred texts with cutting-edge discoveries in science. Both *what was known* and *what is observed and theorized today* are closing the gap that will merge past and present, resulting in innovation for the future.

It is interesting to note that the ancients derived the information in their sacred texts directly from encounters with beings. These ancient sages still had a natural clairvoyance that helped them communicate with the beings in nature (and super-nature) that stand behind the forces of nature. They were able to connect the creative acts of beings with the forces those beings used to manifest the physical world. For the Greeks, lightning was forged in the underworld by Vulcan and then used by Zeus to bring fire down upon the earth. These mythopoetic images can be interpreted as the natural phenomena we see explained by the interaction of beings. Lightning appears to come down from above, but under closer scientific examination, it was found to originate from the earth. The ancients and moderns are both correct; lightning is created in the underworld but seems to come from an angry sky god on the highest mountain.

The unfortunate and narrow-sighted philosophical-theological-scientific circumstance between church and science is that there are few scientists in religion and few religious people in science. The chasm between religion and science widens daily for the person who cannot find a bridge between the two.

A theory of everything is certainly needed, but will not be expressed as a mathematical calculation or a singular revelation. The path to spirit that brings revelations of science into a cosmology that blends the best in both religion and science is a gradual, slow, and measured one. The fusion of spirit and science is what Rudolf Steiner named *spiritual science*, requiring not only the cognizance of all that "has been known" and all that is "known today," but additionally the ability to see the beings behind the forces of nature and find inherent intelligent design to map the contours and motions of the living forces that support all life on Earth and in the cosmos. This requires going beyond Einstein's supposition of the pseudo-magical forces inherent in the hypothetical ether of the ancients. There are now hundreds of new ether theories that go beyond the ancients and Einstein. The old and the new must merge and birth a new ability to objectively observe the forces and beings we encounter in nature.

Einstein's foundation of all cosmic and earthly manifestation was based upon a constant speed of light in the luminiferous ether. Science has now accelerated light many times faster than the known speed of light through experiments with lasers. In just a few short years, Einstein's speed of light theory has been discarded. Many new theories have been proposed to replace Einstein's "scientific fact" turned "erroneous belief." Someday, a science that recognizes ancient aliens, who are none other than spiritual forces, ethers, and deities, will be as cutting-edge as Einstein's light theories once were.

Why wait for materialistic scientists to bridge the chasm between the sacred and profane? For those ready to take the journey, the true nature of the ethers, their genesis, and their immediate connection to human spiritual evolution are revealed through the insights of the ancients and the practical application of modern spiritual scientists who know the power of the ethers. The evolution of the ethers from the past to the present and on into the future is a key element of the Eternal Curriculum.

The Eternal Ethers: A Theory of Everything is based upon an ancient system, updated by spiritual scientists, that for centuries has been seen as one of the first theories of everything. The ancients created cosmologies that embraced what they directly experienced as communion with higher beings and elementals. The modern scientific person often expresses or experiences interaction with divine, hierarchical beings as communication with aliens. In a way, the spiritual hierarchy above us and the elemental kingdoms below us do have an alien nature in that they have a different consciousness and presence compared to the human and his physical world. These alien beings could even be imagined as existing in different dimensions, as long as you consider the consciousness of the solid, fluid, gas, and plasma states of matter to be dimensions.

Science and religion grow closer all the time but are still blind to the knowledge that to get the whole picture, they each have to share with the other. A true synthesis is required to glean the best from both.

One synthesis that can open up the objective thinker to realms beyond the senses is to follow the path of material forces into the realm of the etheric, where forces exist that follow specific patterns that look just like intelligence or thinking. For instance, the modern world is built upon the recent discoveries and innovations of electro-magnetic energy and organized electrostatic broadcasting of those EMF waves (frequencies). A world without electricity is almost unimaginable.

What is electricity? A materialistic answer is that it is generated and sent through copper wires and pulses at 60 hertz per second. This answer describes the effect of electricity, rather than what it is. Who has *seen* electricity? Some might say that it is seen as sparks, but again, this is an *effect* of electricity, not electricity itself. We can create it by having magnets spin, but where does the energy come from? Do magnets suck it out of the air? Is there a limited amount of electromagnetic energy? If so, how much, and how will that be measured?

Soon, the clear thinker must confess that no one has ever seen electricity. Sparks are the substances in air lighting up through the excitation of an electrical discharge. Before long, the scientist may admit that one of the primal forces, electricity, is indeed invisible, intangible, and an unknown force in nature that seems to pervade everything, earth and cosmos, but is not understood except as an outcome or effect of nature. Scientists have built our modern world upon the *effects* of electricity, but do not understand the true nature, origin, or beingness of electricity.

Scientists don't communicate with lightning like the Greeks who worshiped, venerated, and communicated with Zeus. It is fair to say that modern scientists have yet to scratch the surface of the beingness of lightning. Tens of thousands of lightning bolts hit the equatorial regions each day to power the atmosphere, each one of which could power New York City for a year or more; however, scientists have not captured a single one. Nikola Tesla, the inventor of the alternating current system of electricity upon which our electrical grids operate, could make lightning bolts and cast them about his laboratory, yet no other scientist has been able to match his work. Perhaps the secret lies in Tesla's study of Vedic scripture and its spiritual system of ethers as a working cosmology.

Almost no theory of science has remained the same for more than a few hundred years.

Electricity, light, gravity, and nuclear forces (all the forces of modern science) are, in fact, invisible forces that are little understood. Scientific theory is simply another form of belief, and it is no surprise when we hear scientists proclaim that gravity is "nothing like we thought it was." So, I guess it's back to the drawing board. This has often happened in the last few hundred years: everything we knew about a subject is reversed and rewritten and seen, in hindsight, as undeveloped scientific notions and superstitions. Almost no theory of science has remained the same for more than a few hundred years. Seen in this light, science is simply speculation that is not even based upon a solid footing in philosophy. There is no *philosophy of science,* and so there is no true *thinking* in science, just *doing*: i.e., experimentation and theory creation.

How many times have you heard this phrase precede a pontification of a new scientific theory or finding: "We now know through recent discoveries that ...”? Another common technique is to bypass rigorous scientific method by using *scientific consensus* as the basis of what is to be proclaimed. More and more, science seems to be using the language of religion, beckoning the faithful to simply believe their so-called scientific theories.

Spiritual Beings in Nature

Forces in the universe and on the earth are the last shadows or vestiges of living beings. Spiritual beings work through forces in nature, but they do not enter those forces. That is why the forces of nature are alive, animated, and directed by divine wisdom, only later to fall into death. Any person can look at nature and find the patterns of the divine, but not necessarily the divine itself. Even when we consider the far distant spaces where the stars abide, we only find forces and patterns of wisdom that are the insinuation—a shadow—of the divine. When we cast a two-dimensional shadow of ourselves from our three-dimensional form, we are not the shadow that is a semblance of our multi-dimensional beingness. Our physical form created the shadow, but we did not enter the two-dimensional realm where the shadow exists. We are far more than the shadow; we are physical, soul, and spiritual beings, and only one aspect of us (physical) casts its silhouette upon a two-dimensional plane. This is similar to the way that fourth, fifth, sixth, and seventh dimensional beings enter into our earthly (solid) realm of birth and death. If we only have consciousness of our existence in a three-dimensional world, then it is hard to imagine that we were born outside of time and space and entered this realm from our true home: higher dimensions.

But what good are theoretical discussions of dimensions in daily life? What are the practical applications? The answers to these questions are much simpler than science might imagine. Each night when we sleep, we go into these other dimensions. When we die, we enter them and work through them until we are born on Earth again, out of those dimensions. Dreams, communication with the dead, spiritual hierarchies, spiritual consciousness, transcendent experiences, et cetera are far from the domain that science says exists. Theories may include dimensions and time factors in astrophysics and other such fields, but they are still considered superstitious and pseudo-science. Perhaps we need a new approach to understanding the world that can consider the legends of the ancients while embracing the principles and findings of science, yet considering the possibility that higher beings are only casting their shadows in the earthly realm.

The formation of the cosmos is the formation of the human being. We are the microcosm of the macrocosm, if we remember the key factors of space and time. The human being at this point of evolution is not the intended angel that he might become in the future, just as he is not the lower being from which he evolved in the past. It is hoped that each person has a higher vision of humanity in the future: one in which virtues, not vices, guide our lives. In order to see the future nature of the human being, we need a picture or archetype of the future perfected human. We need an image of the divine or the microcosm of the macrocosm.

• • •

*T*rue *spiritual processes and cycles can be detected by scientists if they know where to look to find the beings behind the forces.*

• • •

Although the human being is not, at this moment in evolution, a perfected human, he has the potential to become so in the future, just as the acorn has the force within itself to become a grand oak tree. Keeping this in mind, we need to synthesize a composite picture of the human being evolving over time, until time and space exist no longer—just consciousness. This heavenly image of the human being pictures the full metamorphosis that happens to the human being over the intended course of evolution. There must be an intention of creation for the human being, and this perfected image must be recorded somewhere so that the evolving human being can access it.

Thanks to the work of ancient sages, sacred texts, and the modern spiritual research of theosophists and anthroposophists, we can construct a simple cycle of metamorphic changes that create the framework (forces) for the hierarchy (beings) to help build and create the perfected human inside of us—no matter what our belief system. True spiritual processes and cycles can be detected by scientists if they know where to look to find the beings behind the forces. Scientists might tell us that they already understand DNA mutation and natural selection, but do they tell us who we will become based upon our DNA coding? Does DNA create us, or do we impress onto our DNA who we are and will become? These questions are not being asked by the recombinant DNA experimenters who are playing god with genetically modified organisms, plants, animals, and humans. Will this research cause human spiritual development to evolve or devolve?

Science looks at a living being as it dies and makes theories, just as it arrives at the idea that our universe is a wound-up clock that is unwinding. Seldom do researchers look at the cause, because they are so focused on looking at the effect. For example, there are substances that can damage DNA, causing the telomeres to degenerate, age, and mutate. There are also enzymes, amino acids, and vibrations that can repair telomeres and slow the aging process. If we can manipulate DNA through substance, vibrations, and spiritual development, then what is DNA?

DNA doesn't *create* aging or eternal life, it simply is the *vehicle* for it, just as copper wires are the vehicle for electricity. DNA is an effect, not a cause.

Where does the spiritual scientist find the cause of aging, illness, and suffering—the age-old questions of Buddha? This cause should be found in a theory of everything, since aging happens in the cosmos as well as the human body. Everyday science tells us that all things are dying a slow heat-death in both the cosmos and the human. Most science is based upon entropy. Ectropy is the opposite force of slow heat-death. This word is seldom used in science, and when it is, it is usually called *negentropy*, the opposite of the force of death, which is theorized as the true condition of the physical world. In this idea alone, using concepts of entropy rather than ectropy, we see the true expression of science, which sees destructive rather than creative forces in nature. This idea is reinforced by the general laws of thermodynamics that inform the scientist that nothing new is ever created in the cosmos. All elements, substances, and forces are recycled, but not created anew. This foundational belief of science has blinded scientists to the point where they cannot see new life being created before their blind eyes. These foundational "blinders" of science—speed of light, thermodynamics, entropy— make sure that no cause or being is found behind the forces of nature. These forces of nature are little understood and remain invisible to the scientist.

•   •   •

*I*t will take a new organ of perception, to be able to perceive the living nature of electricity, gravity, levity, sacrifice, or harmony that we witness in nature.

•   •   •

What is the *cause* creating the *effect* of DNA? The ancients would answer that question with one word—ethers. There is one primal ether that created six others. Five of these ethers penetrate earth's atmosphere, and two do not. These primal seven forces are also beings who have a distinct evolution (time) and distinct properties, processes, elementals, and beings they work through to manifest the known world (space). Some aspects of the ethers are tangible. Discoveries have found these forces acting on matter, but they have not named them or recognized that there are seven ethers. Many scientists now acknowledge the existence of the *hypothetical ether* that pervades the entire universe. Again, the effects of these forces have been measured, but no comprehensive theories acknowledge seven ethers or their metamorphosis over time. Ethers also evolve and are moving targets; this is the source of scientists' confusion and their dire need to find "god particles" or eternal etherons that tie the universe together in a cohesive fashion. Scientists may be showing their spiritual anxiety when they cry out for a god particle, turning their longing for cohesion into a prayer for a sign.

Scientists will not figure out the ethers with mathematics or observations based upon the visible spectrum. It will take a new capacity—a new organ of perception—to be able to perceive the living nature of electricity, gravity, levity, sacrifice, or harmony that we witness in nature. What's the point of looking for answers in distant space when we have not found them on Earth? Why would we assume that what we have on Earth is the same in the cosmos?

Suffice it to say that scientists are looking into a mirror when they examine the cosmos with the five senses or devices that serve those senses. It will take new senses to discover the beings behind all that we perceive and experience. It is best to ground all knowledge in the constitution of the human being—the only sure ground we can find.

We will need to use our own beingness to encounter and communicate with the being of Natura. This being is subtle and hidden, but powerful and active. She comes from an invisible place, reveals her visible nature, hides, and then emerges to tend life at every juncture, just to back away again until the cycle runs its course and falls back into the arms of death, pausing long enough to be replenished for another birth.

After a cycle of what seems to be death, Natura springs forth once again through rebirth from the soil of death that has been transformed by some magical power of levity and draws life forth to rise back to its home, the sun. Natura is the handmaiden of birth, death, and rebirth—endlessly, or as far as we can see.

Seven is the magic number of the beings who brought the natural world into existence.

Natura is eternal, with her new buds of spring always deeply hidden in the darkness of earth and restful sleep. Natura accepts death as tranquilly as she does birth. Her beingness is a part of her cosmic whole. She is multiplicity and abundance, by her very nature. It is her shadow that philosophers and sages sought day and night, a being we call Gaia, Mother Earth. Once Natura was anthropomorphized as Gaia, a whole host of scientists and philosophers embraced a renewed morality towards a living Being of the Earth as a biological entity in which humanity has a symbiotic relationship. This is the new direction needed to begin to develop new sense organs, or capacities of soul, that can embrace living concepts warmed through with human love.

Beings of Greek Creation

Some people still have the capacity to clairvoyantly perceive Mother Earth and can dialogue with her in some fashion. The ancient Greeks had a cosmology of creation that is quite instructive, especially in relationship to Gaia and the Greek god Aether—the source of the modern reference to ether. The Greek creation story below shows the metamorphosis of the solar system, where seven is the magic number of the beings who brought the natural world into existence.

As with all stories about the ethers, it starts with one primal ether. In the Greek version, this being is known as Chaos, who is described as being void of air, wherein time (arche) comes into being. From the realm of the eternal, or duration, time comes into being in a physical, linear fashion. Chaos is the primal soup that has all the substance needed for the entire creation of seven stages. Chaos is neither male nor female, neither light nor dark. Chaos gives birth to Erebus (male) and Nyx (female)—brother and sister. Erebus is darkness and the realm of time, while Nyx is night and the female forces of space.

Erebus and Nyx give birth to a most enigmatic being named Aether, who is also known as a son of Chaos and has no mother or father. Aether, or Light, is complete and whole in some versions, and a twin in other versions. Aether's twin was Hermera, the day, seen as male and/or female. Aether is the god of fire, warmth, and light. Aether plays the role of Adam in one sense, in that he is twice created: once male and female, and once just male. In some versions of mythology, there are only three primal gods: Chaos, Aether, and Eros. Aether embodies many of the qualities of Eros. Winged Eros was born from an egg and mated with Chaos. In one version, Eros had a bow and arrow that created earth, water, mountains, animals, and even humans, essentially playing the role of the creator god of the Greeks. Aether is Eros, the creator god. From Aether (and Hemera) come the lower gods and goddesses.

Uranus, the sky god of the heavens who ruled the winds, the sky, the clouds, all the airs, and the movement across Rhea, his mate, also sprang from Aether. The union of Uranus and Rhea gave birth to Chronos, and the old gods were born. From Aether came Ourea, who was the male god of mountains and grew upward out of Gaia.

Oceanus, known as Pontus, or in the female form, Thalassa, the god or goddess of the seas, also came from Aether. Oceanus encircled the whole world and was a shape-shifter like his/her Titan daughters. Thetis, the titan, married Peleus, a human, bringing the primal gods closer to human consciousness.

Gaia, too, came from Aether. She is also known as Rhea, the earth goddess who brought forth the abundance of life on her skin. She is the Mother of All, and her body was the surface of the earth.

With the Greeks, we see a seven-stage unfolding of the beingness of the creatrix, working through Aether to manifest the other primal gods and goddesses. The being of Aether, Eros, is known as the god of love, who "no god or man can resist." Aether is so powerful, in some stories, that although Chaos, his mother, bore him from an egg, he came out of the egg and mated with her to create the other five primal gods. So, no matter how you view the Greek creation stories, seven often becomes the cyclic process that makes the whole, complete evolution of the cosmology, or metamorphosis over time.

The Beings of Greek Creation

Chaos
Erebus and Nyx
Aether (and Hermera) or Eros
Uranus
Gaia
Ourea
Oceanus

Septenary Forces Pervade Nature

The Greek scheme of creation gods is very similar in other cultures. Often, it is the *one* who creates the other *six*, and together the *seven* go through a cycle of seven to perfect creation. The Vedic, Theosophic, and Anthroposophic schemes of these beings will be presented in subsequent chapters. Suffice it to say, they are very similar and carry metamorphic markers that can be found to weave through most traditions as seven breaths, seven seals, seven brothers, seven days of creation, seven spirits before the throne, seven flames, seven heroes, and the like. Seven, the septenary division of creation, is quite common.

Through the analysis of the basic nature of seven, we find the working of the seven planets, one primal (sun) and the other six (planets) working around it. This solar scheme works its forces, processes, elements, and substances into every aspect of the human being and nature. Seven pervades nature on Earth and in our solar system. The Sun is the primal force, and the Moon, Venus, and Mercury create one triangle around the Sun, while Mars, Jupiter, and Saturn create another, juxtaposed triangle around the Sun. Together, the seven planets create the symphony of all that each has to give the Earth. There are septenary correspondences found in all aspects of nature that replicate and resonate with these seven primal forces.

Septenary forces indicate the actions of beings in our solar system who interpenetrate our physical constitution via time, space, consciousness, vibrations, forces, processes, elements, and substances. They have been described by the ancients as beings who have a cosmological plan for humanity, which is not completed yet. These cosmologies always have a goal of the perfection of humanity. Through these cosmologies, we can find where we have been, where we are, and where we are going.

The predicted future in the Greek cosmology indicates that the human being eventually returns to the eternal home from whence he came. The Greek identified with the god Eros in the story of Eros and Psyche to learn about immortality that can be gained after trials and challenges that included going down into the underworld, finding the water of immortality, and staying faithful to those we love. Psyche is the victorious heroine in this story, and she gains immortality, the future goal of Greek cosmology. The story of Psyche and Eros can be found in the first-grade selections in Part Two of this book. It is one of the oldest stories in history and can be found ubiquitously around the world. It is the story of the prodigal son/daughter who leaves his/her father's/mother's home to suffer in the world and eventually return home again. This archetype is the primal message of most ancient cosmologies.

Magic of Seven

"We, together with the earth, are within these interpenetrating spheres. Seven spheres mutually interpenetrate one another, and we grow into this interpenetration in the course of our life, are thus bound up with it. Our life, from birth until death, evolves out of its basic endowment, while the star-spheres in a certain sense draw us on from birth to death."

Rudolf Steiner (GA 234)

Every complete system of the spirit has seven parts. Often, only the first four stages of the seven-fold evolution of a complete system have manifested, because humans are in the fourth large stage of evolution at the current time. We may not see that the stages of a cosmology indicate much about innovation beyond the fifth stage of the seven stages of a complete system. That is because the fifth stage synthesizes the previous four stages and adds novelty, new creation out of nothingness, into the seven cycles. It is this fifth cycle, where the innovation of the progressive spirits is found to manifest most strongly. We are currently in a sub-cycle of five and stand at that moment of innovation to either leap forward with evolution or fall far behind.

Let us imagine this cycle of seven coming into a denser and denser form as it proceeds from the first to the fourth, whereupon it turns upward with the momentum of the pendulum swing built up cumulatively from first to second to third to fourth. At the end of the fourth, the pendulum starts to turn upward with the momentum of the descent of the first four.

The fifth, sixth, and seventh stages of this pendulum swing would, in a way, mirror the descending stages on its upward path. The fifth stage mirrors the third, the sixth mirrors the second, and the seventh stage mirrors the first stage.

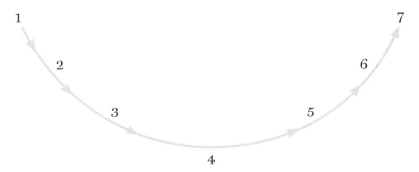

This basic pattern of seven is a limited two-dimensional representation, but it can give us an idea of what it means to "fall into" matter and "rise out" of matter through a descending and ascending cycle of seven stages. This is important to understand in relationship to cosmology. We will be going into each of the stages at great length, but here we will simply point out that the seven-fold path of a complete system implies a mirroring process of previous stages taken to a new level. This is like the way matter comes into being through the seven ethers.

In the first stage of incarnation, we can imagine that the solid or mineral state of physical matter came into existence through warmth. In the second stage, air and light came into existence, along with plants. In the third stage, water and chemical actions came into existence, along with animal life. In the fourth stage, the human being came into existence, along with ego consciousness. Each stage is cumulative.

The human being is surrounded by the *donations* of the solid, fluid, air, and plasma elements that comprise a multi-dimensional, multi-time, multi-consciousness manifestation we call Earth. There are many beings involved in these processes who were active in prior times (and space) to create our surroundings. These surroundings are donations of those beings that have been placed here for humans to use in order to achieve independent consciousness. That is why these beings conceal themselves; they do not want to alarm our materialistic minds with the living revelation of their being until the right organs are developed and the time is right.

Humans cannot, at this time, withstand the full revelation of what the world around them really is. We must learn in small steps to regain our eternal home. We must join with the momentum of the pendulum to swing and carry us along with it to the next stage of evolution. We can align our personal self with the larger scheme of things and find our place among it without being overwhelmed by higher beings or the fascination of elemental beings.

We are embedded in seven cycles within seven cycles within seven cycles. Each of these cycles has a specific aspect of the complete system to contribute. Each cycle, within a greater cycle, within a greater cycle has metamorphic and morphological characteristics that work with each of the seven ethers to manifest one of the seven planetary characteristics (signatures). These cycles can be explained in general tenor and content, but each is still a new manifestation, a living creation that reveals the intent of the big picture—the rhythms of the complete cycle of nature found in the great and the small. Certain qualities, virtues, and ethers enliven each cycle with new forces of growth and information. Each cycle contributes to the whole and is integrally one with the whole.

1 warmth-mineral   7 archai

2 light/air-plant   6 archangel

3 sound/water-animal   5 angel

4 life/earth-human

Humans have been given three kingdoms of nature, as loving donations of the hierarchies, to use for its sustenance. Humans are given a world where we hardly understand the many gifts all around us. Every day, new discoveries in nature bring us closer to wisdom that inherently surrounds us in the world and is found within us. These gifts were donated by higher hierarchies. To go further in this exploration, we should address the hierarchy of beings within us and around us. The schemes of Dionysius the Aereopogite and Trithemeis of Sponheim are quite instructive in this regard.

The Hierarchy

Name	Power	Substance
Seraphim	Love	Image of fire/warmth
Cherubim	Harmony	Image of air/light
Thrones	Willpower	Image of water/sound
Kyriotetes	Wisdom	Donated life ether
Dynameis	Motions	Donated sound ether
Exusiai	Form	Donated light ether
Archai	Time	Works through warmth ether
Archangels	Folk Souls	Works through light ether
Angels	Guardians	Works through sound ether

We can then attribute the specific hierarchy to the stage when they donated substances or came to work through a specific substance.

It is a great leap of imagination to see beings standing behind forces, substances, and elements, but in fact, high spiritual beings have donated their cloaks or shadows to the world so that creation can move through what is needed to create, perfect, and resurrect humanity. The beings of the hierarchy can be described in great detail, and their influence can be mapped over the course of time as an active force in the historical evolution of humanity.

1 Kyriotetes   7 Archai

2 Dynameis   6 Archangels

3 Exusiai   5 Angels

4 Human

Alternative names for these beings are used in other traditions. If you are not willing to suspend your disbelief that there are ethers and angels, then use terminology that is more comfortable for you, like a virtue or a divine quality, instead of Christian angelology. There are many ways to describe these beings and their work in nature. This book will present several approaches to these beings so that their nature may reveal itself in archetypes that are familiar to you.

Going Beyond the Third Dimension

Another approach to the question of human spiritual evolution is found in the seven dimensions of the Theosophists and Anthroposophists, best described by Rudolf Steiner in his book, *The Fourth Dimension*. In this cosmology, there are essentially only three dimensions. The fourth, fifth, sixth, and seventh are obtained by disenchanting or freeing the forces and beings that create the three-dimensional world.

• • •

As we ascend to a higher dimension, we become free of the rules and regulations of the three-dimensional world.

• • •

Let's use some geometric references to begin to understand this process. Imagine that a dot (point) is a place marker with no left/right, up/down, or forward/backward dimension. It represents zero dimensions, but does exist in space. Its only quality is that it exists. In the next dimension, we have a line, which can move along from a point in one direction—perhaps left/right or up/down, but not both. Basically, a line represents one dimension moving forward.

The second dimension is represented by a plane, that mysterious dimension where you have up/down and right/left, like a shadow without depth. A plane can be seen as a two-dimensional object. In the third dimension, which is the world in which we live, we are able to move up/down, right/left, and forward/backward. We are born into a three-dimensional world, and the only way out is to go beyond space and time in dreams, death, or transcendence (ascension).

Imagine, for a moment, that you could eliminate the third aspect of the third dimension: forward/backward. For our purposes of illustration, we show these dimensions as progressing sequentially and chronologically. By eliminating the forward/backward component of our three-dimensional world in this imaginary exercise, where would we be? We would be back in the second dimension, but *with consciousness* that is beyond the second dimension. It would be an entirely different experience of the second dimension than a plane. As we ascend to a higher dimension, we become free of the rules and regulations of the three-dimensional world. We might become free-flowing; we might experience synchronicity and providence, as we are able to transcend the time and space of the three-dimensional world.

In order to create geometric shapes in the fourth dimension, we would need more than one two-dimensional plane. We would need other *conscious* two-dimensional planes to create a platonic solid, like a cube. We would need five other planes, or conscious entities, to join us at the same moment to create the outside of the six-sided cube. However, the timing would have to be synchronized and cohesive, and it would only last for a moment, because we are planes with only one side.

Steiner provides an exercise to help us imagine the infinite number of planes that it takes to make a cosmic sphere. In projective geometry, a sphere may be referred to as an infinite amount of planes raying in towards a center point. This exercise prepares the mind for imagining what the fourth dimension might look like, because it has characteristics of the plane as a model for what the hierarchy does to create the third dimension.

To reach the fourth dimension, we annihilate the third dimension; we explode it by going beyond space into a *time perception* of space. Space appears over time as distinct points in time. If space were imagined not to exist, we would become beings who were not limited by the spatial reference to time. For instance, when we study a human biography thoroughly, we can develop a timeless perspective of that human life; we can see the whole picture without the restrictions of time and perhaps even find deeper meaning in that life. This is the view seen from the fourth dimension: a view that collapses space and finds the meaning of time through consciousness that is usually blinded and confused by space and time.

Truly, attaining a timeless consciousness is the foundation of many religious practices, gaining immortality after death, or life from one human incarnation to another. It is this spaceless perspective that allows us the consciousness to see life from the dimension of time. This can develop later into the eternal perspective we wish to attain as the culmination of our incarnations. This is, essentially, resurrection or life reborn, a liberation from this muddy vesture of decay. If you can dissolve the three-dimensional space realm with consciousness, you can attain the spaceless dimension of time: the fourth dimension.

To reach the timeless realm of the fifth dimension, we destroy or dissolve, *with full consciousness*, one-dimensional time, which is a one-direction timeline. To reach the sixth dimension, where even duration no longer exists, we must consciously dissolve the dimension of a dot, zero dimensions, or simple existence in the physical world. When we do that, we attain the ability to realize the illusion of duration. The eternal then appears before us: the home we left long ago and are now returning to at the end of the seven stages. We end up at the beginning, but *with consciousness* that has been developed enough to become co-creators with the divine.

Stage 1: point

Stage 2: line—1D

Stage 3: plane—2D

Stage 4: solid—3D

Stage 5: spaceless—4D

Stage 6: timeless—5D

Stage 7: duration-less—6D

The cycle of wholeness is impressed into a complete cycle of seven. We can give each stage a different name and describe it from many viewpoints. The core characteristics of each stage can be found everywhere in nature, from butterfly metamorphoses to the life cycles of the growing human being. From Greek myth to modern gravity theories, we find these mysterious seven cycles for those with eyes to see.

Take, for example, the life cycle of a monarch butterfly, a most wondrous creation of nature filled with wisdom and mystery. The butterfly is the best example of metamorphosis and has great secrets to share about the present evolution of humanity. For instance, the butterfly starts as a dot (egg) on a leaf: a simple placeholder filled with the secrets of what it will become. Often, there are seven raised lines cross the top of the egg—perhaps a sign of what is to come. The egg is what we previously called zero dimensions: just a placeholder.

The egg hatches and the caterpillar emerges, first eating the remains of the egg, and then eating voraciously in one forward direction. The caterpillar is somewhat one-dimensional at first. It sheds its skin five times in this stage, a type of sub-stage of the larger stage of the one-dimensional caterpillar.

After a while, the caterpillar finds a nice, two-dimensional underside of a leaf to attach its back legs to while it begins to spin its thread into a cocoon that resembles a crude sphere. The butterfly encloses itself in the tomb of the chrysalis, becoming a womb for the next stage of evolution. Its new home, the sac of the chrysalis, turns a one-dimensional caterpillar into a two-dimensional chrysalis of potential. The one-dimensional caterpillar passes through the two-dimensional chrysalis and then into the three-dimensional butterfly that commands the three dimensions of space.

These first three stages are much like the three dimensions of space, but as a living metaphor. The butterfly dies and is reborn in the process of being birthed into the third dimension.

Then, a marvelous example of metamorphosis happens with the *fourth generation* of butterfly. The archetypal butterfly, the monarch, emerges from the chrysalis stage and lives for a few weeks, wherein it reproduces the next generation. At the fourth generation, the monarch does something remarkable: it flies back south to winter, often thousands of miles, and returns home to lay eggs on the same milkweed plant upon which it was born. Its lifespan in this generation is a remarkable six to eight months. Here is how it looks:

Generation 1 Monarch	Egg-cocoon-butterfly-reproduction-death (life cycle is a few weeks)
Generation 2 Monarch	Same as generation 1
Generation 3 Monarch	Same as generation 1
Generation 4 Monarch	Egg-cocoon-butterfly-flies thousands of miles to winter—returns to birth location to reproduce—death (life cycle of six to eight months)

The first-generation butterfly lays eggs within a few weeks, and then dies. The second-generation monarch does the same, and so too for the third generation. The first three generations of monarchs only have short lives of about four to six weeks. Only the fourth generation has the encoded message to fly south for the winter and return six to eight months later in an extended life cycle.

This is a perfect picture of human evolution through the seven stages of incarnation and resurrection. In this analogy, humans are the butterflies that don't really come into existence until the fourth stage: butterfly. Therefore, the mineral stage is likened to the egg, the plant stage to the caterpillar, the animal stage to the chrysalis, and the butterfly stage to the human.

The next three stages of human development might be likened to the three further generations the butterfly needs to complete the cycle of seven. Humans are, perhaps, butterflies coming out of the chrysalis before they have spread their wings and filled them with air. After that, we can imagine that the *awakened initiate* might be the fourth-generation butterfly that flies south and then returns home to lay eggs and complete the cycle. It is easy to see why the butterfly is such an excellent example of the seven stages of metamorphosis and can lend great insight into where humans are in relationship to the monarch.

Are you the first or fourth generation monarch? Do you feel that insatiable longing to return home to a place you seemingly have never been before? Perhaps you are the high flier that the species depends upon to evolve and carry on. The analogy, as you can see, is metaphorical, but borders on literal. These processes can be found everywhere in nature. It is our task to awaken to our stage of evolution, take our own spiritual development seriously, and align it with higher forces and beings who can lead us across the quantum gaps in evolution that come between each new stage.

When approaching the sacredness and primal nature of the beingness of seven, the words of the enigmatic thinker, C. G. Harrison, come to mind as a firm foundation and show us where to begin the ascent of the ladder to heaven, or the Seven-Story Mountain. In *The Transcendental Universe,* Harrison tells us that there are Three Axioms at the foundation of spiritual science that are universal truths:

The Three Great Axioms

1. Seven is the perfect number.
2. The microcosm is a copy of the macrocosm.
3. All phenomena have their origin in vortices.

Harrison tells us that the number seven is distinguished in the laws regulating the harmonious perception of forms, colors, sounds, and taste. There is a periodical septenary return of cycles in insects, reptiles, fishes, birds, mammals, and man himself. All evolution proceeds in cycles of seven. During the first half of each cycle, its rate is subject to a gradual diminution; it then increases in the same proportion that it diminished. Its end corresponds with its initial velocity, and the whole series is expressed in multiples of seven.

Harrison asks the question:

> Now if the mysterious Septenary Cycle be a law in nature, if it is found controlling the evolution and involution (or death) in the realms of entomology, ichthyology, and ornithology, as in the kingdoms of the animal, mammals, and man, why cannot it be present and active in the cosmos in general, and why should not an occultist be able to trace the same law in the life of the solar system, the planet and the races of men which inhabit it?

The number seven is the key factor in spiritual science and in every ancient religion because it is the primal element in nature, the septenary constitution of the universe. Every series of which seven is the numerical ration is a cosmos which is found in the great or small. The highest expression of this law is the individual human being who is the microcosm of the macrocosm.

The God-Idea evolves through seven forms in the theosophical "Fifth Root Race," and they correspond roughly, in their order, to the evolution of the seven sub-races: the former is an intellectual, and the latter a physical evolution. Harrison tells us:

> The Powers of Light are the Elohim (gods) of the first chapter of Genesis, who speak in the first person plural ("Let *us* make man in *our* own image"), and the seven spirits (or breaths) of God mentioned in the Apocalypse. They are, in a certain sense, the creators of the world; the world proceeded from them. Each of the seven breaths is correlated to the sevenfold occult forces of nature operating on different planes of consciousness, and these occult forces are correlated, in their turn, to potentialities inherent in every human being. The Powers of Light, though one in their

essence, as the manifested Logos, are reflected in time as seven, which emanate from, and return into, the Logos, each in the culmination of its time.

Theosophical Cosmology of Seven

Every world system, including our present one, consists of seven planetary or consciousness stages. Within our world, called the Planetary Incarnation of Earth, they carry the names: Saturn—Sun—Moon—Earth—Jupiter—Venus—Vulcan. *These names are not synonymous with the planetary bodies we see in our current solar system.* These planetary conditions (also called incarnations, rounds, or globes) have stages of consciousness that involve the Holy Trinity, the nine hierarchy, the elementary kingdoms, humanity, the elements, elementals, sub-elementary beings, and the kingdoms of nature. These seven planetary incarnations are also called Great Cycles. Each planetary incarnation has an associated stage of consciousness. Humanity only came into waking consciousness during the fourth incarnation of Earth, which corresponds to the consciousness stage of Ego-Consciousness, which is the particular element of the human being.

The following successive stages of consciousness are true for all hierarchies: trance, dreamless sleep, dreaming, ego-consciousness, imaginative consciousness, inspirational consciousness, and intuitive consciousness.

Planetary Incarnation	Consciousness Stage	Element
Saturn	Trance	Mineral
Sun	Dreamless Sleep	Plant
Moon	Dreaming	Animal
Earth	*Ego-Consciousness*	*Human*
Jupiter	Imagination	Angel-Imagination
Venus	Inspiration	Archangel-Inspiration
Vulcan	Intuition	Archai-Intuition

Every planetary incarnation is comprised of seven smaller cycles called life-conditions, or epochs. In this way, our world system is comprised of forty-nine epochs (7 x 7) in the complete cycle. We are currently in the fifth epoch of the fourth planetary incarnation, Earth, which is the Post-Atlantean epoch.

Earth Epochs

Polarian
Hyperborean
Lemurian
Atlantean
Post-Atlantean (our epoch)
Sixth Epoch
Seventh Epoch

Every epoch is comprised of seven smaller cycles called sub-epochs. There are 343 sub-epochs in the complete cycle (7 x 7 x 7). The sub-epochs are also known as the seven root-races, or ages:

Post-Atlantean Sub-Epochs	Age Began	Zodiacal
Ancient Indian	7227 BC	Leo
Ancient Persia	5067 BC	Gemini
Egyptian/Chaldean/Sumerian	2907 BC	Taurus
Greco-Roman	747 BC	Aries
Anglo-Germanic	*1413 AD*	*Pisces*
Future Russian	3573 AD	Aquarius
Future American	5733 AD	Capricorn

There are also seven sub-conditions below the sub-epochs. Each sub-epoch, or root-race, is comprised of seven archangelic rulership periods that last around 360 years for each of the seven archangels, totaling approximately 2160 years for the complete archangelic rulership cycle. These archangelic rulership periods were developed in Europe by Johannes Trithemius, Abbot of Sponheim (1462–1516) in his work, *A Treatise on the Seven Secondary Causes, Intelligences, or Spirits, Who Move the Spheres According to God. A Little Book or Mystical Chronology.* It is believed that when each archangel becomes the ruling archangel of a period, it ascends to the next higher hierarchical rank to carry out its duties. Ascended archangels become archai, Time Spirits, during the course of their rulership, or what is called "The Spirit of the Times" or Zeitgeist. Here are the archangelic rulership periods according to Trithemius:

Ruling Archangel	Began	Planetary Rulership
Uriel	246 BC	Saturn
Anaeal	109 AD	Venus
Zachariel	463 AD	Jupiter
Raphael	817 AD	Mercury
Samael	1171 AD	Mars
Gabriel	1525 AD	Moon
Michael	1879 AD	Sun
Uriel	2233 AD	Saturn

We can see by these charts that the world has cycles of seven within cycles of seven, within cycles of seven. Seven is the reflection of the solar system as a holographic image of the whole that impresses its harmonics in all aspects of nature. These planetary morphological resonances manifest in the natural world through what are called correspondences, or planetary signatures. Whether a metal, tree, sound, color, hierarchical being, planetary condition, or years in the human life cycle, seven is the magic weaving resonance that ties the heavens above to the earth below.

The chart below gives some of the correspondences of seven in the natural world that can illuminate the associative aspects of one substance to another. The spectrum of seven spans the exact amount of stages to make metamorphoses effective.

Planet	Metal	Tree	Organ	System	Color	Day
Moon	Silver	Cherry	Brain	Reproduction	Purple	Monday
Venus	Copper	Birch	Kidneys	Elimination	Green	Friday
Mercury	Mercury	Elm	Lungs	Respiration	Yellow	Wednesday
Sun	Gold	Ash	Heart	Circulation	White	Sunday
Mars	Iron	Oak	Gall Bladder	Reproduction	Red	Tuesday
Jupiter	Tin	Maple	Liver	Nourishment	Orange	Thursday
Saturn	Lead	Pine	Spleen	Preservation	Indigo	Saturday

The seven planetary correspondences are found in music, speech, philosophy, liberal arts, and practically everything else imaginable. They are not just forces (or streams) we find in nature but are also found in the human biography as seven-year stages of development that relate to the planets. Even these seven-year periods can be seen to be comprised of yet another set of seven stages.

Beredene Jocelyn gives a beautiful description of these seven-year cycles in the human life in her book, *Citizens of the Cosmos*, which is one of the finest books on this topic and is recommended to every reader. She points out that life involves a series of births that are correlated to these planetary cycles. Each seven years brings the birth of another aspect (body) of the human being. Our physical birth was only the first of numerous other births we have in life.

From birth to seven, the moon rules physical development. The child separates from the maternal organism and leaves the hereditary body behind by age seven. The moon promotes growth primarily through the mother, and then through the home in general. This seven-year period is dreamlike and has an instinctive consciousness that is nurtured by imitation. The organs are given form during this period with the dentition of the second teeth: a sign that the molding of the physical organism is completed.

The second seven years begins with the birth of the child's etheric body out of the sheath of universal ether, comparable to the birth of the physical body out of the physical maternal sheath. The etheric formative forces that had been active in molding the organs are then free to be used for learning and memorizing during the next seven years of the Mercury cycle (7 to 14). These are the seven years of elementary school: grades one through seven. (Grade eight is a summary of the previous seven years.) Rudolf Steiner indicated that these seven years should be taught by the same teacher to the same class of growing students. During those crucial years of etheric body development, the teacher becomes the messenger, like Hermes (Mercury), mediating between the child and the world, or a midwife birthing the etheric body.

Planet	Vehicle	Age	Developed During
Moon	Physical Body	B–7	Atlantis
Mercury	Etheric Body	7–14	Ancient India
Venus	Astral Body	14–21	Ancient Persia
Sun	Sentient Soul	21–28	Ancient Egypt-Chaldea
Sun	Intellectual Soul	28–35	Greco-Roman Civilization
Sun	Consciousness soul	35–42	Present Anglo-Saxon-Teutonic
Mars	Spirit Self	42–49	Future Age
Jupiter	Life Spirit	49–56	Future Age
Saturn	Spirit Man	56–63	Future Age

The unique contribution of Jocelyn's work is that it goes beyond the unfolding of the seven-year life cycles. It subdivides each seven-year period, allotting a year to each of the seven planets in the same sequence as in the larger seven-year ordering.

The first of each seven is a Moon year, the second is a Mercury year, the third is a Venus year, and so on. The first three years are ruled by the three inner planets and confer to each life cycle what is comparable to infancy (Moon: a new beginning, adjustment, and growth), childhood (Mercury: learning), and adolescence (Venus: love and beauty).

The fourth, the central year of every seven, is always ruled by the Sun, which strengthens ego awareness and promotes ego activity. The Sun's influence is so mighty that it extends beyond a single year into three years (Sentient, Intellectual, and Consciousness Soul). It overlaps with the last two-thirds of the previous Venus year, and the first two-thirds of the following, fifth year.

The demarcation between all years, and between the seven-year cycles, is not rigid. As between day and night there is twilight, so between all periods there is a flexible and gradual transition. The fifth, sixth, and seventh years of every seven-year period are ruled by the outer planets: Mars (energetic activity), Jupiter (expansion), and Saturn (culmination, completion, stability, and maturity). This gives the key to life's year-by-year unfolding, as well as to the successive seven-year cycles of the entire earth-life.

The second period of seven years, the Mercury cycle, covers the time between two significant events: the change of teeth and puberty. These are the physical manifestations of the birth of the etheric body at seven and of the astral body at fourteen. At seven, the function of the etheric body changes from an essentially physical to a soul nature. After seven, the individual etheric body is born and is free for soul activity and development. The Mercury cycle is a time of learning by means of pictures and through the authority of the teacher.

When a person looks back over her life, she can see the sections or phases of seven-year stages, or seven chapters. Each life period responds in its own way; each period has its own power. The seven-year rhythms of life can become gateways of vision into macrocosmic realms. Likewise, the reverse is true, and planetary forces can stream into humans through these rhythmic gateways. The life cycles are the creative work of the planetary spheres. The quality of each cycle and the forces and aptitudes unfolding from within are manifestations of cosmic influences raying in from without. The sequence of the planetary spheres, as they expand into the cosmos, is the same sequence that unfolds within the successive life-periods.

Concerning the processes and manifestations of the cycles of seven in the seven ethers, we can turn to Guenther Wachsmuth's seminal work, *The Etheric Formative Forces*, for great insight into the overall importance of the processes of seven:

> Thus the states of consciousness, the etheric formative forces, and the processes connected with substance are all linked up in man through harmonious relationships with processes in the cosmos and in the earth organism.
>
> This important rhythm of 1=7; 2=6; 3=5; 4 lies at the base of the etheric structure of the earth organism and also plays an important role in the origin of other organisms and other phenomena of our cosmic system. A general principle of conformity to law can also be followed out through all the kingdoms of Nature—indeed, even into—the laws of evolution and the rhythms in periods of human culture.
>
> | | |
> |---|---|
> | Sphere 1 = 7 | Warmth ether |
> | Sphere 2 = 6 | Light ether |
> | Sphere 3 = 5 | Chemical ether |
> | Sphere 4 | Life ether |
>
> If we observe the interior and the exterior of the earth, we may say that the inner earth presents, in respect to the distribution of its etheric forces, a complete reversal, a turning upside down, of the etheric structure of the earth organism prevailing outside the shell of the earth.
>
> This primal phenomenon, the reversal, the turning upside down, of the etheric structure from without inwards is repeated in the case of other macrocosmic and microcosmic organisms. The phenomenal world of our sense organs, the world of matter is at every moment of its existence in eternal motion, transformation, evolution, metamorphosis.
>
> It is interesting to trace the way in which the evolving human being as an embryo, as a child, and then during the change of

teeth about the seventh year, and at puberty about the 14th year that is, in the upper and the lower pole—is seized upon and influenced by the etheric formative forces in ever new forms and with higher functions in the growing organism. These organic processes complete themselves in seven-year rhythms (about the seventh year, change of teeth; fourteenth year, puberty; twenty-first year, maturity of understanding, the "majority").

Wonderfully harmonious and absolutely self-evident, the etheric formative forces bring about in great rhythms the formation of our macrocosmic system with its seven planets, its seven-toned musical scale, its seven-colored light spectrum, its seven-staged arrangements of the chemical elements and also maintains similar rhythms when they create the architecture and evolution of the microcosm of the human organism which is woven with these rhythms of the universe and the earth. The human body is part of these great rhythms and processes of the cosmos and earth, into which, man is involved as a being living in the world of substance.

Understanding the evolution of the embryo, the child, and the human life-stages with their reciprocal action of spiritual, soul, and bodily metamorphoses is of decisive importance especially for a pedagogy which shall enter into the being of the child. The same harmonious laws lie at the basis of the evolution of the planetary bodies and the evolution of man."

Rudolf Steiner describes the sevenfold division of the human being as the meshing of the physical, soul, and spiritual aspects of the human being. Sometimes he also uses a scheme of nine bodies to further elucidate the nature of the soul as threefold. This scheme is usually described as follows:

Seven Human Bodies

Physical Body
Etheric Body
Astral Body
Ego/I
Spirit Self
Life Spirit
Spirit Human

Music and the Planets

Music is another clear representation of the power of seven. The seven notes of the scale are reflected in the seven groups of the periodic table and the processes of evolution. Evolutionary processes manifest through seven stages, much like the seven notes that resolve in the octave. Human evolution is also reflected in the capacity to hear and appreciate more refined aspects of the interval between notes. Even the division of the scale into seven steps happened over time, as human hearing evolved. To speak of the notes of the Eternal is to also speak of the evolution of the elements, the planets, and humanity. As Rudolf Steiner wrote in the *Course for Young Doctors* (GA 316), "The human being, when making the transition to activity, is actually structured like a musical scale."

Our modern experience of the seven-interval scale shows Earth at the fourth stage of development, or the fourth interval. The fifth, sixth, and seventh have yet to evolve. The first four intervals have brought creation to this point and have correspondences with the physical body, etheric body, astral body, and the ego/I consciousness. The interval of the fifth is the new impulse for the future—the awakened ego/I consciousness. The mood of the fifth is openness and wakefulness to the world.

Planetary Stages	Interval
Saturn	Prime
Sun	Second
Moon	Major third
Earth	Fourth
Jupiter	Fifth
Venus	Major sixth
Vulcan	Major seventh
New cycle	Octave

The future mood of the interval of the sixth is felt as a longing for love that moves outward into the world. The mood of the seventh is felt and experienced as a further reaching out into the world to bridge the gap between ego/I consciousness and the world itself. When the connection is made, the person can grapple with the world and transform it—recreate it anew through reimagination. The sixth and seventh intervals are the expression of human willpower acting on the world. Once the octave is reached, the feeling of accomplishment surrounds activity. The willpower of the sixth and seventh become accomplished fact in the outer world. In the octave, action has joined with world process; a completed cycle of seven comes home again.

Dr. Steiner pointed out in the *Warmth Course* (GA 321) that:

> The image of the octave can help us visualize the arrangement of elements in the periodic system. We see an analogy between the inner laws of pitch and the structure of matter as it prepares to be active in chemical processes. Accordingly, we are justified in seeing the processes of union and dissolution in material only in one particular instance.

Matter is music slowed down, according to Steiner; architecture is frozen sound. Atoms and elements all seem to dance to the music of the spheres in their chemical exchanges that happen harmoniously throughout nature. The elements are a symphony of harmonious sharing that reflects cosmic order through the processes of a complete cycle of seven and its metamorphic power over time. We find this manifesting in all aspects of nature, from caterpillars and rainbows to life cycles and planetary manifestations. In his book, *Supersensible Knowledge* (GA 55), Steiner writes: "Thus we have seven colors in the rainbow, just as there are seven notes in the scale and seven levels of atomic weights in the atomic realm."

The chemical ether is also called atomic, valence, sound, and number ether, and numerous other names that indicate the power of sound to create harmonious exchange between atoms in chemical reactions. Geometry, proportions, ratios, and mathematics all demonstrate the same forces of give and take that make life possible. The sound ether is imagined as music, whereas the life ether is sometimes described as the word ether, denoting conscious meaning and form. Sound becomes structured when the life ether enters into chemical exchanges and builds cohesive organisms.

The sevenfold forces of the planets raying into the earth and the human body donate the harmonic music of the spheres as the formative forces to build the ethers into cohesive life. These sounding ethers are cosmic mathematics that continually stream living sound into life. Steiner speaks of them as "The mathematical proportions of chemistry are really expressions of the mathematical proportions of the music of the spheres, which has become mute by condensing into matter" (Rudolf Steiner, *The Mission of Christian Rosenkreutz* (GA 130)).

The music of the spheres creates the balanced proportions between the planets and manifests in the organs of the human body and the structure and form of DNA and other such mechanisms. Through morphic resonance, the organs receive and broadcast the same music, or vibrations, that keep the organs in alignment, with healthy formative forces streaming into the organ from the planetary spheres. This communication between the heavenly and earthly realms is the source of cohesive life on earth. The combined forces of the seven planets, the seven intervals, the seven organs, the seven levels of atomic weights, and the many other complete cycles of seven found in the human environment are all linked together in a grand symphony of music that is produced by a heavenly harp with seven strings. The human constitution is a symphony of beings, sounds, and life that make it an instrument for the gods to play.

In *Art in the Light of Mystery Wisdom* (GA 220), Steiner tells us much the same thing:

> If I were to describe everything to you, I would describe a wonderful music within the human body; music that is not heard, but is nonetheless experienced inwardly. What we experience musically is essentially nothing other than outer music meeting with the inner singing of the human organism. This human organism is a reflection of the macrocosm, which we carry within us as Apollo's lyre, in the form of concrete laws that are much stronger than natural laws. In us, the cosmos is playing Apollo's lyre. The human body is more than simply the aspect that biology recognizes; it is also a most wonderful musical instrument

Music is the gift of the planetary spheres to humans. It draws us into heavenly harmonies, bringing higher consciousness and health. We don't need to travel to the planets because they are in our organs, sounding the music of the spheres as the metamorphic life-pattern of the harmony and resonance that designs and creates the morphological development of the cosmos and humanity.

Seven Hierarchical Virtues and the Planets

The Seven Virtues that are outlined in *The Gospel of Sophia* trilogy relate to the planets via time—through the morphological development of our solar system. This development is almost inconceivable to human thinking at this point of evolution. Rudolf Steiner tells us how the planets actually came to be as they appear to us now. The heavenly and human virtues arise out of these stages. Developing the virtues is like climbing a ladder to heaven; conversely, the seven deadly sins have been pictured as a ladder descending in the opposite direction. The concept of *falling into matter* applies here—or as William Erwin Thompson, a renowned cultural historian, calls it, "the time it takes falling bodies to alight."

The planets are the leftover signs of the development of space through time, or the Temple of Wisdom described in *The Gospel of Sophia* trilogy. The outer planets of Saturn, Jupiter, and Mars represent a spatial reminder of three great cycles of the process of seven that the solar system has already gone through (Ancient Saturn, Ancient Sun, and Ancient Moon). The current physical Earth and Moon represent the Earth's planetary incarnation, or the fourth stage of the seven. The current physical planets of Venus and Mercury—as well as our current Sun—represent the future stages that will complete the Great Cycle of seven as Future Jupiter, Future Venus, and Future Vulcan.

Essentially, the seven hierarchical virtues are the gifts of the higher hierarchies through time that leave a donation or shadow of their activity in this realm. The hierarchy has donated virtues to us, such as selfless sacrificing, bestowing grace, renunciation, consciousness, wisdom, harmonious order, love, the ego/I of the individual human being, Imagination, Inspiration, Intuition, and other such higher virtues. These virtues translate to humans as stages of development, either rising to heaven or descending to hell.

The hierarchical stages are given cosmological names: Saturn, Sun, Moon, Earth, Jupiter, Venus, and Vulcan. These names are not the same as the planets we commonly reference, and should not be confused with them. These cosmological names address the inner characteristics of each period in the cycle of seven. We are currently in the fourth cycle, called Earth, which more or less coincides with the planet Earth in relationship to the current configuration of the solar system.

There is another way to look at the *space* manifestation of the virtues instead of a *time* manifestation. There are no indications or ancient traditions to support an exact scheme of the virtues as they relate to space. *The Gospel of Sophia* trilogy presents a more complete elucidation of this idea. Each virtue is related to a pillar based upon the spatial markers that the aspirant travels through in the spiritual world at night or after death. This expanding sphere of consciousness grows outward through the current planetary spheres based upon proximity.

Aspirants learn that there are two initial doors into the Temple: either the Moon or the Sun. The choice of which door to enter is based upon the spiritual development of the individual. The scheme of associations is listed below:

Pillar One	Humility-Compassion	Moon or Sun
Pillar Two	Love	Moon or Sun
Pillar Three	Purity	Venus
Pillar Four	Generosity	Mercury
Pillar Five	Temperance	Mars
Pillar Six	Diligence	Jupiter
Pillar Seven	Patience	Saturn

Seven in Relationship to Planetary Formation

As we look again and again at the tessellations of seven, we find endless ramifications and applications that help illuminate the nature of all complete systems around us. One of the grander applications of the metamorphic process of the cycle of seven is found in the cosmology of theosophy and anthroposophy in relationship to our solar system. This cosmology takes supple thinking to imagine. Metaphorically, it requires the faith of the caterpillar that spins itself into a chrysalis, falling into deep sleep, not knowing its next transformation. Surely, if a butterfly can metamorphose, the solar system can, too. This is what we discover in this grand cosmological scheme of seven stages.

• • •

*B*ehind all matter is donated spirit which is held suspended *in space and time for the purpose of humans birthing independent consciousness.*

• • •

The solar system is a living being with a life cycle that has births, deaths, and rebirths—seven in the full cycle. In other words, the planets and the central sun as we know them now have changed dramatically, which creates a stark contrast to the current ideas of what matter is. The spiritual cosmology of the solar system is directly connected to hierarchical beings and their metamorphic ascension into the higher hierarchy above them. Even the gods evolve, and their process is intimately connected to ours. As the hierarchy evolved, donations of grand virtues of sacrifice, wisdom, and love have woven our solar system into one that currently looks somewhat fixed and stable. This is an illusion of space and time that is created as multi-dimensional inter-weavings that create many different, independent, and concurrent perspectives of reality.

An Eternal Curriculum for the Etheric Body

"One of the finest, most highly attenuated substances within the reach of human faculties is called Akasha. The manifestations of beings and of phenomena in the Akasha are the most delicate and ethereal of any that are accessible to humans. What a person acquires in the way of occult knowledge lives not only in their soul but is inscribed into the Akasha-substance of the world."

Occult Science and Occult Development (GA 152)

Behind all matter is donated spirit that is held suspended in space and time so humans can birth independent consciousness. In the beginning, human consciousness was child-like and directly "tied to its mother's apron strings." Our consciousness and the consciousness of the divine were one.

If we were to become independent beings with full spiritual consciousness, we would need to experience free will, which meant leaving our mother behind and setting out on our own journey. Over the eons, we fell into matter, until we now find ourselves on Earth, having experiences in the physical realm. Our suffering leads us to a desire to find our way back to the mother, but this time joining her with our hard-earned, but fully awake consciousness. We suffer in order to awaken to our consciousness and find our way back home. This is the story of the prodigal son/daughter.

Currently, humans are in danger of falling deeper into matter through pride, greed, and the other deadly sins and losing their desire to find the way back to spirit-mother-home. Our consciousness becomes engrossed in the physical, sensational, and digital realms. We fall into matter until we are buried, and all light shining upon our way back home is darkened.

Humans are immortal beings. That is the lesson of life: to know that we keep on living in other forms after death, until the next birth. Birth and death are illusions of space and time; they are the cyclic patterns found in all nature: birth, death, rebirth. This is also true for the grand stages of morphological development of our solar system. Our solar system was not created by a gradual and sequential slowing down of matter from a "big bang" that just happened randomly. Instead, it was a "big birth" that keeps unfolding wisdom in the world, from the intricate way a cell is organized to the dance of the planets around the sun.

Ancient Wisdom from Clairvoyants

To consider spiritual cosmology, we first must give the disclaimer that we will not be considering the currently named outer planets of Uranus, Neptune, and Plato. These planetoids were not part of our solar system in the first three stages of the cycle, but joined our solar system in the fourth stage, and then, only as a shadow of the seven planets. The asteroid belt between Mars and Jupiter is included in this process of development. Anything beyond our solar system is extremely difficult to explain with human thinking, or even imaginative thinking. A full explanation arises out of the work of Rudolf Steiner, but the indications he gives insinuate that we are looking into a mirror when we look out into space beyond our solar system. We have yet to understand our solar system, let alone the universe.

Steiner's indications about the solar system and universe continue to be proven true. In his *Astronomy Course* (GA 323),

Steiner describes the nature of light, the center of mass of the solar system, the nature of the interior of the sun, the presence of arsenic in comet tails, the zodiacal degree of the galactic and super-galactic centers, and many other ideas that have been validated by scientists like Theodor Landscheidt and Ervin Laszlo.

Steiner was a great astrophysicist who has not been given credit for some of the most important insights in the field. Even the true motion of the planets was explained by Steiner and later proven with mathematical equations. The list of profound insights from Steiner concerning cosmology make him one of the most effective sources to find new discoveries in science through his indications. Therefore, what is about to be shared is not theoretical speculation, but ancient wisdom that has been known by clairvoyants for millennia and confirmed by Steiner, who was also clairvoyant. He was able to reaffirm ancient teachings and clothe them in spiritual scientific terms that, like Nikola Tesla's, will keep being applied for centuries to come.

We would do well to imagine each complete system in the world as being a whole unto itself. Our solar system is one of those complete systems in the process of seven stages. We need not, at this point, consider anything outside of this system, but if you were to take everything outside of our solar system and imagine it to be a complete system, it would be found to follow the same cycles and patterns.

In other words, what is happening in the universe is also happening in our solar system; they mirror one another. Therefore, the consideration of our solar system's metamorphosis is most easily imagined as somewhat independent of all the fantastic and incorrect ideas of modern science about the universe that minimalize the importance and centrality of our system's development.

If the story of the solar system were told the way Steiner explains it, it would sound something like this:

In stage one, called Saturn, there were no suns, planets, light, or time as we know it. Only the hierarchy, who do not take on physical form, brooded over this amorphous potential. Then, the hierarchy's plan of seven stages was created out of love and harmony. Once this plan was communicated to the hierarchy of willpower, creation came into being as a mood of holy self-sacrifice. This sacrifice broke into two, and the world of substance and the world of time (as a sequential process) came into being.

*M*atter appears during a Manvantara period of manifestation and disappears during the Pralaya period of non-manifestation.

Space was not yet created, but the substance of sacrifice became warmth, and the beings that lived in this warmth clustered together in bundles and manifested time as living beings.

The human being also came into existence at that time as a seed. In each seed, a human existed in all of its forms, from animal-like characteristics with a physical body, to the future nature of humans as angels without physical form, in the perfect cosmological shape of a sphere. The area, or sphere, of this ancient Saturn condition was the size of the orbit of our current planet Saturn as it moves around the sun.

The second stage of the solar system's metamorphic development comes after what we might call a chrysalis stage of disincorporation, which remembers the past and reorganizes for the future. This "falling back" into non-manifestation is a condition where no *matter* exists. This is the largest jump of imagination required in understanding the process of the cycle of seven as it concerns the solar system.

Between each stage is a sleep, a sort of death to the previous stage, but a cognizant remembering of the past development that is able to create a new synthesis and re-organization of the past that is more in line with future needs still exists. In Vedic literature, this is called a Pralaya, or period of non-manifestation. Matter appears during a Manvantara period of manifestation and disappears during the Pralaya period of non-manifestation.

Movement and manifestation congeals matter and then later dissolves it again to be used in the next phase of development, just as the caterpillar goes through a chrysalis stage of dis-corporation and then re-incorporation to become a butterfly.

The concept of cycles of manifestation and non-manifestation flies in the face of materialistic science because science has made *matter* its holy grail and the *speed of light* the only nourishment coming from this grail.

Matter is not truly solid. Atoms are mostly space with organized particles spinning around that space, much like we envision our solar

Space is a conscious, remembering substance.

system. To picture a Pralaya, imagine that the spinning particles in an atom become motionless and fall into the empty space that they once filled. If we also imagine that the "space" is a living being that remembers all that the particles do, then we start to approach the true reality of matter from a spiritual perspective.

Matter is congealed spirit, or spirit that has fallen or been donated to the physical realm. This constitutes a type of creation out of the vacuum of space, which is where most modern theories are leading. Space is a conscious, remembering substance that is no-substance. It is then only a small step to take to imagine that a conscious, spiritual space might not only hold and know the past, but through projective metamorphosis of the cycle of seven, can also predict the future.

A seed remembers the past of all of its parent plants and also knows the future nature of the growth of root, stem, leaf, blossom, and new seed again. Each seed must go through death (pralaya) to be born again in a new form. The process of seven that is found in the metamorphosis of a complete cycle is found everywhere in the plant kingdom, and also in the human being that relates to the plant kingdom.

Another place that space is overthrown by time is through repeated human earthly incarnations. Each human will grow through many stages of development and through many incarnations. The newborn appears out of an invisible world with memories or capacities from past lives. The lessons and advancement of the current life are taken into an invisible world after death, and from there, reborn again. These cycles have similar stages of manifestation and non-manifestation in the physical world.

It is the invisible world that fills in the blanks of what will come about through metamorphosis. Often, the stages are evidently connected and clearly evolve into the next form, but at others, it seems indistinct and nebulous—or even shocking—in the dramatic transformation from blossom to seed.

From Pralaya to Manvantara, non-manifestation to manifestation, the seven-cycle grows dynamically and then falls back and rests. This cycle can be witnessed as growth spurts in human development. In a plant, it manifests as a burst of growth that then falls back and recedes before the next burst of growth. Plants, animals, and humans all have these metamorphic cycles, both in the physical and non-physical realms. The visible world is penetrated thoroughly by the invisible, which seems to move the physical towards progressive spiritual development. Some call these *forces*, while others call them *beings*. It is, in fact, a mixture of both, with an accompanying complex system to support the physical foundation built up from the seven ethers.

The ethers themselves follow these same cycles of morphological metamorphosis. Each of the seven ethers is based upon the development of the previous one. One of these ethers was created during each of the cosmological stages of development.

On Ancient Saturn, for instance, warmth ether came into existence, and the element of heat was born at that time. Warmth ether was donated by the Beings of Willpower—the beings called Thrones, in the Christian enumeration of the hierarchy. In stage one, the Beings of Willpower were the prime movers who brought warmth into existence, wherein the Beings of Time found their personal expression, similar to the current consciousness of humans. All of the beings, ethers, forces, substances, and currents evolve from one stage to the next, after a rest-period. Therefore, at the next stage of the cycle of seven, there is a rebirth from non-manifestation that brings all of the growth and evolution from the prior period forward.

The warmth from the Ancient Saturn period was brought into the next period, called the Ancient Sun Planetary Condition. During this stage, the Beings of Wisdom donated space as a defined place where light could be born. This light continued to warm space, and the substance that was luminous filled the area of the orbit of the current planet Jupiter. The Beings of Wisdom, called Kyriotetes, filled this space with the living substance of wisdom. Beings of Inspiration, archangels, populated this wisdom-filled space and experienced their human stage during Ancient Sun. The name Ancient Sun was given to this stage because the sphere of light that was as large as the current Jupiter sphere glowed like our current Sun.

Then, time and space begin to work together, along with the beings who work through time and space. The substance of this stage would later become plants, just as the substance of Ancient Saturn became what we now know as the mineral kingdom. All beings and substances continued to evolve. Then, another rest-period came to re-organize substance for future needs.

The third stage of cosmological metamorphosis is called Ancient Moon. During this stage, the Beings of Motion, the Dynameis, donated a fluid substance similar to water, and the Beings of Imagination, the angels, experienced their human stage in this fluid world. Later, this substance became the animal kingdom. This stage of Ancient Moon inscribed the sphere of the current planet Mars. No physical substance was yet present, even though the atmosphere was similar to water.

Humans continued to watch these three stages of development from the non-manifested realm as the substance that would later become their bodies continued to reorganize again and again at higher levels. Each new stage developed substances, forces, and associations of beings who evolved into the realm of the current Earth. During Ancient Moon, the angels felt a moving, weaving world of fluid pictures that answered their longing for the spirit. The virtue of renunciation was practiced by the Beings of Motion as they helped create the relationships between all forces, beings, substances, times, and spaces.

The fourth stage of cosmic metamorphoses is called the Earth Planetary Condition. It is the stage we find ourselves in currently, even though prior recapitulations of the three previous stages took place before any true physical substance as we know it came into being. In this stage, humans were brought out of the non-manifestation realm into the solid, physical world of manifestation. Humans now benefit from the efforts of the three previous stages. The fourth stage is the densest stage and the middle of the seven-stage cycle. It is in this stage that the true intent of the full process of the seven stages manifests. The Earth Planetary Condition (or Incarnation) is the culmination of the full cycle of seven. The creation of humanity, as we now know it, is the fulfillment of evolution. All prior stages exist in our stage of the Earth Incarnation, but not until a recapitulation of Ancient Saturn, Ancient Sun, and Ancient Moon occurred.

The past, present, and future are found in the workings of the etheric body.

The three stages of Ancient Saturn, Ancient Sun, and Ancient Moon have condensed and congealed repeatedly, as each new stage has come to birth after recapitulating the development of the whole. Thus, the Earth Incarnation recapitulated, or repeated at a higher vibration, the Ancient Saturn stage and was as large as the orbit of the current planet Saturn. As this recapitulation happened, the current planet of Saturn was left in its current orbit as a physical marker of that ancient stage of development. The virtues, gifts, donations, and experiences of that first stage of development are concurrently available for humanity as different aspects of the constitution of the human being and the natural world.

Ancient Saturn gave us warmth that evolved into light on Ancient Sun, and then into sound or fluid during Ancient Moon, and eventually into life as we know it now, in the Earth Incarnation. Warmth ether evolved into light ether, then into sound/chemical ether, and then into life ether. The warmth of

ancient Saturn evolved through four stages into what we now
know as minerals. Light evolved through three stages into plants,
sound into animals, and now life brings forth humanity on a
planet that is filled with ancient donations that have evolved into
the natural kingdoms of nature.

Ancient Saturn	Ancient Sun	Ancient Moon	Earth Incarnation
			Life ether
	Sound ether	Sound ether	Sound ether
	Light ether	Light ether	Light ether
Warmth ether	Warmth ether	Warmth	Warmth
Heat	Heat	Heat	Heat
	Air	Air	Air
		Liquid	Liquid
			Solid

Humans have each of these stages of metamorphosis inscribed
into the workings of the etheric formative forces found in the
human etheric body. This etheric body provides the patterns,
substances, currents, donations of beings, and associations with
living hierarchical beings as the blueprint of life and a well-spring
of living energy. The past, present, and future are found in the
workings of the etheric body.

As the Earth Incarnation continued in its recapitulation of
the prior periods, it separated the luminous substance, which
continued to contract into our current Sun from the denser
material. The current planet Jupiter was left behind as a marker
of that period and remnant of denser matter that separated from
the newborn Sun. Then, a most wondrous thing happened: there
was a "war in heaven" wherein some beings wanted to create
a physical planet too soon, before it was called for in proper
evolution. These beings congealed the denser substances and
attempted to create the Earth too soon.

A planet was created that subsequently dis-incorporated as a planetoid and fell into pieces, and now inscribes a circular plane between the current Jupiter and current Mars that we know as the asteroid belt. This "almost" planet was the scene of the war in heaven—and the heavens won, casting some beings further down into congealing substance who were not part of progressive evolution. These beings are called Luciferic, after their leader, Lucifer. The asteroid belt was left as a marker of that development and a sign of the war in heaven.

After each of the recapitulations of Ancient Saturn, Ancient Sun, and Ancient Moon, there were small rest periods where substance was once again reorganized and transformed into the new material needed for future evolution. After the recapitulation of Ancient Saturn, we find the current planet Saturn congealing into its current form. After the Ancient Sun recapitulation, it congealed as the current planet Jupiter, and Ancient Moon is the current planet Mars. In between the recapitulation of the Ancient Sun and Ancient Moon Conditions, we have the war in heaven and the marker of the asteroid belt left in the space between current Mars and current Jupiter. The current planets of Venus, Mercury, and the Moon also condensed and formed into spheres at the same time as the earth was doing the same.

Christ descended through time and space and demonstrated how to conquer this realm of death with consciousness, wisdom, and love.

The next stage of Earth Incarnation was no longer a recapitulation. It was new and brought the virtue of *consciousness* to human beings. Consciousness is the gift of the Spirts of Form who donated the substance of the ego, or I consciousness, to the human being. This ego/I still had to go through evolution to develop into a self-conscious, independent human being. The leader of the Spirits of Form is the second person in the Holy Trinity, Christ, who is the perfected model of the developed human ego/I. Christ held humans back as seeds to be planted at the right moment in spiritual development in the donated realms of planet Earth.

Death is the result of the physical, solid world coming into being. Death is found only in the shadow cast by spirit into this realm; it is an illusion of time and space. Christ descended through time and space and demonstrated how to conquer the realm of death with consciousness, wisdom, and love. Christ is the template or model of the perfected human ego/I—the divine human.

As the current Earth was condensing and congealing, after the recapitulations, the physical, solid world came into existence. The Earth Incarnation is now undergoing smaller sub-stages of cycles of seven. These stages are little known or understood by current science. Each of these sub-cycles also recapitulates the standard metamorphic influences found in the cosmological morphology of our solar system. Similar forces and patterns can be found in these sub-cycles.

Intent of Evolution

It is not only the past that we find woven into the wisdom of nature that surrounds us. The future is also imprinted in the etheric body and lies as potential patterns of metamorphosis that will unfold as the future of humanity. Through the insight of Rudolf Steiner and other great clairvoyants, we understand what the future will look like and what hierarchies will be involved in bringing forth future evolution. This is very difficult for the materialist to imagine, let alone comprehend or apply.

The future stages of human evolution are found within us as potential capacity. Some advanced spiritual souls can already embody these future stages in our current time. They are utilizing future capacities in the present moment. These capacities or stages are called Imagination, Inspiration, and Intuition.

Humans can experience the past through the material substances found in our physical realm. By embodying the capacities that will develop naturally in the future of human beings, we can experience the future in this lifetime. Through substance (space), we experience the past; through elevated consciousness (time), we can experience the future. Once a full cosmology is developed by the human being, space and time can be dissolved by consciousness, and the individual may receive the future gifts of the spirit in the present time. This makes humans immortal, and no longer impinged upon by the death forces of space and the limiting forces of time. Consciousness is beyond space and time, and it is the intent of evolution that humans evolve into spiritual beings who are not limited by either space or time.

Consciousness is beyond space and time, and it is the intent of evolution that humans evolve into spiritual beings who are not limited by either.

The full scope of the cycle of seven is to bring forth new creations from seeming nothingness. This process is happening all the time in human thinking, feeling, and willing as it evolves into Imagination, Inspiration, and Intuition. Humans become conscious co-creators in spiritual evolution with their hierarchical creators. All beings participate in this process of development. This is the magic of the metamorphic processes of the cycle of seven found in all complete living systems.

The chart of the Incarnations of the Earth below illustrates the seven stages of cyclic metamorphosis, even into the future. Each hierarchical virtue of those stages is given in the second column. The human virtues that relate to the ancient incarnation stages of development are listed next, and then the beings associated with experiencing their human consciousness in the different stages.

Note that once humans become fully human, conquering death, space, and time, they become more than the humans we are today; we take on the characteristics and virtues of the next rank in the hierarchy as angels, and so on. It is also important that the new impulse for the future comes out of the fifth stage of development. To find the new forces of evolution, we should look to the developing capacity of Imagination that supports this new growth and evolution.

Incarnation	Hierarchical Virtue	Human Virtue	Beings
Saturn	Sacrificing	Humility	Archai (Time Beings)
Sun	Bestowing	Love	Archangels
Moon	Renunciation	Purity	Angels
Earth	Consciousness	Generosity	Humans
Jupiter	Imagination	Temperance	Humans as Angels
Venus	Inspiration	Diligence	Humans as Archangels
Vulcan	Intuition	Patience	Humans as Archai

By this time in our evolution (currently), we should be developing a certain *sense* for the cycle of seven. These cycles are the currents through which the ethers flow and transform themselves by metamorphosis in the human etheric body. Warmth, light, sound, and life may not sound like a theory of everything, even if we add the mysterious Akasha ether of the ancients, and the two higher ethers above it. When we add the three missing ethers to the standard four ethers, we have a complete septenary system. But to continuously refer to a nebulous "etheric body of seven ethers" or "body of etheric formative forces" will not please the modern scientist. We need to delineate exactly what these etheric components are and precisely how they function.

Later in this book, a plethora of explanations and definitions of the ethers will be presented. Below is a quick reference guide to the ethers to help create a picture of these substances and enumerate the forces, elements, states of matter, and other correspondences that relate to the four ethers as they manifest in the world.

The Four Ethers

The Tree of Knowledge of Good and Evil—Levity

Warmth Ether—fire ether, chaotizing ether, primal beginnings, Thrones first offering, human consciousness, soul realm, waking consciousness, willing, thermal action, salamanders, ego, red circle forms

The Tree of Life—Gravity

Sound Ether—chemical ether, number ether, form ether, tone ether, harmony of the spheres, folk spirits, inspiration, feeling, dreamless sleep, plants, valence, magnetism, Ahriman, undines, fluids, organs, glands, archangels, sub-atomic, hydraulics, blue semi-circular forms

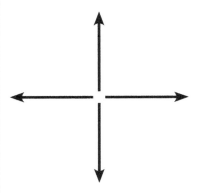 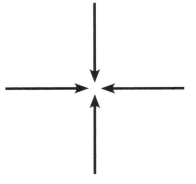

Light Ether—radiance, illumination, imagination, angels, Lucifer, phosphorous, nerves, ATP (adenosine triphosphate), astral, fallen astral, dream consciousness, animals, sylphs, air, pneumatics, electricity, yellow triangle form

Life Ether—word ether, spoken creation, limbs, archai, intuition, time spirits, trance consciousness, minerals, meaning, willing, physical, asuras, radioactivity, gnomes atomic ether, gravity, the third force, solids, fusion, red square forms

The scheme above demonstrates that four simple ethers encompass a living, pulsing world of forces and activities that are much like the pulsing heart that circulates human blood and performs many complex functions: systole and diastole, in and out. The two ethers of warmth and light expand, whereas the ethers of sound and life contract. This is none other than levity and gravity. Even beings, conditions, forms, states of consciousness, and most everything in the physical world are found to relate to these four ethers. The akasha ether moves between the four other ethers as a *mother* who is present whenever any two ethers yearn to touch. Complimentary opposites create polarity that the mother is always rectifying.

These four ethers are active throughout the body, but especially in the etheric body, which is where ethers flow in and out of etheric currents based upon the time of day and the rising and falling of each ether cycle. These etheric currents are like the currents described in Chinese acupuncture. The ethers flow along these meridians and in and out of the chakras as they send energy up and down the channels and the spinal column.

Curriculum for the Etheric Body

The etheric body is always moving. It is fluid and flowing, always changing from minute to minute. It follows certain regular patterns and can be nourished with what it needs to keep the human physical body supple and alive. This body of formative forces builds up the physical body in somewhat magical ways. After the waking hours of activity, the physical body is rejuvenated by the etheric body during sleep. The etheric body is a time body that works in cadences that resonate with cosmic rhythms. This etheric organ of time works with regular, rhythmic up-building that may seem insignificant, but actually holds the keys to the harmonic timing that tunes the temporal aspects of the etheric body. Rhythms of waking and sleeping may seem unimportant and can be taken for granted, but, in fact, they hold the secret to resetting the pineal and pituitary function each night, bringing nourishment to the physical body and psychological condition of the soul.

To help our children and ourselves fully nourish the etheric body, we need to provide the etheric body with the food it requires: a curriculum full of wisdom.

Sleep is the panacea of the soul and produces the states of consciousness that relate directly to the etheric body's timing functions of renewal and rebuilding. These are called states of consciousness: dreaming, dreamless sleep, and trance consciousness. Science concurs that good sleep depends on reaching each of these three states within a given time-frame during the night. Going without one stage or not spending enough time in another stage can cause deep psychological stress, and even illness.

The etheric body also rejuvenates itself in a larger way through the development that occurs during ages seven through fourteen. This seven-year cycle, if properly prepared in the educational environment, nourishes the eternal, ever-renewing forces of the etheric body. This nourishment is called the *eternal curriculum,* or the education of the etheric body of *wisdom children.* To help our children and ourselves fully nourish the etheric body, we need to provide the etheric body with the food it requires: a curriculum full of wisdom.

Waldorf Curriculum and the Education of the Etheric Body

This book presents images to elucidate the timing and nature of the etheric body and offers a theoretical and practical methodology to recognize the etheric and how to feed it for human spiritual development. The Waldorf curriculum of Dr. Rudolf Steiner will be used as the model to nourish the etheric body because it is the best curriculum available for those purposes. Waldorf provides a key to understanding the stages of growth of the etheric body and the cultural images and stories of the past, present, and future that relate to those stages. The Waldorf curriculum presents the best that each particular stage of human development has added to the collective evolution of humanity. It also gives ideas for the future by using the works of advanced souls, forerunners of human development, to insinuate the future stages of the cycle of seven.

In a companion book entitled *The Eternal Curriculum for Wisdom Children: Intuitive Learning and the Etheric Body,** stories and literature from the different periods of human development that Steiner related to the individual stages of human development in the child from age seven to fourteen will be presented. Additionally, literature is offered to the adult or teacher who might be presenting this literature to the children, whether in a classroom or at home. Hopefully, by offering both a child and an adult perspective, a more well-rounded picture of any stage is presented. There are many suitable selections for each grade, but only a handful at each stage will be offered as a sample of what might be presented to the student or used to expand the experience of the teacher or parent.

Images from literature are a major part of the curriculum, but in a Waldorf school, the children fully experience each cultural period through a host of direct activities that relate to each culture through song, dance, illustrations, architecture, or any cultural experience that might help the child know what it was like to be a Greek, an Egyptian, or a Persian. For a time, the child is fully immersed in the culture being studied or lived into. Passing through the stage of intellectual and spiritual development of mankind at the right stage of child development is the key, and Steiner gave us that key in his Waldorf curriculum, which maps out past and future cultures.

Using daily rhythms to reinforce learning is vital to memory development, and through good study habits, the elementary teacher teaches and nourishes the etheric body of the students. Far more than a course on study skills, which can be simple rote memory training, the Waldorf student "becomes" the cultures they study through eating the food, wearing their clothes, and living the lives of the culture being studied. This type of full immersion into a subject teaches deep knowledge that is project-based learning at its best.

Waldorf educational methodologies, in Rudolf Steiner's age, were far ahead of their time and now align with many new educational methodologies. The Waldorf teacher is taught that children learn through the three soul forces of thinking, feeling, and willing; too much focus on one capacity of learning can harm the other capacities. A balance of all three capacities is needed to engage in effective learning, no matter what type of curriculum is being used. Waldorf schools do this inherently to allow students more freedom in the experience of the cultural phenomena of the ages.

---

* *The Eternal Curriculum for Wisdom Children: Intuitive Learning and the Etheric Body* by Douglas Gabriel is a practical book for teachers and parents that provides applications for implementing the eternal curriculum in a classroom or home learning environment.

ᴛhe Ever-Changing
Understanding of the Ethers

"Nature is a perpetual circulatory worker, generating fluids out of solids, fixed things out of volatile, and volatile out of fixed, subtle out of gross, and gross out of subtle . . . thus, perhaps, may all things be originated from Ether."

Isaac Newton, *Hypotheses of Ether and of Gravitation*

The ethers are the great secret the Mystery Schools of antiquity. It is by the knowledge of ethers and their operation that the spiritual scientist comes to understand the workings of spiritual forces in the material world and his bodily constitution. The ancients recognized etheric forces as *binders* between the spiritual energies of the divine and the physical substances through which they operate. To the spiritual scientist, the ethers are the secret of all life functions and growth.

The etheric realm is invisible to physical perception, but may be examined by those possessing etheric vision. When seen, it resembles a slightly luminous, thin haze that is dimly stratified. Its lower parts are placid and unchanging, but its upper layers are in a state of constant agitation. Many beings inhabit this etheric realm, and there are highly refined areas that are used for spiritual development.

Ethers have laws governing them and have qualities inherent in their natures that every spiritual scientist should learn to know and use. A considerable part of physical sickness and disease originates in the etheric body's activities. In the normal state of health, the physical body is surrounded by etheric currents that flow in and out through the skin, and enclose the body in a flickering aura. This aura is a natural defense, repelling contagion and infection, and destroying any germs that come within its field.

*T*he etheric body was known among the ancients as the water of life.

The etheric body of the human being is a brilliant complex of radiant energy. Etheric force flows along every nerve, so that each fiber seems to be filled with an internal light. It glistens in the cell tissue, and the minute particles appear like tiny stars. In pulsing waves, it pours out from the nerve ends and extends several inches beyond the skin. Ethers fill all organisms with vitality and life.

The essential functions of life, respiration, growth, reproduction, assimilation, excretion, and circulation are maintained by the forces flowing through the etheric body, which regulates life energy and sustains all organic structure, maintaining the functions of living tissue. The etheric body was known among the ancients as the "water of life."

The etheric body is closely involved in all the processes of human growth, and is especially active from the seventh to the fourteenth years, the period of most rapid physical development. Nature has entrusted the perpetuation of the species to the etheric body, and it is the nature of this substance in seeds, eggs, and cells that makes them fertile. Although much ether is derived from the sun, the etheric body's activity in the human physical body is most intense during sleep. It sustains and regulates the automatic and involuntary functions and repairs daily wear and tear.

Most of the ailments involving the etheric body are the result of the failure of the human being to cooperate with the natural harmony of his physical body. The effort necessary to mend the damage done by wrong habits, improper diet, overwork, and physical exhaustion may tax this energy flow beyond its capacity. In addition, the etheric body must cope with the depressing and demoralizing effects of destructive mental patterns and emotional excesses that react harmfully upon the physical body.

The powers of the ethers depend upon proper food, relaxation, sleep, sunlight, exercise, the normal expression of the emotions, and the right attitude of mind. Many spiritual aspirants fail in their search for higher truths because they neglect or even ignore the physical foundation of spiritual regeneration in the etheric body. While the perfection of the physical body is not the principle end of philosophy, the release of the transcendental powers in man depends to a considerable degree upon the health of the etheric body.

The ethers have been revered in the past by the great sages, who saw them as the quintessential manifestation of spirit in matter. The most ancient texts refer to the ethers as the creators of the cosmic and earthly realms. They are known by many names, such as Swara, El Eloa, AEther, Divine Eros, Phanes, Protogous, and a host of others. H. P. Blavatsky names this divine force in *The Secret Doctrine*—Fohat. She wrote extensively about the ethers and the spiritual elements, as she calls them, and the seemingly magical being Fohat. Who or what Fohat is remains uncertain in Blavatsky's theosophical writings, but Fohat holds the highest position in her cosmology.

Blavatsky's Theosophical teachings were a foundation upon which Steiner built. Steiner was well aware of the debate between Blavatsky and a student of hers, Rama Prasad, who wrote the book *Nature's Finer Forces*, an exposition of the ancient Shivite Tattvic (etheric) philosophy of the science of breath. Blavatsky felt that misuse of the information in Prasad's book could lead to black magic and harm the unwitting aspirant who tried to carry out experiments with the tattvas (ethers). Great debates ensued for years in both theosophic and anthroposophic circles concerning whose view was correct.

Rudolf Steiner worked with his secretary, Guenther Wachsmuth, to create a seminal work on the ethers entitled *The Etheric Formative Forces in Cosmos, Earth and Man*. Although this work is similar to Prasad's interpretation of *The Science of*

Breath, it is different in some areas. In his book, Wachsmuth attempted to consciously connect the reader to current scientific theories and did not use Prasad's book as a basis; instead, it was developed out of research done at the anthroposophical headquarters in Dornach, Switzerland.

Modern ether theorists find difficulties with both Prasad and Wachsmuth and tend to use the similarities found in both, thereby allowing for cross-pollination of ideas. Milner and Smart wrote *The Loom of Creation* in 1976 as a modern exposition on the ethers' cosmological development and their role as forces of nature that effect human cultural development. The use of Kirlian photography and other methods of "seeing" the ethers were presented in a bold and wonderful way in Milner and Smart's presentation. Not surprisingly, disputes ensued because they did not adhere to previous forms of presentations of etheric science.

It is instructive to view the differing opinions about the ethers to corroborate our own spiritual scientific research in this most important area of cosmology. We will take Blavatsky's presentation of the content of the most ancient *Stanzas of Dyzan* (from the *Secret Doctrine*) as a point of departure on this amazing path to the ethers. But first, let us review the classical and modern views of the ethers before delving into the most ancient views of aethers—the tattvas. What we will see in the end is that both views converge into similar descriptions. Cutting-edge theories concerning the ethers even use the terms the ancients employed to describe these same phenomena.

Classical View of the Aethers

The ancients believed in an *aether* (old spelling) in the universe above the earthly sphere. They called it *quintessence,* and it was used to explain light and gravity. Another name for aether is *apeiron,* as named by Anaximander in Greece. He believed creation is eternal and infinite, or boundless (*apeiron*), subject to neither old age nor decay. The apeiron perpetually yields fresh materials from which everything we can perceive is derived. Apeiron generated the polarities that acted on the created world. Everything is generated from apeiron, and then it is destroyed by going back to apeiron, according to nature.

Greek society could perceive gods everywhere; therefore, the first glimmerings of the observed laws of nature were derived from divine laws created by divine beings. The Greeks believed that the universal principles could also be applied to human societies and the human individual.

In the mythical Greek cosmogony, the beginning of the universe is Nyx, the Void, who is considered a divine being. One can also name Her the Abyss. Thales called this first principle water. This apeiron is the primal chaos. It acts as a foundation by which all of the forms of creation arise.

Plato mentions aether, but Aristotle added aether to the system of the classical elements as the *fifth element*. Aether, located in the celestial regions and heavenly bodies, moves in circles and has none of the qualities of terrestrial elements. Aristotle believed that crystalline spheres made of aether held the celestial bodies, explaining the orbits of planets in circular motion in the crystalline aether.

*A*ether theories were superseded by the General Relativity Theory of Einstein.

Quintessence is the Latin name of the fifth element used by medieval alchemists for a medium similar to the heavenly bodies. There was very little presence of quintessence within the alchemical terrestrial sphere. Quintessence became synonymous with elixirs of life, medicinal alchemy, and the philosopher's stone.

In the modern age, aether theories began to spring up to explain the propagation of electromagnetic and gravitational forces. Newton used the idea of aether to help match observations to strict rules of physics. Einstein himself noted that his own model, which replaced these theories, could itself be thought of as an aether.

Aether theories were superseded by the General Relativity Theory of Einstein. Some physicists have tried to reintroduce the concept of aether attempting to address perceived deficiencies in current physical models.

The use of aether to describe the motion of light was popular during the 17th and 18th centuries. Johann Bernoulli, a Swiss mathematician, postulated that all space is permeated by aether containing "excessively small whirlpools." This theory of "luminiferous aether" would influence the wave theory of light proposed by Christiaan Huygens, a Dutch astronomer and mathematician, in which light traveled in the form of longitudinal waves via an "omnipresent, perfectly elastic medium having zero density, called aether."

Sir Isaac Newton used aether in his theory of gravitation. He based the whole description of planetary motions on a theoretical law of dynamic interactions and introduced a mechanism of propagation through an intervening medium called aether. In his aether model, Newton describes aether as a medium that "flows" continually downward toward the Earth's surface and is partially absorbed and partially diffused. This "circulation" of aether is what he associated the force of gravity with in order to explain the action of gravity in a non-mechanical fashion. His theory also explains that aether was dense within objects and rare outside of them. As particles of denser aether interacted with the rare aether, they were attracted back to the dense aether, much like cooling vapors of water are attracted back toward each other to form water.

Modern Scientific Theories of the Aethers

Aether (ether) theories in modern physics generally propose the existence of a medium that is a space-filling substance or field, necessary as a means of transmission for the propagation of electromagnetic and gravitational forces. There are many theories of aethers, including Albert Einstein's (1879–1955) luminiferous aether, which was a theorized medium for the propagation of light.

Sir Isaac Newton, the English physicist (1642–1726) postulated in his *Third Book of Opticks* (1718) that an *aethereal medium* transmits vibrations faster than light, by which light, when overtaken, is put into "fits of easy reflection and easy transmission," causing refraction and diffraction. As Newton wrote, "And is not this medium the same with that medium by which light is refracted and reflected, and by whose vibrations light communicates heat to bodies?"

Albert Einstein wrote in *Ether and the Theory of Relativity* (1920): "The velocity of a wave is proportional to the square root of the elastic forces which cause its propagation, and inversely proportional to the mass of the aether moved by these forces."

After Einstein completed his foundational work on general relativity, Hendrik Lorentz (1853–1928), a Nobel Prize–winning Dutch physicist who Einstein conferred with in developing his relativity theories, wrote a letter to Einstein in which he speculated that within general relativity, the aether was re-introduced. In his response, Einstein wrote that one can speak about a new aether, but one may not speak of motion in relation to that aether.

Responding to Lorentz, Einstein wrote, "I agree with you that the general theory of relativity is closer to the ether hypothesis than the special theory. This new ether theory, however, would not violate the principle of relativity, because the state of this ether would not be that of a rigid body in an independent state of motion, but every state of motion would be a function of position determined by material processes."

In a lecture given at the University of Leiden, Germany on May 5, 1920 and entitled Ether and the Theory of Relativity, Einstein indicated,

> It would have been more correct if I had limited myself, in my earlier publications, to emphasizing only the non-existence of an

ether velocity, instead of arguing the total non-existence of the ether, for I can see that with the word ether we say nothing else than that space has to be viewed as a carrier of physical qualities. To deny ether is ultimately to assume that empty space has no physical qualities whatever. The fundamental facts of mechanics do not harmonize with this view. Besides observable objects, another thing, which is not perceptible, must be looked upon as real, to enable acceleration or rotation to be looked upon as something real. The conception of the ether has again acquired an intelligible content, although this content differs widely from that of the ether of the mechanical wave theory of light.

Between 1892 and 1904, Hendrik Lorentz created an electron/aether theory in which he introduced a strict separation between matter (electrons) and aether. In his model, the aether was completely motionless and it would only be set in motion in the neighborhood of ponderable matter. The work of Lorentz was mathematically perfected by Henri Poincaré, a French mathematician (1854–1912) who proposed the "relativity principle" as a general law of nature and tried to harmonize it with electrodynamics. However, he used the notion of an aether as a perfectly undetectable medium and distinguished between apparent and real time.

In the 1920s and '30s, Einstein labored to develop a unified field theory that would re-cast all things, including space, as a manifestation of the "total field," a synonym for his "new ether." In 1920, Einstein indicated in lectures and writings that

> We may say that according to the general in such space there not only would be no propagation of light, but also no possibility of existence for standards of space and time (measuring-rods and clocks), nor therefore any space-time intervals in the physical sense. But this aether may not be thought of as endowed with the quality characteristic of ponderable media, as consisting of parts which may be tracked through time. The idea of motion may not be applied to it.

In another paper, entitled *Concerning the Aether* (1924), Einstein argued that Newton's absolute space is the "Aether of Mechanics." Within the electromagnetic theory of Lorentz, one can speak of the "Aether of Electrodynamics," in which the aether possesses an absolute state of motion. However, the difference lies in the fact that because it was no longer possible to speak, in any absolute sense, of simultaneous states at different locations in the aether, the aether became, as it were, four-dimensional, since there was no objective way of ordering its states by time alone.

Einstein stated in his 1938 book, *The Evolution of Physics*: "This word ether has changed its meaning many times in the development of science." Its story, by no means finished, is continued by the relativity theory. The "aether of general relativity is not absolute, because matter is influenced by the aether, just as matter influences the structure of the aether."

Aether Theorists throughout History

Aether is a philosophic and scientific concept denoting the existence of an imponderable substance underlying all of nature. In Greek mythology, Aether is mentioned by Hesiod as a figure of the Highest Heaven. The only things higher than Aether are mother Nix ("The Night") and father Erebus ("The Dark"). Aether issued forth from the dark of the night and the dark of the cosmos. Aether's sister is Hemera ("The Day"). It is Chaos that precedes everything, but it is from the Aether that Heavens, Earth, and Sea arise. Aristotle treated the Aether as the finest of substances that filled up space—a fifth element alongside Air, Water, Fire, and Earth. The Aether thus became known as "Quintessence."

The birth of the scientific concept of the Aether can be traced to Renaissance thought—in particular to the *one-all* substance of Spinoza, Descartes' notion of a vortical occupation of space, and Leibniz's theory of monads. These different systematic thoughts share the concept of an imponderable substance that animates all physical reality, and are precursors to modern theories of a dynamic Aether. Robert Fludd suggested that the Aether was "subtler than light," and cites the 3rd century views of Plotinus on the ubiquitous and non-material properties of this subtle substance.

The notion of a static aether—a mechanical, jelly-like aether—finds its classical origins in Newton. In 19th century physics, the positing of a luminiferous aether was used to reconcile Maxwell's electromagnetic theory and Newtonian mechanics. This inaugurated the brief age of the *Classical Aether* embraced by Young, Maxwell, Kelvin, Lodge, Lorentz, and others.

The failure to detect the motion of the Earth through the aether called the classical concept of the aether into question, and it was formally dispensed with for the first time in Albert Einstein's theory of Special Relativity. The demise of the *Classical Aether* was equally due to the rise of the field concept—from Faraday through Maxwell to Einstein and Quantum-Dynamics. Space now becomes treated as a given, and as being permeated by fields present and propagating even in the vacuum, which is devoid of ordinary matter. The fields may be electromagnetic, gravitational, or supermassive, and more recently have been belabored as a "quantum foam," a "space-foam," a "zero-point field" or the "dark energy" of the missing Higgs particles.

The first attempt at a theory of the *Dynamic Aether* was Nikola Tesla's hypothesis that propagation of electric signals was distinct from the generation of electromagnetic signals, and made the latter possible. Tesla envisioned an *Electrical Aether* with incompressible and radiative properties. He presented experimental evidence for this physical reality in his studies on the wireless transmission of power and the resonant states of the longitudinal electric radiation that has become known as *Tesla Radiation*.

The modern scientific development of aether theories points to both dark and subtle properties of the aether—it points towards the concept of a mass-free energy medium that has "a-photic" or non-electromagnetic properties. The aether's "subtlety" results from its mass-free or non-inertial property, and the "invisibility" from its non-photonic or dark nature.

New scientific theories bring us back to the Greek scientist Aristotle, who wrestled the original concept of the Aether from the heavenly world of Greek mythology and brought it down to bind the four elements in the first inklings of modern science.

Aristotle (384–322 BC) was a Greek philosopher. He founded the Academy at Athens. Aristotle believed the heavens (that region beyond the sphere of the moon) are made of a fifth substance called aether. Unlike the other four substances, which can be transformed into one another, aether is unchanging and indestructible.

> *Corpus Aristolelicum*
>
> *Categories*
>
> *On Generation and Corruption*
>
> *On the Heavens*
>
> *On Interpretation*
>
> *Metaphysics*
>
> *Physics*
>
> *On Sense and Sensible*

René Descartes (1596–1650) was a French philosopher, mathematician, and scientist. Descartes maintained that the world is a plenum, and there is no true vacuum or void. He believed in a continuous aether that completely fills the space not occupied by solid bodies and mediates their interactions by means of a system of vortices—the whole universe was a system of interlocking vortices or *tourbillons*. The planets are carried around by a sea of aether moving in whirlpool fashion, producing what we would call gravitational effects. All space was a sea filled with matter that swirled around in large and small vortices (forming the Cartesian Vortex universe). Descartes referred to the aether as the "second matter" and "second element."

1626   *Rules for the Direction of the Mind*

1630   *The World*

1637   *Discourse on the Method*

1641   *Meditations on First Philosophy*

1644   *Principles of Philosophy*

1649   *Passions of the Soul*

Sir Isaac Newton (1642–1727) was an English physicist and mathematician whose ideas laid the foundations of classical mechanics. Newton's force-law of gravity lacked a causal mechanism, and an explanation of how such a force could be transmitted over vast distances through apparently empty space was sought. Newton, at times, thought universal gravity might be caused by the impulses of a stream of aether particles bombarding an object or by variations in an all-pervading aether. Newton held the view that light particles stimulated, or were accompanied by, vibrations in an all-pervading aether. Newton theorized his views on the transmission of gravity and other forces through a tenuous medium, filling all space, which he called the luminiferous aether. It conveyed the forces of cohesion and repulsion by which matter was maintained in ordered systems. He believed the aether to be denser in empty space than in the vicinity of massive bodies, thereby providing a mechanism for gravitational attraction. The earth then moved towards the sun under the pressure of the aether.

1669   *De analysi per aeuqationes numero*
       terminuorum infinitas

1671   *Method of Fluxions*

1684   *De motu corporum in gyrum*

1687   *Philosophiae Naturalis Prinicipia Mathematica*

1704   *Opticks*

Christiaan Huygens (1629–95) was a Dutch mathematician, astronomer, physicist, and mathematician who discovered the moon Titan and the pendulum clock. Huygens proposed a wave theory of light in which waves propagated longitudinally through a stationary aether. The speed of propagation was finite. This aether was continuous throughout space and consisted of hard elastic particles that transmitted impulses without being displaced themselves. Gravity was "the action of the aether."

1651   *Cyclometriae*

1654   *De circuli magnitudine inventa*

1659   *Systema saturnium*

1690   *Traite de la lumiere*

1698   *Cosmotheoros*

1703   *Opuscula posthuman*

Georges-Louis Le Sage (1724–1803) was a Genevan physicist most known for his theory of gravitation and the invention of telegraph. Le Sage proposed an aether consisting of tiny particles. He called them ultra-mundane corpuscles—streaming in all directions with enormous speed, a kinetic theory of gravity. The "ultra-mundane corpuscles," moving at high speed and coming from all directions, are continually impacting all material objects. Le Sage's aether may be considered the first to serve in a theory of the cause of gravity.

1748   *Essai sur l'origine des forces mortes*

1758   *Essai de Chymie Mechanique*

1758   *Lucrece Newtonien*

1818   *Physique Mecanique de George Louis Le
        Sage* (posthumously)

Leonhard Euler (1707–1783) was a Swiss mathematician,
physicist, astronomer, logician, and engineer most noted for his
work in mechanics, fluid dynamics, optics, astronomy, and music
theory. He conjectured that the aether transmits not only heat
and light, but also magnetic and electric forces and gravitation.
Euler was a notable adherent of the aether-wave theory of light,
as opposed to Newton's corpuscular version.

1736   *Mechanica*

1748   *Introcution in analysin infinitorum*

1765   *Elements of Algebra*

1755   *Institutiones calculi differentialis*

1768   *Institutionum calculi integralis*

Pierre-Simon marquis de Laplace (1749–1827) was a French
mathematician, statistician, and astronomer noted for his
development of probability. Laplace investigated the ideas
that the density of the aether was proportional to the radial
distance from the center of a body and that the force of gravity is
generated by the impulse of such an aether medium.

1799   *Celestial Mechanics*

1809   *The System of the World* (2 volumes)

Thomas Young (1773–1829) was an English polymath and
physician who made contributions to the fields of vision, light,
solid mechanics, energy, physiology, language, musical harmony,
and Egyptology. Young's wave theory of light consisted of
longitudinal vibrations (similar to sound waves) in a luminiferous
aether. A gas, of course, readily conducts such waves.

1807   *A Course of Lectures on Natural
        Philosophy and the Mechanical Arts*

1855   *Miscellaneous Works of the Late Thomas
        Young* (posthumously)

Augustin-Jean Fresnel (1788–1827) was a French engineer and physicist who helped establish wave optics. He introduced the transverse wave theory of light, which could account for all the known phenomena of optics; consequently, the aether became solid-like and rigid, yet allowed the free passage of heavenly bodies. The aether flowed through the interstices of material bodies, even on the smallest scale.

1819   *Memoir on the Diffraction of Light*

1819   *The Wave Theory of Light*

Nikola Tesla (1856–1943) was a Serbian-American inventor, electrical engineer, physicist best known for his invention of the alternating current (AC) electricity supply system. Tesla wrote in *My Inventions: The Autobiography of Nikola Tesla*:

There manifests itself in the fully developed being, Man, a desire mysterious, inscrutable and irresistible: to imitate nature, to create, to work himself the wonders he perceives. Long ago he recognized that all perceptible matter comes from a primary substance, or tenuity beyond conception, filling all space, the Akasha or luminiferous ether, which is acted upon by the life-giving Prana or creative force, calling into existence, in never ending cycles all things and phenomena. The primary substance, thrown into infinitesimal whirls of prodigious velocity, becomes gross matter; the force subsiding, the motion ceases and matter disappears, reverting to the primary substance. Ere many generations pass, our machinery will be driven by a power obtainable at any point in the universe. This idea is not novel. We find it in the delightful myth of Antheus, who derives power from the earth; we find it among the subtle speculations of one of your splendid mathematicians. Throughout space there is energy. Is this energy static or kinetic? If static our hopes are in vain; if kinetic—and this we know it is, for certain—then it is a mere question of time when men will succeed in attaching their machinery to the very wheelwork of nature.

1888	*A New System of Alternate Current Motors and Transformers*
1891	*Phenomena of Alternating Currents of Very High Frequency*
1893	*On Light and Other High Frequency Phenomena*
1904	*The Transmission of Electrical Energy Without Wires*
1915	*How Cosmic Forces Shape Our Destinies*
1919	*My Inventions*
1935	*The New Art of Projecting Concentrated Non-Dispersive Energy through Natural Media*
1935	*A Machine to End War*

Peter Higgs (1929) is a British theoretical physicist and Nobel Prize laureate for his work on the mass of subatomic particles. The Higgs boson is a key particle in the Standard Model of particle physics. The theory predicts the presence of the Higgs boson as a necessary ingredient for imparting mass to particles. The Higgs field has brought back the notion of an ether and earned the Nobel Prize.

Frank Wilczek, a Nobel Prize-winning physicist at MIT, writes in his 2008 book, *The Lightness of Being: Mass, Ether and the Unification of Forces*:

No presently known form of matter has the right properties to play the role of the ether. So, we don't really know what this new material ether is. We know its name: the Higgs condensate [or Higgs field], after Peter Higgs, a physicist who pioneered some of these ideas. The simplest possibility is that it's made from one new particle, the so-called Higgs particle. But the ether could be a mixture of several materials. There are good reasons to suspect that a whole new world of particles is ripe for discovery, and that several of them chip in to the cosmic superconductor, a.k.a. the Higgs condensate.

Wilczek argues from many lines of evidence that there is in fact an ether that undergirds space, which he calls alternately the *Ether*, the *Grid*, or the *Cosmic Superconductor*. The recent evidence regarding the Higgs boson lends support to Einstein's *New Ether* concept and, more generally, to the idea that there is a ground of being that undergirds our reality.

1964   *Broken Symmetries, Massless Particles and Gauge Fields*

1966   *Spontaneous Symmetry Breakdown Without Massless Bosons*

1979   *Dynamical Symmetries in a Spherical Geometry*

Ervin Laszlo (1932) is a Hungarian philosopher of science, systems theories, and integral theories, and an advocate of quantum consciousness. In his book, *Science and the Akashic Field—An Integral Theory of Everything,* Ervin Laszlo reveals the nature and workings of the primal ether of akasha, or what he calls the *A-field Theory*. He defines akasha as a Sanskrit word meaning "ether": all-pervasive space. Originally signifying "radiation" or "brilliance," akasha in Indian philosophy was considered the first and most fundamental of the five elements: akasha, fire, air, water, and earth. Akasha embraces the properties of all five elements; it is the womb from which everything we perceive with our senses has emerged and into which everything will ultimately re-descend. The *Akashic*

Record is the enduring memory of all that happens, and has ever happened, in space and time.

Laszlo highlights the *Akashic Field Theory's* central idea: the revolutionary discovery that at the roots of reality, there is an interconnecting, information-conserving, and information-conveying cosmic field. The A-field works on the principles of quantum vacuums or zero-point energy fields that fill all of cosmic space, where nothing disappears without a trace, and where all things that exist are, and remain, intrinsically and intimately interconnected. The effects of the Akashic Field are not limited to the physical world; the A-field informs all things—the entire web of life. It also informs our consciousness. Evidence of the A-field is arising in the fields of quantum physics, cosmology, biological sciences, and consciousness research.

The A-field conveys the most direct, intense, and therefore evident information between things that are similar to one another, that are isomorphic or have the same form. A-field information is carried by superposed vacuum wave-interference patterns that are equivalent to holograms. We know that in a hologram, every element meshes with isomorphic elements—with those that are like itself. This meshing is called "conjugation." A holographic pattern is conjugate with similar patterns in any assortment of patterns, however vast. This is similar to resonance. Tuning forks and strings on musical instruments resonate with other forks and strings that are tuned to the same frequency, or to octaves that are higher or lower, but not to different frequencies. Information conveyed through the A-field subtly tunes all things to all other things and accounts for the coherence we find in the cosmos, as well as in living nature.

Through torsion waves in the vacuum, the A-field links things and events in the universe at staggering speeds: a billion times the velocity of light. The interference patterns of torsion waves create cosmic-scale holograms—the holograms of stars and entire stellar systems. They extend throughout our universe and correlate its galaxies and other macrostructures. In the domains of life, the individual holograms of the molecules and cells of an organism conjugate with the encompassing hologram of the whole organism, producing nearly instantaneous coherence within the organism.

An informed universe is rooted in the rediscovery of the ancient tradition of the Akashic Field as the vacuum-based holofield. The universe is a highly integrated, coherent system, much like a living organism. Its critical feature is information that is generated, conserved, and conveyed by and among all its parts. Space is the origin and memory of all things that exist and have ever existed. This cosmic information field, the Akashic Field, connects organisms and minds in the biosphere, and particles, stars, and galaxies throughout the cosmos.

2004　*Science and the Akashic Field: An Integral Theory of Everything*

2008　*Quantum Shift in the Global Brain: How the New Scientific Reality Can Change Us and Our World*

2013　*Dawn of the Akashic Age New Consciousness, Quantum Resonance, and the Future of the World*

Helena Blavatsky
on the Ethers

"The primordial Seven, the first seven breaths of the Dragon of Wisdom, produce in their turn from the holy circumgyrating breaths— the fiery whirlwind."

H. P. Blavatsky, *The Secret Doctrine*

H. P. Blavatsky, the notable theosophist of the late 1800s, was enigmatic because she had access to wisdom from the Near and Far East that others seemed to lack. Her two primary books, *Isis Unveiled* and *The Secret Doctrine*, are still marvels of scholarship, even with our modern access to the internet. Blavatsky helped found the Theosophical Society in America as a turning point in East-West esoteric development. Her understanding of comparative religions, mythologies, and mystery teachings is still unparalleled in our day. It was through her efforts that many of the New Age movements have arisen. They have used her insights and groundbreaking efforts to open the field of comparative spiritual science.

Blavatsky is relevant in a review of the ethers because she was an early commentator on the subject from a theosophical, rather than scientific, point of view. Her descriptions of the aethers, tattvas, and fohat can only be matched by the scientific theories of aethers found in the descriptions in the section above (and also in the appendix of this book under New Theories of the Aethers).

The newest theories, as described by Einstein, Tesla, and Newton, describe ether as intangible forces that border on the divine. According to Eastern teachings found in the Hindu Vedanta, creation is attributed to an entity called the Aether. Blavatsky calls this invisible being who works through the forces of the cosmos *Fohat*. She doesn't tell the reader how she chose this name, but she is describing what some term the "Solar Logos." Blavatsky writes that the aether leads to the beingness of the cosmos, and thus to a hierarchy of invisible beings who have created our known universe from a few basic substances interwoven with great wisdom, purpose, and love.

Let's examine some of Blavatsky's remarks from her work, *The Secret Doctrine* concerning the primacy of these forces and beings who have brought all creation into being and sustains it to this very moment. All quotes in this section are taken from H. P. Blavatsky's principle work, *The Secret Doctrine*.

> Occult Science recognizes Seven Cosmical Elements—four entirely physical, and the fifth (Ether) semi-material, as it will become visible in the air towards the end of our Fourth Round, to reign supreme over the others during the whole of the Fifth. The remaining two are as yet absolutely beyond the range of human perception. These latter will, however, appear as presentments during the 6th and 7th Races of this Round, and will become known in the 6th and 7th Rounds respectively. These seven elements with their numberless sub-elements far more numerous than those known to science are simply conditional modifications and aspects of the ONE and only Element. This latter is not Ether, not even Akasa but the Source of these.

This is the only time that Blavatsky addresses this mystery. These remarks could take volumes to explain, because the implications are tantamount to saying that the seven cosmical elements (ethers) hold the key to spiritual development. The sixth and seventh are beyond human perception, though in the near future (sixth and seventh races), we will be able to perceive them.

Rudolf Steiner refers to the sixth and seventh ethers as the "unfallen ethers" that will become accessible in the future and do indeed relate to future conditions of human spiritual development. The sixth and seventh ethers are often ignored as the ether scientists focus on are the four or five ethers they wish to study that are cognizable currently in evolution. The fifth ether, Akasa (also known as Akasha), now "reigns supreme" over the other ethers. Therefore, Steiner indicates, the Akasa ether is the ether we should be focusing on at this time in evolution.

The new *Akashic Field Theory* of Ervin Laszlo has opened the door for an understanding of this ether in our time. In his book, *Science and the Akashic Field, An Integral Theory of Everything*, he demonstrates an interconnecting cosmic field at the roots of reality that conserves and conveys information. It is also called the *Zero-Point Field* that underlies space itself. This type of scientific work is moving in the right direction to reveal the ethers in a scientific manner.

Blavatsky's description of the Divine as one element (akasha) is generally pantheistic. This revelation of the divine is profound and without comparison, as she writes below in *The Secret Doctrine*.

> Metaphysically and esoterically there is but ONE Element in nature, and at the root of it is the Deity; and the so-called seven elements, of which five have already manifested and asserted their existence, are the garment, the veil, of that deity; direct from the essence whereof comes Man whether physically, psychically, mentally or spiritually considered. Four elements only are generally spoken of in later antiquity, five admitted only in philosophy. For the body of ether is not fully manifested yet, and its noumenon is still "the Omnipotent Father—Ether, the synthesis of the rest."

The Omnipotent Father, Ether, is the source and end of the manifest world, plus the future of the manifest world to come. Ether, then, is the alpha and the omega, the beginning and the end, or what we might call eternity. This description makes

Ether (the one element) the singular divine being, quickly going
from *forces* to *beings* to *timelessness* to *humanity's evolution* to
the *mysteries of the Father God*, to a *perfect synthesis of ONE.*
What Blavatsky describes is the entire path of the "prodigal son."
Humanity, over time, is connected to the evolution of the ethers
like the spiritual student re-enacts the evolution of the prodigal
son. This is most significant and a worthy reason to study the
ethers and unveil their many mysteries.

> The hierarchies of those potencies or Forces have been classified
> on a graduated scale of seven from the ponderable to the impon-
> derable. They are Septenary,—not as an artificial aid to facilitate
> their comprehension—but in their real Cosmic gradation, from
> their chemical (or physical) to their purely spiritual composition.

This aspect of the *one*, to become the *seven*, is the key to
understanding our solar system and its reflection in the human
body. Six planets sing together, with the sun in the middle: the
one who contains the *seven*. This organizing force of the *one* ether
produces the manifold associations of creation that resonate
with this symphony. The human organs, chakras, bodily systems,
chambers of the heart and head, and the many other sevenfold
aspects of the human being are maintained by these forces, who
are, in fact, beings.

> The four-fold Jupiter, as the four-faced Brahma—the aerial,
> the fulgurant, the terrestrial, and the marine god—the lord and
> master of the four elements, may stand as a representative for
> the great Cosmic gods of every nation. While passing power over
> the fire to Vulcan, over the sea, to Neptune, and over the Earth,
> to Pluto—the Aerial Jove was all these; for AEther, from the first,
> had pre-eminence over, and was the synthesis of, all the elements.
>   Chaos (space) is called senseless by the ancients, because
> it represented and contained in itself all the Elements in their
> rudimentary, undifferentiated State. They made of Ether, the fifth
> element, the synthesis of the other four.
>   Akasa—of which Ether is the grossest form—the fifth univer-
> sal Cosmic Principle (from which proceeds human Manas-Spirit

Self) is, cosmically, a radiant, cool, diathermanous plastic matter, creative in its physical nature, correlative in its grossest aspects and portions, immutable in its higher principles. In the former condition it is called the Sub-Root; and in conjunction with radiant heat, it recalls "dead worlds to life." In its higher aspect it is the Soul of the World; in its lower—the Destroyer.

All too soon Blavatsky leaves her descriptions of the *one* and the *seven* and says that the aether itself is fourfold, held together by one being with numerous faces. This is the standardly accepted approach to the ethers—four in nature, held together by the one primal ether called Akasa (Akasha-variate spelling). This Akasa is even higher than "ether" and is the source of humanity's future spiritual body, called Manas, or Spirit Self. This Akasa ether has unparalleled powers to manifest physical, soul, and spiritual aspects of the Divine in the earthly realm. Even life and death arise from the ethers, and somehow the Akasa creates the Soul of the World.

> The aether and chaos, or, in the Platonic language, mind and matter, were the two primeval and eternal principles of the universe. The former was the all-vivifying intellectual principle; the chaos, a shapeless liquid principle, without 'form or sense,' from the union of which two sprung into existence the universe, or rather the universal world, the first androgynous deity—the chaotic matter becoming its body, and ether its soul. According to the phraseology of a Fragment of Hermias, "chaos, from this union with spirit, obtaining sense, shone with pleasure, and thus was produced the Protogonos (the first-born) light." This is the universal trinity, based on the metaphysical conceptions of the ancients, who, reasoning by analogy, made of man, who is a compound of intellect and matter, the microcosm of the macrocosm, or great universe.

Christians are all familiar with chaos as the "waters of creation," but the use of ether as the original "creative force" is a bit of insight worth savoring. Ether is the "all vivifying intellectual principle" or the "soul" of creation. Then, Blavatsky jumps to the

idea of ether as the 'universal trinity' as chaos and ether give birth
to light. This aside, concerning Greek aether and creation, is most
mysterious and shows the genesis of the idea of a Divine Trinity
in Blavatsky's mind.

> From ether have come all things, and to it all will return. The
> images of all things are indelibly impressed upon it; and it is the
> store-house of the germs or of the remains of all visible forms, and
> even ideas.

The concept that information is "indelibly impressed" upon
ether and that that information remains and can be accessed
has been demonstrated with Laszlo's *Akashic Field Theory*. The
Eastern idea of the Akashic Ether being a Hall of Memory, or the
Akashic Records, is in keeping with the later ideas of Steiner, who
could access these Akashic Records in a conscious fashion and
retrieve information from the past, or even look into the future.

Tattvic Correlations with the Aethers

According to Blavatsky, we find seven forces in nature, or seven
centers of force. Everything seems to respond to that number: for
instance, the septenary scale in music, or the septenary spectrum
of color. There are several reasons why only five tattvas were
given in the Indian systems. This is owing to our having reached
only the Fifth Race and being endowed with only five senses. The
two remaining senses (and ethers) are still latent in man. The five
physical senses correspond with the five lower tattvas; the two
that are yet undeveloped can only be recognized through spiritual
science. It is easy to see that these two tattvas and the two senses
(the sixth and the seventh) correspond to the two highest human
principles (buddhi/atman, or life spirit and spirit man).

Unless we open in ourselves, by occult training, the sixth
and seventh senses, we cannot correctly comprehend their
true nature. Thus, the statement in *Nature's Finer Forces* by
Rama Prasad that, in the tattvic scale, the highest tattva of all is

akasha, followed by four, each of which becomes grosser than its predecessor, if made from the esoteric standpoint, is erroneous. Once akasha, an almost homogeneous and universal principle, is translated simply as "ether," then akasha is dwarfed and limited to our visible universe. Ether is differentiated substance; akasha, having no attributes save one—sound, of which it is the substratum—is no substance, but rather chaos, or the Great Spatial Void.

Esoterically, akasha alone is *Divine Space*, which becomes ether only on the lowest and last plane, or our visible universe and Earth. The primal correlation of akasha is its primordial manifestation, the *Logos*, or *Divine Ideation* made *Word*, and that *Word* made flesh. Sound may be considered an attribute of akasha only on the condition of anthropomorphizing the latter. It is not a characteristic of it, though it is certainly as innate in it as the idea "I am I" is innate in human thought.

Akasha contains and includes the seven centers of force. There are seven tattvas, of which akasha is the seventh—or rather, their synthesis. Akasha is universally omnipresent, which places its commencement beyond the four planes of our *Earth Chain*, the two higher tattvas being as concealed to the average mortal as the sixth and seventh senses are to the materialistic mind. Therefore, while Hindu, Sanskrit, and Puranic philosophy speaks only of five tattvas, spiritual scientists name seven, making them correspond with every septenary in nature. The tattvas stand in the same order as the seven macrocosmic and microcosmic forces. These are as follows:

1. *Adi Tattva* is the primordial universal force, issuing at the beginning of manifestation from the eternal immutable Sat, the substratum of all. It corresponds with the "Auric Envelope" (Atman) or "Brahma's Egg," surrounding every globe, and every man, animal, and thing. It is the vehicle containing potentially everything: spirit and substance, force and matter. It is the *Force* which proceeds from the *First* or *Unmanifested Logos*.

2. *Anupapadaka Tattva* is the first differentiation on the plane of being—the first being an ideal one—or that which is born by transformation from something higher than itself. It is "parentless," born without father or mother, from itself, as a transformation. It is the *Force* that proceeds from the *Second Logos*.

3. *Akasha Tattva* is the point that all the exoteric philosophies and religions start from. Akasha Tattva is the etheric force, ether. Hence the name given to Jupiter, the "highest" god, or Pater Aether; Indra, once the highest god in India; Uranus, as the etheric or heavenly expanse; Pneuma, or the Biblical Holy Ghost, rarified wind or air. It is the *Force* of the *Third Logos* and is the creative force in the manifested universe.

4. *Vayu Tattva* is the aerial plane where substance is gaseous.

5. *Taijasa Tattva* is the plane of our luminous atmosphere and light.

6. *Apas Tattva* is watery or liquid substance or force.

7. *Prithivy Tattva* is solid earthly substance, the terrestrial spirit or force, lowest of all.

All these correspond to our principles, and to the seven senses and forces in man. According to the tattva or force generated or induced in us, so will our bodies act. Those who practice meditation, those trying to learn the "science of breath," will find that it is by utilizing the five tattvas only that this science is described. The "Five Breaths," or rather the five states of the human breath, correspond in Hatha-Yoga to the terrestrial plane. They are the very reverse of the plane of spirit, or the higher macrocosmic plane, reflected as they are in the astral light, upside down. The macrocosm is divided into seven great planes of various differentiations of substance—from the spiritual, or subjective, to the fully objective or material, and from akasha down to the sin-laden atmosphere of our earth.

The *Science of the Five Breaths* has a twofold significance and application. It is accepted literally by the Hatha-Yogis, as relating to the regulation of the vital, lung breath, but by the ancient Raja-Yogis, it was understood as referring to the mental or "will" breath, which alone leads to the highest clairvoyant powers: to the function of the third eye and the acquisition of the true Raja-Yoga occult powers. The former use the five lower tattvas; the latter begin by using the three higher alone—for mental and will development—and the rest only when they have completely mastered the three; hence, they use only one out of the five (akasha tattva). The Raja-Yogi does not descend to the planes of substance beyond subtle matter, while the Hatha-Yogi develops and uses his powers only on the material plane.

The Raja-Yogi knows that the tattvas are the modifications of Svara, which is the root of all sound, the substratum of the Pythagorean *Music of the Spheres*. Svara is beyond spirit, the spirit of the spirit, or the "current of the life wave," the emanation of the *One Life*. Svara threw itself into the form of akasha, and thence successively into the forms of vayu (air), agni (fire), apas (water), and prithivi (solid matter).

The two channels of energy, Ida and Pingala, are simply the sharp and flat of Svara, the keynote and the middle key in the scale of the septenary harmony of the principles—which, when struck in a proper way, awakens the sentries on both sides, the spiritual Manas (higher thought), and the physical Kama (desire), and subdues the lower through the higher.

Seven chakras are situated in the head, and these master chakras govern and rule the seven principal plexuses in the body. Physiology shows septenary groups all over the exterior and interior of the body: the seven head orifices, the seven organs at the base of the brain, the seven plexuses (chakras), etc. The seven plexuses, or tattvic centers of action, are the centers where the seven rays of the Logos vibrate.

In *The Secret Doctrine*, it is revealed that the "Sons of Fohat" are the personified forces known as motion, sound, heat, light, cohesion, electricity, and magnetism. Every impulse or vibration of a physical object producing a certain vibration of the air—that is, causing the collision of physical particles, the sound of which can affect the ear—produces, at the same time, a corresponding flash of light, which will assume some particular color. An audible sound is but a subjective color, and a perceptible color is but an inaudible sound. Both proceed from the same potential, plastic substance, which is invisible space. Every human passion, every thought and quality, is indicated in the aura by corresponding colors and shades of color, and certain of these are sensed and felt rather than perceived. As a string vibrates and gives forth an audible note, so the nerves of the human body vibrate and thrill in correspondence with various emotions under the general impulse of the circulating vitality of prana, thus producing undulations in the psychic aura of the person that result in chromatic effects. The human nervous system may be regarded as an Aeolian harp, responding to the impact of the dynamic vital force and manifesting the subtlest shades of the individual character in color phenomena.

Blavatsky's Concept of Fohat

Blavatsky continues to elucidate the Eastern ideas concerning the original elements and ethers in *The Secret Doctrine* and leads the reader to the *Being of Fohat*. As Blavatsky writes, Fohat may be the most important being in cosmology and holds the secrets to human spiritual evolution. At first, Fohat seems to be the source that akasha, the primal ether, originated from. Fohat is at once an unmanifest force that creates all forces, the forces themselves, the effects on the mediums the force acts within, and the consciousness of both the divine and human affected by Fohat. Fohat even seems to be the image of what a human being was created to become. Fohat is our past, our present, and our future, simultaneously.

• • •

*F*ohat is cosmic electricity, primordial light, the ever-present electrical energy, the universal propelling vital force, the ceaseless destructive and formative power, the synthesis of the many forms of electrical phenomena.

• • •

It is nearly impossible to summarize what Blavatsky wrote and said about this magical force. This author dares to say that in all that he has read of Blavatsky's work, the following description of Fohat is the most beautiful and comprehensive picture of the Divine. Fohat seems to be the Father, the Son, and the Holy Ghost, along with all human spiritual evolution. Fohat is the quintessential understanding of cosmology, and essential in understanding the development of the ethers and their application. Blavatsky writes in *The Secret Doctrine*:

In the manifested Universe, there is "that" which links spirit to matter, subject to object. This something, at present unknown to Western speculation, is called by the occultists "Fohat." It is the bridge by which the Ideas existing in the Divine Thought are impressed on Cosmic substance as the laws of Nature. Fohat is thus the dynamic energy of Cosmic Ideation; or, regarded from the other side, it is the intelligent medium, the guiding power of all manifestation, the Thought Divine transmitted and made manifest through the Angel Hosts, the divine architects of the visible world.

Thus, from Spirit, or Cosmic Ideation, comes our consciousness; from Cosmic Substance the several vehicles in which that consciousness is individualized and attains to self—or reflective—consciousness. Fohat, in its various manifestations, is the mysterious link between Mind and Matter, the animating principle electrifying every atom into life.

In *Stanzas of Dyzan,* which is part of *The Secret Doctrine*, she writes:

Darkness radiates light, and light drops one solitary ray into the Mother-Deep. The ray shoots through the virgin egg causing the eternal egg to thrill, and drop the non-eternal germ, which condenses in the world-egg. Then the three fall into the four. The radiant essence becomes seven inside, seven outside. The luminous egg, which in itself is three, curdles and spreads in milk-white curds throughout the depths of Mother, the root that grows in the depths of the ocean of life. The root remains, the light remains, the curds remain, and still Oeaohaa is ONE. The root of life was in every drop of the ocean of immortality, and the ocean was radiant light, which was fire, and heat, and motion. Darkness vanished and was no more; it disappeared in its own essence, the body of fire and water, or Father and Mother.

Behold, Oh Lanoo! The radiant child of the two, the unparalleled refulgent glory: bright space son of dark space, which emerges from the depths of the great dark waters. It is Oeaohoo the Younger, he shines forth as the son; he is the blazing divine dragon of wisdom; the one is four, and four takes to itself three, and the union produces the Sapta, in whom are the seven which become the hosts and the multitudes. Behold him lifting the veil and unfurling it from east to west. He shuts out the above, and leaves the below to be seen as the great illusion. He marks the places for the shining ones, and turns the upper into a shoreless sea of fire, and the ONE manifested into the Great Waters.

The germ is that, and that is light, the white brilliant son of the dark hidden Father. Light is cold flame, and flame is fire, and fire produces heat, which yields water: the Water of Life in the Great Mother.

Father-Mother spin a web whose upper end is fastened to spirit—the light of the ONE darkness—and the lower ONE to its shadowy end, matter; and this web is the universe spun out of the TWO substances made in ONE, which is Svabhavat.

It expands when the breath of fire is upon it; it contracts when the breath of the Mother touches it. Then the sons dissociate and scatter, to return into the Mother's bosom at the end of the great day, and re-become ONE with her; when it is cooling it becomes radiant, and the Sons expand and contract through their own selves and hearts; they embrace infinitude.

The Svabhavat sends Fohat to harden the atoms. Each is a part of the web. Reflecting the "Self-existent Lord" like a mirror, each becomes in turn a world.

Listen, ye Sons of Earth, to your instructors—the Sons of Fire. Learn, there is neither first nor last, for all in one: number issued from no number.

Learn what we who descend from the primordial Seven, we who are born from the primordial flame, have learnt from our Fathers.

From the effulgency of light—the ray of the ever-darkness—sprung in space the re-awakened energies. And these are the essences, the flames, the elements, the builders, the numbers, the form, the formless, and the forces of Divine Man—the sum total. And from the Divine Man emanated the forms, the sparks, the sacred animals, and the messengers of the sacred Fathers within the Holy Four.

This was the army of the voice—the Divine Mother of the Seven.

The primordial Seven, the first seven breaths of the Dragon of Wisdom, produce in their turn from the holy circumgyrating breaths the fiery whirlwind.

They make of him the messenger of their will. The Dzyu becomes Fohat, the swift Son of the Divine Sons whose sons are the Lipika, runs circular errands. Fohat is the steed and the thought is the rider. He passes like lightning through the fiery clouds.

The celestial Ocean, the Ether is the Breath of the Father, the life-giving principle, the Mother, the Holy Spirit, for these are not separated, and their union is Life. It is the breath of the Father (or Spirit) and the breath (or heat) of the Mother (matter).

The *Stanzas of Dzyan* are from the most ancient Eastern texts that produced the contents of the mystery schools as spiritual science. These mystery images were the science of their day and accurately explained the forces of nature and their genesis to the clairvoyant sages of the past. These images are hardly imaginable to us, let alone the secret mysteries behind them. We have in this one section many names for Fohat: Dzyu, Svabhavat, Self-existent Lord, the Divine Son, the Breath of the Father, the Breath of the

Father, the Mother, the Celestial Ocean, the Holy Spirit, Oeaohaa the Younger, the Blazing Divine Dragon of Wisdom, the Radiant Child of the Two, the Unparalleled Refulgent Glory, and Bright Space Son of Dark Space, who emerges from the depths of the great dark waters. These appellations suggest the highest position for Fohat in the cosmology of the East. Surely, Fohat can be seen as the third person of the Trinity of Father, Mother, Child. Fohat is suggestive of the forces, and being of the Solar Logos, the second person in the Divine Trinity of Christians. As Blavatsky continues to explain:

> All the Kabbalists and Occultists, Eastern and Western, recognize the identity of "Father-Mother" with primordial AEther or Akasa, (Astral Light); and its homogeneity before the evolution of the "Son," cosmically Fohat, for it is Cosmic Electricity. Fohat hardens and scatters the seven brothers; which means that the primordial Electric Entity—for the Eastern Occultists insist that Electricity is an Entity—electrifies into life, and separates primordial stuff or pre-genetic matter into atoms, themselves the source of all life and consciousness. There exists an universal agent unique of all forms and of life, that is called Od, Ob, and Aour, active and passive, positive and negative, like day and night: it is the first light in Creation:—the first Light of the primordial Elohim—the Adam, "male and female"—Electricity and Life. The expanding and contracting of the Web—the world stuff of atoms—expresses here the pulsatory movement; for it is the regular contraction and expansion of the infinite and shoreless Ocean of that which we may call the noumenon of matter emanated by Svabhavat, which causes the universal vibration of atoms. It is through Fohat that the ideas of the Universal Mind are impressed upon matter. Some faint idea of the nature of Fohat may be gathered from the appellation "Cosmic Electricity" sometimes applied to it; but to the commonly known properties of electricity must, in this case, be added others, including intelligence.

Here we have the explicit naming of Fohat as the "Son" and as "Cosmic Electricity" as an "entity." This cosmic electricity, or "primordial Electric Entity" brings life through electricity and separates atoms that create life and consciousness. Here again, forces and beings are interwoven as naturally as water flowing downhill. The male and female of "Electricity and Life" weave the web of life through expansion (warmth and light ether) and contraction (sound and life ether), creating the pulsations and vibrations of atoms. This living world of forces and beings becomes personal through the imagery and language of the mysteries. Electricity even takes on intelligence and other characteristics not known to modern science.

Fohat, being one of the most, if not the most important character in esoteric Cosmogony is one thing in the yet un-manifested Universe and another in the phenomenal and Cosmic World. In the latter, he is that occult, electric, vital power, which, under the will of the Creative Logos, unites and brings together all forms, giving them the first impulse which becomes in time law. But in the un-manifested Universe, Fohat is that potential creative power in virtue of whose action the noumenon of all future phenomena divides, to reunite in a mystic supersensible act, and emit the creative ray. When the "Divine Son" breaks forth, then Fohat becomes the propelling force, the active Power which causes the ONE to become TWO and THREE—on the Cosmic plane of manifestation. The Triple One differentiates into the many, and then Fohat is transformed into that force which brings together the elemental atoms and makes them aggregate and combine.

From the Unknown ONE, the Infinite totality, the manifested ONE, Deity, emanates; and this is the Universal Mind, which, separated from its Fountain-Source, is the Demiurgos or the creative Logos of the Western Kabbalists, and the four-faced Brahma of the Hindu religion. In its totality, viewed from the standpoint of manifested Divine Thought in the esoteric doctrine, it represents the Hosts of the higher creative Dhyan Chohans (angelic hosts). Simultaneously with the evolution of the Universal Mind, the concealed Wisdom of Adi-Buddha—the One Supreme and eternal—manifests itself as Avalokiteshwara, which is the Osiris of the Egyptians, the Ahura-Mazda of the Zoroastrians, the Heavenly Man of the Hermetic philosopher, the Logos of the Platonists, and the Atman of the Vedantins.

Again, beautiful names for the Divine are given by Blavatsky as: Unknown ONE, Infinite Totality, Universal Mind, Demiurgos, Creative Logos, and even the Unmanifest Universe. Fohat is manifest and unmanifest, which makes him/her/it the most pervasive Deity described in Eastern cosmologies. When Fohat is a manifest Deity, the entire angelic hosts come from him as Divine Thought. The entire evolution of Universal Mind comes forth from Fohat. Fohat has many names in different beliefs, and the solar hero traditions are a picture of Fohat manifesting as Osiris, Ahura-Mazda, the Heavenly Man, the Logos, and the Atman of Hindu traditions.

Ultimately, the picture that Blavatsky has painted of this being is equivalent to the Christian view of Christ as the second person in the Trinity of Father, Son, and Holy Ghost. Christ is the universal plan that was created in the unmanifest but now unfolds in the manifest universe. The pre-Christian solar-hero gods are, similarly, a clairvoyant description of Christ descending from the Sun as *Son of God* to become the redemption, salvation, and future model of every human's spiritual self as the *Son of Man*. It seems that even though Blavatsky was "blocked" from a current "etheric clairvoyance" of the etheric world, she did have a very clear understanding of the descent of the logos.

Blavatsky continues to describe Fohat in celestial language that is given to no other deity, god, or element in creation. She says that Fohat sets the laws of macrocosmic and microcosmic evolution in motion, in concert with the Universal Mind, to make our bodies copies of the solar system. Seven is the principle that manifests both the macrocosm and the microcosm through harmonic resonance.

- Fohat is the personified electric vital power, the transcendental binding unity of all energies and forces, on both the unmanifested and manifested planes.
- Fohat is a living force created by divine willpower.
- Fohat is a living being who is the creator, the created, and the vessel that holds both.

- Fohat is an electric, vital fluid that flows out from the sun that is invisible, but takes on material form and beingness.

- Fohat is the principle of the Animal Soul of nature and is associated with the Hindu god Vishnu—the great Sustainer.

- Fohat is called the Pervader and Manufacturer, and is a manifestation of solar energy. Fohat can take three steps (gunnas) and stride through the Seven regions (tattvas) of the universe.

- Fohat is called Divine Love and equated with the Greek creator gods Eros and Phanes as an electric power of affinity and sympathy—like Eros's (Cupid's) arrows bring uncontrollable love.

- Fohat tries to bring the pure Spirit from the ONE absolute into the souls of humans as the spiritual ego.

- Fohat is a personal god who came from the ONE source and manifests through the principle of seven.

Just as a human being is composed of seven principles and differentiated matter in the solar system existing in seven different conditions, so Fohat is ONE and Seven. On the cosmic plane, Fohat is behind all such manifestations as light, heat, sound, adhesion, levity, and gravity, and is the "spirit" of electricity, which is the life of the universe.

There is a septenary scale of manifestation, which begins at the upper rung with the "One Unknowable Causality," and ends as "Omnipresent Mind" and "Life Immanent" in every atom of matter. Fohat is called the "Builder of the Builders" or "Great Architect of the Universe," and is the force that built our septenary scale. There is intelligent law and sentient life throughout the universe, and Fohat is the Guiding Spirit of all of it.

Fohat, is said, metaphorically, to have sprung from the brain of the Father and the bosom of the Mother, and then to have metamorphosed itself into a male and a female—positive and negative—electricity. Fohat has seven sons, who are his brothers, and he/she/it is forced to be born time after time, whenever any two of his sons/brothers indulge in close contact—whether an embrace or a fight. To avoid conflict, Fohat binds together and unites those of unlike nature and separates those of similar temperaments.

There is a fountain of life in the bowels of the earth that arise to the magnetic North Pole. It is the electromagnetic current that circulates through all the arteries, and that is said to be found stored in the "navel" of the Earth. The agitation of the fohatic forces at the two cold ends (North and South Poles) of the Earth results in a multi-colored auroral radiance that contains several of the properties of akahsa. Sound is the characteristic of akasha: it generates air, the property of which is touch, and which, through friction, produces color and light. The Aurora Borealis and Aurora Australis take place at the very centers of terrestrial electric and magnetic forces. These two poles are said to be the store-houses, the receptacles, and the liberators of cosmic and terrestrial vitality (electricity) at the same time. Had it not been for these two natural "safety-valves," the earth would have been rent to pieces long ago.

The *First-Born* are the life, the heart, and pulse of the universe; the *Second-Born* are its mind or consciousness. Creation commences with the re-awakening of the universal mind concurrently with, and parallel to, the primary emergence of cosmic substance. Then, absolute wisdom mirrors itself in its ideation, which results in cosmic energy called Fohat. Thrilling through the bosom of inert substance, Fohat impels it to activity, and guides its primary differentiations on all the seven planes of cosmic consciousness.

Fohat is the key that reveals symbols and allegories in the mythology of every nation. Fohat, shown in her/his/its true character, proves how deeply versed all those nations were in the science of nature, and natural philosophy. In India, Fohat is the scientific aspect of both Vishnu and Indra. In Egypt, Fohat was known as Toum, who is spoken of as the protean god who generates other gods and gives himself the form he likes, as the "master of life giving his vigor to the gods." He is the overseer of the gods, and he "creates spirits and gives them shape and life." He is the "North Wind and the Spirit of the West" and the "Setting Sun of Life," or the "Vital Electric Force" that leaves the body at death. Fohat is the "Fiery Waters of Space" and the "Son of Ether" in its highest aspect: akasha, the Mother-Father of the Primitive Seven.

Theosophical View of Fohat

In theosophy, Fohat is cosmic life or vitality: bipolar cosmic vital electricity, equivalent to the light of the Logos, Eros, the fiery whirlwind. As the bridge between spirit and matter, Fohat is the "collective intelligent forces" through which cosmic ideation impresses itself upon substance, thus forming the various worlds of manifestation. In the manifested universe, it is that occult, electric, vital power which, under the will of the Creative Logos, unites and brings together all forms giving them the "first impulse," which, in time, becomes law. Fohat becomes the propelling force, the active power which causes the one to become two and three. Then, Fohat is transformed into that force which brings together the elemental atoms and makes them aggregate and combine.

Fohat is the primordial force or vitality in the cosmos. It is that which links spirit and matter in the first stages of differentiation. In the manifested stages of the universe, Fohat is the force that causes the differentiation from the one to the many, while at the same time, it is the power that unites and combines the various units and atoms of the cosmos. Fohat can be described as "cosmic vitality," or the *prana* of the universe. It has been considered the universal energy that includes all the forces of nature. It is the energizing force of the universe. Force is often seen as blind energy, but Fohat is not blind; it is a directed and intelligent power. In other words, it is power imbued with purpose.

The manifested universe is the result of the interaction of Cosmic Ideation with Cosmic Substance, and Fohat originates from that interaction. Fohat represents or corresponds in nature to the force which generates tension, and yet is still the resultant tension itself.

Fohat is power in a dynamic form and is the creative purpose flowing through the manifested universe, but it can, in contrast to "creativity," manifest as a fierce destructive force. Thus, it can be regarded as a duality, Fohat being both the active "male and female" potency. *Shakti* (female) is the capacity to take up an impression, inherent in wax and in other plastic and pliant materials, while Fohat is the potency that makes the impression, the seal or stamp imprinting a replica of its own characteristics upon the receptive wax. Both Fohat and Shakti represent differentiations of the larger universal Fohat as the One Force.

It is possible to picture Fohat on a wide scale as a dynamic pulsating energy, not unlike electricity, but not identified with it. Unlike electricity, Fohat has rather been seen as some vast and cosmic consciousness operating at every "level" of the cosmos and linking each plane to the other; spirit to mind and mind to matter. In such a sense, Fohat might be described as the "law-giver" of the universe.

It is necessary to outline, as clearly as possible, a picture of how Fohat manifests and works, keeping in mind the fact that it is not that which manifests, but the invisible energy behind that manifested form. In the mineral kingdom Fohat emerges as such phenomena as electricity although the actual work done by electricity is by the movement of electrons. It also appears on the material level as prana (breath) where it organizes matter as living material. In the sentient animal form Fohat is very complex, for superimposed on Shakti and Fohat is the creative reproductive power of *kundalini*, the serpent of wisdom.

We might consider the situation when matter existed in its most basic form. Some purposeful force is needed to stir this basic matter to build more complex forms and combinations— that force is Fohat; that force continues to be present as more and more complex forms emerge, although Fohat, of necessity, changes its character to suit the needs of each level of being. It is through Fohat that the Ideas of the Universal Mind are impressed upon matter.

Let us work this out in the macrocosm and microcosm: Fohat, prana, electricity, magnetic fluid, are all terms used for this one vitalizing life. The microcosm is animated and vitalized by prana, and its actions controlled by the indwelling thinker. The macrocosm is animated and vitalized by Fohat; its actions are controlled by the informing intelligence we call the Solar Logos (spirit of the Sun). Fohat is divine thought or energy (Shakti) as manifested on any plane of the cosmos. It is the interplay between spirit and matter. Blavatsky gives us a scheme of Fohat's manifestation. The seven differentiations of Fohat are:

1. The Plane of divine life:	Adi	Sea of fire
2. The Plane of monadic life:	Anupadaka	Akasha
3. The Plane of spirit:	Atma	Aether
4. The Plane of the intuition:	Buddhi	Air
5. The Plane of mind:	Mental	Fire
6. The Plane of desire:	Astral	Astral Light
7. The Plane of density:	Physical	Ether

Alice A. Bailey on Fohat

Alice Bailey, a student of Blavatsky, states in *A Treatise on Cosmic Fire* that Fohat is agni, the threefold energy (emanating from the logoic ego) which produces the solar system, the physical vehicle of the Logos, and animates the atoms of substance. Fohat is the basis of the evolutionary process, or the cause of the psychic unfoldment of the Logos, and he is the vitality that ultimately brings about a divine synthesis in which the form approximates subjective demand and, after being consciously directed and manipulated, is finally discarded.

Fohat is cosmic electricity, primordial light, the ever-present electrical energy, the universal propelling vital force, the ceaseless destructive and formative power, and the synthesis of the many forms of electrical phenomena.

Akasha, in manifestation, expresses itself as Fohat, or divine energy, and Fohat, on the different planes, is known as aether, air, fire, water, electricity, ether, prana, and similar terms. It is the sum-total of that which is active, animated, or vitalized, and of all that concerns itself with the adaptation of the form to the needs of the inner flame of life.

Agni, the Lord of Fire, rules over all the fire elementals and devas on the three planes of human evolution: the physical, the astral, and the mental. He rules over them not only on this planet, called Earth, but on the three planes and in all parts of the system. He is one of the seven brothers who each embody one of the seven principles, or who are, in themselves, the seven centers in the body of the cosmic Lord of Fire. He is that active, fiery intelligence who is the basis of the internal fires of the solar system. In their totality, these seven Lords form the essence of the cosmic Lord, called Fohat in the occult books.

The major seven planes of our solar system being but the seven sub-planes of the cosmic physical plane, we can consequently see the reason for the emphasis laid by Blavatsky upon the fact that matter and ether are synonymous terms and that ether is found in some form or other on all the planes, and is but a gradation of cosmic atomic matter called mulaprakriti or primordial pregenetic substance when undifferentiated. When differentiated by Fohat (or the energizing Life, the third Logos or Brahma), it is termed prakriti, or matter.

This is a great mystery and is allied to the mystery of electricity (or of fohatic life) that Blavatsky refers to. The Messengers, the Builders, the Devas, are flaming fire, radiant electric matter, and only in time and space, only during manifestation, and only through the cycles of objectivity is such an entity as man possible, or can a Heavenly Man come into existence. It is a force, working through a dual manifestation of differentiated force, through the energy of matter, the coherency of forms, through force centers, and force points. It is Fohat in triple demonstration, of which the final or third is unknown and inconceivable.

Only the very strong, refined physical body; the controlled, stable, and equalized emotional body; and the properly striated mental body can enter the subtler planes and literally work with Fohat to develop a path of spiritual development. In referring to this path, those who find their way on to this path work with Fohat, or with the essential energy of our solar system, which differentiates into seven major types of energy.

The energies which utilize the akasha (ether) in the universe are divided into three main divisions, according to the ageless wisdom. Fohat is analogous to what Christians regard as the spirit. It is the will-to-exist, the determining life principle of God, who, we can predicate, is the sum of all forms, and of all states of consciousness; it is divine purpose, actively functioning— the breath of life. It is the connecting, electrical, spiritual chord between the intelligence in the one universal life and its reflections as it breathes outwards.

Hindu Tattvas

"The universe came out of tattva or the tattvas; it goes on by the instrumentality of the tattvas; it disappears in the tattvas; by the tattvas is known the nature of the universe. Unmanifested, formless, one giver of light is the great Power; from that appeared the soniferous ether (akasa); from that had birth the tangiferous ether. From the tangiferous ether, the luminiferous ether, and from this the gustiferous ether; from thence was the birth of the odiferous ether. These are the five ethers and they have five-fold extension. Of these the universe came out; by these it goes on; into these it disappears; even among these it shows itself again. The body is made of the five tattvas; the five tattvas, O Fair One, exist therein in the subtle form; they are known by the learned who devote themselves to the tattvas."

The Science of Breath and the Philosophy of the Tattvas, Kapila

We have looked at the tattvas, ethers, and Fohat from the perspective of H. P. Blavatsky and her Eastern approach to the concepts. Now we will examine the work that arose from Rama Prasad, a fellow Theosophist of Blavatsky's, who attempted to elucidate what Blavatsky brought forward in *Isis Unveiled* and *The Secret Doctrine* concerning the ethers. His book, *Nature's Finer Forces*, was the Bible of the ethers for Theosophists who wanted more information on these important ideas. But not all Theosophists were convinced that Prasad's commentary on the great Sankhya teacher Kapila's work entitled *The Sivagama, The Science of Breath and the Philosophy of the Tattvas* was accurate in all its details.

Blavatsky herself said the following about Prasad and his book. "The *Saivagama (Nature's Finer Forces)* in its details is purely Tantric, and nothing but harm can result from any practical following of its precepts. I would most strongly dissuade a member of the Esoteric Section from attempting any of these Hatha-Yoga practices, for he will either ruin himself entirely, or throw himself so far back that it will be almost impossible to regain the lost ground in this incarnation. The translation referred to has been considerably expurgated, and even now is hardly fit for publication. It recommends Black Magic of the worst kind, and is the very antipodes of spiritual Raja-Yoga. Beware, I say."

One can only wonder what would make Blavatsky so adamant about this book, and yet she still allowed Prasad to remain in the Theosophical Society and teach in India. Prasad had a substantial following then, and many Theosophists still find his book quite helpful. Perhaps Blavatsky herself was reacting to her own limited understanding of this topic. Blavatsky may have accurately described the Christ's descent in mythologies and religious traditions, but she did not understand Christianity and left that domain to the English Theosophists Anna Bonus Kingsford and Edward Maitland, who had delineated a beautiful theology of Christ in their book, *The Perfect Way*. Blavatsky was clear that she did not bring the message of Christianity in her teachings, which focused primarily on Eastern traditions. Therefore, a complete understanding of the manifestation of the ethers would include the role of Christ's appearance in the etheric realm, and Blavatsky does not include that in her view.

It is true that the use of the tattvas is magic; therefore, the misuse of them would constitute "black magic." Rudolf Steiner has indicated that breath exercises from the East are not appropriate for Westerners and can lead their spiritual development in the wrong direction. Therefore, all references to breathing exercises have been left out of this free-rendering of the content of Prasad's book. Steiner teaches that only natural breathing is used in current spiritual exercises and meditation. The aspirant should "free" the breath and not "control" it.

The translation of *The Science of Breath and the Philosophy of the Tattvas* that Prasad made was from the *Sivagama* of Kapila, the founder of the Sankhya Tattvic School of Philosophy. Kapila was considered an incarnation of the Hindu god Vishnu. The *Sivagama* was purportedly spoken by Shiva directly to Kapila and is considered the sacred teaching of the creator Brahma.

In Kapila's teachings, we have the Hindu Trinity of Brahma, Shiva, and Vishnu. These teachings are a description of the creation story and the spiritual science of the ancients, not exclusive to Hinduism and the Vedas. The origin of these teachings is unknown, but some scholars believe they are the remnants of the teachings of Tonpa Shenrab Miwoche, who is the principal originator of the most ancient Tibetan teachings on the tantras called Dzogchen, or the "highest path." Shenrab was the first Buddha and was the teacher of Sakyamuni (Gautama) Buddha, who we generally accept as the founder of Buddhism.

Blavatsky's tattvic philosophy is derived from the *Book of Dzyan*, a purportedly Tibetan text written in a secret language called Senzar from a collection of books entitled, *The Books of Kiu-Te* (rGyud-sde in Tibetan). These texts have yet to be found in the Tibetan cannon of sacred literature. Some theorize that

Blavatsky confabulated the entire thing and simply rewrote *The Hymn of Creation* from the *Rig Veda*. Close examination shows that the *Stanza of Dzyan* only slightly resembles this much later philosophical writing. The *Stanzas of Dzyan* appear to be extremely ancient and are either real or a tremendously good forgery fraught with wisdom.

Dzyu is described by Blavatsky as "the one real (magical) knowledge, or Occult Wisdom, which, dealing with eternal truths and primal causes, becomes almost omnipotence when applied in the right direction. Dzyu is the expression of the collective Wisdom of the Dhyani-Buddhas." Remember that Dzyu becomes Fohat, that most mysterious of all of Blavatsky's cosmological beings. The Vedic equivalent of Fohat has not been found, and the detailed descriptions of this being even span into the far future. Blavatsky goes far beyond the standard tantric view of cosmology. Even if Blavatsky utilized existing sources that are known, she added amazingly detailed descriptions that appear nowhere else. The most ancient tantric verses describing creation were from Aryadeva's four verses of commentary on Nagarjuna's work, *Pancakrama*. The reader can see that these verses could not have been the source of Blavatsky's cosmogony.

> The entire world is dependent on a cause, for something independent can never arise. The world's cause is luminosity; luminosity is the universal void. From luminosity arises the great void, and from that is the arising of means. From that, wisdom is arisen. From that is the arising of air. From air is the arising of fire, and from fire is the arising of water; and from water, earth is born. This is the arising of living beings. The earth element dissolves in water. Water dissolves in fire, and fire in air. Air dissolves in mind. Mind will dissolve in the mental derivatives, and the mental derivatives in ignorance. This, too, will go to luminosity. That is the cessation of the triple world.

This passage surely was not the source of *The Stanzas of Dzyan* any more than the *Rig Veda's* "*Hymn of Creation*" was.

Blavatsky had some source of spiritual science that was derived from an ancient source that had great detail about matters of the highest order. Fohat, as a force or being, along with Dzyu, cannot be found or compared to other Eastern philosophies. Rama Prasad does not discover either of these beings in his translation of one of the most complete Sivagama Tantras.

Rama Prasad's View of the Ethers (Tattvas)

The following is a condensed extract from the book *Nature's Finer Forces* by Rama Prasad. Prasad set a new standard in the Theosophical Society of H. P. Blavatsky by releasing a translation of a principal tantric text in the tattvas (ethers). Blavatsky and others were not pleased with Prasad's translation, nor his commentary on the text. Much controversy arose from this publication, and you are advised to keep an open mind whenever considering "theories" about the ethers. Make sure not to carve anything into stone unless it directly agrees with your own perception and experience.

For Prasad, the tattvas are the five modifications of the Great Breath. Acting upon Prakriti, this Great Breath throws it into five states, having distinct vibratory motions, and performing different functions. The first outcome of the evolutionary state is the akasa tattva. After this comes, in order, the vayu, the taijas, the apas, and the prithivi. The word akasa is generally translated into English as the word "ether." We might call akasa the sonoriferous (sound) ether, vayu the tangiferous (touch) ether, apas the gustiferous (taste) ether, and prithivi the odoriferous (smell) ether. Just as the luminiferous ether—an element of refined mater without which the phenomena of light find no adequate explanation—exists in the universe, so do the four remaining ethers: elements of refined matter without which it will be found that the phenomena of sound, touch, taste, and smell find no adequate explanation. It is not the vibrations of the ethers—the subtle tattvas—that cause our perceptions, but the ethereal vibrations transferred to different media, which are so many modifications of gross matter. Ethers produce vibrations similar to their own in gross media. Every succeeding tattvic state has the qualities of all the foregoing tattvic states as they evolve.

Svara

The tattvas are the modifications of Svara. "All the world is in the Svara; Svara is the spirit itself." The proper translation of the word Svara is "the current of the life-wave." It is that wavy motion that is the cause of the evolution of cosmic, undifferentiated matter into the differentiated universe. The primeval current of life-wave is, then, the same one that, in man, assumes the form of inspiratory and expiratory motion of the lungs, and this is the all-pervading source of the evolution and the involution of the universe.

> It is the Svara that has given form to the first accumulations of the divisions of the universe; the Svara causes involution and evolution; *the Svara is God Himself,* or more properly the great Power.

The Svara is the manifestation of the impression on matter of the power that in man is known to us as the power that knows itself. It is to be understood that the action of this power never ceases. It is ever at work, and evolution and involution are the very necessity of its unchangeable existence. The Svara has two different states. The one is known on the physical plane as the *sunbreath*, and the other as the *moon-breath*. The period during which this current comes back to the point from whence it started is known as the night of parabrahma.

The current of the Great Breath works into these five ethers. With the beginning of the vayu tattva, these elementary ethers are thrown into the form of spheres. This was the beginning of formation, or what may also be called solidification. This sphere is the self-conscious universe.

It will thus be seen that the whole process of creation, on whatever plane of life, is performed most naturally by the five tattvas in their double modifications: the positive and negative. There is nothing in the universe that the *Universal Tattvic Law of Breath* does not comprehend.

The akasa is the most important of all the tattvas. It must, as a matter of course, precede and follow every change of state on every plane of life. Without this there can be no manifestation or cessation of forms. It is out of akasa that every form comes, and it is in akasa that every form lives. The akasa is full of forms in their potential state. It intervenes between every two of the five tattvas. The tattvas exist in the universe on four planes. The higher of these planes differ from the lower in having a greater number of vibrations per second. The four planes are:

1. Physical
2. Mental
3. Psychic
4. Spiritual

Action of the Etheric

From the Sun, a "solar wind" constantly streams forth called the sunbreath. It is a partially electro-magnetic nitrous gas, which is very subtle and non-physical in nature. This is part of the Prana (Life Matter) of the Eastern Mysteries. The Earth's magnetic field captures this incorporeal nitre as the solar wind streams past our planet. This unmanifest substance circulates around the planet in a series of fivefold waves, each of which comprises five sub-waves. This bundle of magnetic streams has been detected entering the magnetic north pole, but there is no comprehensive theory about their nature or working. These currents are constantly rising and falling in intensity and have an unknown source of energy.

The *Tattvic Flow* starts at sunrise and proceeds from akasha, to air, to fire, to water, to earth. It takes 24 minutes for each tattva in the cycle. Thus, it takes a total of two hours for a primary flow of all five tattvas to transit the complete *Tattvic Flow* cycle. The Earth's electromagnetic field (Van Allen Belts) and ley lines are vitalized by these incoming etheric currents.

Tattvas are a mode of motion—the central impulse, which keeps matter in a certain vibratory state, or a distinct form of vibration. Every form and every motion is a manifestation of these tattvas singly or in conjunction. This is the intent of the alchemical transformation: to raise the vibrations of matter and thus bring it into the condition of harmony or quintessence.

Types of Tattvas

Akasha (space) Sonoriferous (sound) ether or akasa (thought) tattva is said to move by fits and starts, and to move in all directions. Akasa is all-pervading, and the original impulse falls back upon itself along the line of its former path. Space is a quality of the akasa tattva. The vibration of this ether is shaped like the hole of the ear. It represents the womb of the Universal Mother or Spirit. Akasa is symbolized by an oval or egg shape and is every color, black, or clear, and its flashing is luminous. It can be used as a doorway to allow an initiate to look for information within the "Akashic Records." The akasa ether contains all forms and could be called the collective memory of the universe. It contains all memories of human experience in the past, but also the future in seed form. If the akasa predominates in the soul, then happiness ensues. Misuse of this ether leads to the sin of Pride.

Vayu (fire) Tangiferous (warmth) ether or vayu (touch) tattva or agni tattva. The vibrations of this ether are described as being spherical in form, and the motion is said to be at acute angles to the wave. Locomotion is its quality, and spherical its motion. Vayu is a form of motion itself, for motion in all directions is motion in a circle, large or small. It is the main motive energy in the body and our personal power—digesting our food to produce prana, producing blood and other fluids, and sustaining the nourishment and growth of the body. Just as the heat of the Sun makes life possible on Earth, the heat of the agni tattva sustains life in the body. Though we cannot see it, we feel its touch. The main center of operation for the vayu is the chest region, which includes the principal organs. Anger is the sin of fire.

Teijas (air) Luminfierous (light) ether or taijas (sight-color) tattva. Expansion is the quality of the taijas tattva following from the shape and form of motion which is given to this ethereal vibration. The luminiferous ether is present just as much in a darkened room as in the space without. Our ordinary vision does not see the vibrations of the luminiferous ether; it only sees the vibrations of the media that the ether pervades. Gluttony is the sin of air.

Apas (water) Gustiferous (chemical) ether or apas (taste) tattva is said to resemble the half moon in shape. It is said to move downward, opposite the luminiferous ether. Therefore, this force causes contraction. The direction of this ether is the reverse of the Agni, and it is therefore easy to understand that contraction is the result of the play of this tattva. Smoothness is its quality. As the atoms of any body in contraction come near each other and assume the semi-lunar shape of the apas, they must easily glide over each other. The very shape secures easy motion for the atoms. Apas is a manifestation of the forces of both forcefulness and will, and dullness and attachment. Lust is the sin associated with apas.

Prithivi (earth) Odoriferous (life) ether or prithivi (smell) tattva is said to be quadrangular in shape, and thus is said to move in the middle. It moves neither at right angles, at acute angles, upwards, nor downwards; it moves along the line of the wave. Cohesion is the quality of the prithivi, which is the reverse of akasa. Akasa gives room for locomotion, while prithivi resists it, which is the natural result of the direction and shape of this vibration. Prithivi covers up the spaces of the akasa. It is the basic element of earth. It is an expression of dullness, unawareness, and attachment, and functions only from need and instinct. It mainly operates through our sense of smell. The foundation of the physical structure of the body—bones, skin, flesh, teeth, and marrow—originates from this physical element of earth. Greed is the sin associated with prithivi.

Nature of Prana

Every point of Prana is a perfect picture of the whole ocean; every other point is represented in every point. Every atom has, therefore, for its constituents, all the four tattvas, in varying proportions according to its position with respect to others. The different classes of these solar atoms appear on the terrestrial plane as the various elements of chemistry. The spectrum of every terrestrial element reveals the color or colors of the prevalent tattva or tattvas of a solar atom of that substance. The greater the heat to which any substance is subjected, the nearer the element gets to its solar state. Heat destroys, for the time being, the terrestrial coatings of the solar atoms.

Prana is that state of tattvic matter that surrounds the Sun, and in which the Earth and other planets move. It is the state next higher than matter in the terrestrial state. The terrestrial sphere is separated from the solar prana by an akasa. This akasa is the Mother of the terrestrial vayu (warmth). At this point in the heavens, the prana changes into akasa, which gives birth to the terrestrial vayu, the rays of the Sun that fall on the sphere from without. They are not stopped in their inward journey. Through these rays, the ocean of prana, which surrounds our sphere, exerts an organizing influence upon it.

The terrestrial prana—the earth-life that appears in the shape of all the living organisms of our planet—is a modification of the solar prana. The influence of this terrestrial prana develops two centers of work in the gross matter that is to form a human body. Part of the matter gathers round the northern center, and part round the southern center. The northern center develops into the brain, and the southern into the heart. The column along which the positive matter gathers runs between these foci.

Origin of the Universe

In the beginning, there was an immense potency of dormant energy in which everything existed in a latent state of potentiality, like a caterpillar inside the cocoon before it differentiates into a butterfly. As creation began, the divine, all-encompassing consciousness took the form of the first and original vibration manifesting as the word AUM—without beginning or end, the Divine Self of the Universe. The all-encompassing mantra AUM is the "name of God," the vibration of the Supreme. The essence of all wisdom has its roots in this sound. In the triad AUM the divine energy is united in its three aspects as: the creative power that manifests all, the preserving power that sustains all, the liberating power that brings about transformation and renewal raising the vibrations of all.

At the beginning of creation, as the sound of AUM divided the unity, two powers emerged from it: purusha—original consciousness and prakriti—primordial nature. Prakriti is the eternal stream of divine energy and purusha is the divine self, the unchanging, omnipresent and omniscient witness of all events and mutations of prakriti. The cosmic forces that create the desire for union and the striving for expansion are intrinsic dualistic impulses of nature. Why does the seed sprout? Love contains the impulse for development and expansion, and this love is part of the Divine Being's natural cosmic nature.

In a progressive sequence, the three gunas (essential qualities) and the five tattvas (elementary principles) emanated from prakriti. These form the basis of all manifestations, of all subtle and gross forms. Without some impetus the tattvas cannot unite. For that they require the participation of the gunas, which are characterized by the following qualities: *rajas*—activity, movement, restlessness, passion; *tamas*—rigidity, laziness, darkness, ignorance; *sattva*—harmony, light, purity, knowledge.

Tattvas and gunas are the primordial forces that have an effect on both the physical and astral planes. They influence all forms of life physically, psychically, and spiritually from the beginning of their earthly existence to their end. Through the multi-layered combinations of these basic powers, the human body, with its highly complex organs, nerve and brain functions, comes into existence and the psyche and mind are formed.

The most highly developed and most powerful center on earth is the human. Just as bees collect around the queen bee, all forces and tattvas follow when the atman (ego) enters the embryo. For a human form to be constructed, the orderly combination of an immense number of effects is necessary. In the same way, but at a lower intensity, animal and plant life come into being. The cosmic forces are collected within the human body at certain central points, the chakras; these function like power stations. They draw in tattvic energy; transform, store, and distribute it; and then radiate it out into the cosmos again.

As we can derive from the freely rendered summary of some of the salient points about the tattvas from both Blavatsky and Prasad, the ethers are the primal forces of creation. Blavatsky did not rewrite either the *Sivagama* or any other extant Tibetan text, like Prasad did to authenticate his viewpoint. Blavatsky's source, *The Stanzas of Dzyan*, is insightful and more complete than any other commentary on the Tattvic Philosophy of India. Prasad's commentaries are standard Vedic beliefs that do not stray far from the usual translations or interpretations, whereas Blavatsky created Fohat as a new principle to describe the living substance of the ethers. Blavatsky is singular in her approach to ancient wisdom and comprehensive in her pre-Christian scholarship concerning ancient wisdom. We can learn a great deal from both authors, as long as we put them in perspective and glean a modern application for such ancient principles.

The Etheric Land
of Shamballa

Eastern traditions speak of a land where the aspirant can directly encounter the "rarified" ethers that are only referred to in the highest tantric teachings. This "land" is spoken of in many fashions and throughout almost all mythologies, religions, and spiritual teachings. This land is often called, Shamballa, Tushita, Heaven, New Jerusalem, or Eden Regained. In this land, the higher ethers of the Tree of Life are available as nourishment for those who are invited into this sacred domain, the holy of holies. Great Masters are found in this realm, and the lucky visitor is asked to drink a heavenly nectar and eat a divine ambrosia. These spiritual foods are the gifts of the higher ethers that nourish the etheric and physical bodies of the aspirant as a heavenly dew that blesses the efforts of the aspirant. Reaching this land is the goal of the path of self-development.

To find Shamballa, we can look again into the profound work of H. P. Blavatsky in *The Secret Doctrine* to start the search. Blavatsky teaches that a series of seven root-races or humanities will develop during the present fourth round of the Earth's evolution. Each lives on its own continent; just as the root-races overlap, so parts of the continents of one root-race become incorporated into the continental system of the next.

The first continent is known as the *Imperishable Sacred Land* and is the most mysterious of the seven continents. It is said to be located in the region of the North Pole. This Sacred Land is stated never to have shared the fate of the other continents because it is the only one whose destiny it is to last from the beginning to the end of the Manvantara, throughout each Round. It is the cradle of the first man and the dwelling of the last divine mortal. Of this mysterious and sacred land, very little can be said except, perhaps— according to a poetical expression in one of the *Commentaries on the Secret Doctrine*—that the "polestar has its watchful eye upon it, from the dawn to the close of the twilight of the Great Breath."

According to the Hindu Kurma Purana, an island called Shveta-Dvipa, or White Island, lay in the northern sea, the paradisiacal homeland of great yogis possessing supreme wisdom and learning. Blavatsky writes: "According to Tibetan tradition the *White Island* is the only locality which escapes the general fate of other continents and can be destroyed by neither fire nor water, for—it is the 'eternal land.'"

North of the Himalayas, possibly in the Tarim Basin, lay Uttarakuru or northern Kuru, a version of Shambhala which the Mahabharata describes as the blissful land of the sages towards which Arjuna, the warrior prince of the Bhagavad-Gita, travelled in search of enlightenment. It is described as a place of marvels where magic fruit trees yield the nectar of immortality. It is said to be one of four regions surrounding Mount Meru like the petals of a lotus and to be the homeland of the siddhas: enlightened yogis famed for their miraculous powers.

Tibetan View of Shamballa

Tibetan sacred texts speak of a mystical kingdom called Shamballa, hidden behind snow peaks somewhere north of Tibet, where the most sacred Buddhist teachings—the *Kalachakra* or

Wheel of Time—are preserved. It is prophesied that a future king of Shambhala will come with a great army to free the world from barbarism and tyranny, and will usher in a golden age. Similarly, the Hindu *Puranas* say that a future world redeemer—the Kalki Avatara, the tenth and final manifestation of Vishnu—will come from Shamballa. Both the Hindu and Buddhist traditions say it contains a magnificent central palace radiating a powerful, diamond-like light.

The mythical paradise of Shamballa is known under many different names: the Forbidden Land, the Land of White Waters, the Land of Radiant Spirits, the Land of Living Fire, the Land of the Living Gods and the Land of Wonders. Hindus have known it as Aryavarsha, the land from which the Vedas come; the Chinese as Hsi Tien, the Western Paradise of Hsi Wang Mu, the Royal Mother of the West; the Russian Old Believers knew it as Belovodye; and the Kirghiz people as Janaidar. But throughout Asia, it is best known by its Sanskrit name, Shamballa, meaning "the place of peace, of tranquility."

It is regarded by most esoteric traditions as the true center of the planet, as the world's spiritual powerhouse and the heartland of a brotherhood of adepts from every race and country who have been influential in every major religion, every scientific advance, and every positive social development in history.

Buddhist texts say that Shamballa can be reached only by a long and difficult journey across a wilderness of deserts and mountains, and warn that only those who are called and have the necessary spiritual preparation will be able to find it; others will find only blinding storms, empty mountains, or even death. One text says that the kingdom of Shamballa is round, but it is usually depicted as an eight-petalled lotus blossom—a symbol of the heart chakra. Indeed, an old Tibetan story states that "The kingdom of Shamballa is in your own heart."

According to Lama Kunga Rimpoche, "Shamballa is probably at the North Pole, since the North Pole is surrounded by ice, and Shamballa is surrounded by ice mountains." A few lamas believe that Shamballa exists outside the earth, on another planet or in another "dimension." Other Tibetans believe that "Great Shamballa is far beyond the ocean. It is the mighty heavenly domain. It has nothing to do with our Earth. Only in some places, in the Far North, can you discern the resplendent rays of Shamballa." The lamas concede that the heavenly Shamballa has an earthly counterpart. Indeed, the expression "the resplendent rays of Shamballa" seems to be a reference to the aurora that manifests in the polar region. The ruler of Shamballa is "ever vigilant in the cause of mankind."Hhe sees all the events of earth in his "magic mirror," and "the might of his thought penetrates into far-off lands." The inhabitants of Shamballa are uncountable. The splendid new forces and achievements that are being prepared there for humanity are numerous. Messengers from Shamballa are at work in the world, and the ruler himself sometimes appears in human form. They stress that the secrets of Shamballa are well guarded, and that it is impossible for anybody to reach Shamballa unless their karma is ready and they are called.

The Theosophical View of Shamballa

Theosophists recognize that Shamballa is a real place: Shamballa is an actual land or district, the seat of the greatest brotherhood of spiritual adepts and their chiefs on earth today. From Shamballa, at certain times in the history of the world, come forth the messengers or envoys for spiritual and intellectual work among men. This Great Brotherhood has branches in various parts of the world, but Shamballa is the center or chief lodge. We may tentatively locate it in a little-known and remote district of the high tablelands of central Asia—more particularly, in Tibet.

Tibet is surrounded by an akashic veil of invisibility; an army of airplanes might fly over it and not see it. All the armies of all the nations on earth might pass it and not know that it existed. It is quite an extensive tract of country. In it are gathered some of the most valuable records of the human race. There, surrounded by the greatest and most evolved human beings, the Silent Watcher of the Earth has his invisible abode.

Shamballa, our spiritual home, is said to comprise two localities on earth. One of them is "situated in the highlands of Asia, somewhere to the westward of the meridian line passing through Lhassa." Long ago, this locality was a sacred island in a vast Central Asian inland sea, known as the "abyss of learning" or "sea of knowledge," and was accessible via subterranean passages. According to tradition, this place exists to this day as an oasis surrounded by the Gobi desert.

In other words, Shamballa, in one of its meanings, is the Sacred Imperishable Land. Theosophical literature also states that there is an even higher Shamballa located in the Sun, and that all these different localities are inhabited by classes of entities with which the human race is spiritually and intellectually connected.

Traditions of a paradisiacal, primeval land in the far north are universal. Sometimes this sacred land is said to be located in the center or navel of the earth. In one sense, this refers to the North Pole, which appears to be in the center of the earth if the planet is viewed from above the pole. The northern paradise is often associated with a world tree, a world mountain, or a pillar from which four rivers emerge, and a world-engirdling ocean or serpent. The pillar, mountain, or tree links our own middle earth with the upper and lower worlds. All these symbolic features can be interpreted on different levels—terrestrial, astronomical, and spiritual—but clearly are descriptions of the tattvas or ethers. The World Tree is the akasha ether branching out as four rivers in the other four ethers.

What Is Shamballa?

The above references are a testament to the fact that most major religions have an unusual belief about the North Pole as the original home of humanity and the continued home of higher

spiritual beings. These purified realms where higher beings reside
are also the home of the ethers. It is through the North Pole and
South Pole that the magnetic dynamics of the Earth's Van Allen
Belts interact with solar wind. These electric and magnetic forces
and their interaction with the Sun are only partially understood
by scientists. A great deal of modern research is focused on this
interaction.

Rudolf Steiner tells us that we should study the Finnish
national epic, *The Kalevala*, as a soul exercise of the greatest
importance for our time. *The Kalevala* is a most wondrous
fairytale-like story that directly addresses the longings of soul that
a modern person feels. The main task of the story is that three
great heroes must go "to the Northland—Kalevala" and battle with
the Old Woman of the North to win one of her daughters who
ride on the "rainbow of the north"—ostensibly, the aurora borealis.
The "ancient smithy," Ilmarinen, forges the great desire of the Old
Woman of the North, the Sampo, to win one of her daughters.

Harald Falck-Ytter, a student of Rudolf Steiner's teachings,
tells us in his brilliant book on the aurora, entitled *Aurora The
Northern Lights in Mythology, History and Science*, that the
aurora borealis is the same as the Sampo from *The Kalevala*. He
reminds us that the Sampo was created by the divine-human
smith Ilmarinen in the dark land of the North. It was forged with
cunning art:

On One side was a corn-mill

On another side a salt-mill

And upon the third a coin-mill.

Now was grinding the new Sampo,

And revolved the pictured cover.

The corn, salt, and coin are the life-processes of body, soul,
and spirit, which are brought forth by the Sampo as it grinds. The

Sampo is topped by a many-colored lid that also revolves and is called the "vaults of heaven" or "heavenly spheres." It is defined as "colorful, embroidered with rune and script," or the revolving vault of the heavens filled with brilliant stars and colored northern lights, upon which a variety of runes and written signs and forms are visible. Whoever could interpret the "many colored lid" would be able to read the heavenly script.

An elemental-supersensory sheath of forces surrounding the earth dips down to earth at the poles. The elemental sphere of forces does not move with the earth, but remains in a kind of static relationship to the Sun. The structure of its forces is able to influence the earth-elements so that, for example, it can give rise to fluctuations in atmospheric pressure. In this way, a sort of friction is generated on the earth: a perpetual grinding between this sheath of forces and the Earth's sphere.

A picture arises that the Sampo is the visible land of Shamballa covering the northernmost pole where the ethers rush into the atmosphere of the Earth, mitigated by the magnetic torus field of the earth. "Winning" this Sampo is the ultimate prize for gods and men. It is a sort of "marriage" to another part of yourself that is transmitted from the Sun and the cosmos through the currents that bring the etheric, formative forces into play in the etheric bodies of the Earth and humans.

This region of the Earth is a crucial connecting point between Earth and Sun. Spiritual scientists describe these etheric forces as a rope, or masonic cable tow, that reaches from the Sun to Earth and "pulls" the Earth behind the space that the sun has previously traversed. This rope or cable is tantamount to a magnetic tractor beam that is the source of ethers directly flowing into the Earth's etheric body. This concept was laughed at in the past, but now makes for the best of science. Four space satellites have now been put into orbit around the Earth to study these phenomena, which esotericists have known about since ancient times.

A NASA-funded researcher, C. Q. Wei, at the University of Iowa has figured out how to find doorways that directly connect the Earth to the Sun. He calls them X-points, or electron diffusion regions, where the magnetic field of Earth connects to the magnetic field of the Sun, creating an uninterrupted path leading from our own planet to the sun's atmosphere 93 million miles away, like a giant rope pulling the Earth behind the Sun.

Researchers have long known that the Earth and Sun must be connected. Earth's magnetosphere (the magnetic bubble that surrounds our planet) is filled with particles from the Sun that arrive via the solar wind and penetrate the planet's magnetic defenses. They enter by following magnetic field lines that can be traced from *terra firma* all the way back to the Sun's atmosphere.

On the dayside of Earth (the side closest to the sun), Earth's magnetic field presses against the Sun's magnetic field. Approximately every eight minutes, the two fields briefly merge or "reconnect," forming a portal through which particles can flow. The portal takes the form of a magnetic cylinder about as wide as Earth. The European Space Agency's fleet of four *Cluster* spacecraft and NASA's five *Themis* probes have flown through and surrounded these cylinders, measuring their dimensions and sensing the particles that shoot through them. The cylindrical portals tend to form above Earth's equator and then roll over Earth's winter pole. In December, Flux Transfer Events roll over the north pole; in July, they roll over the south pole.

Flux Transfer Events and interplanetary magnetic clouds may be associated with magnetic flux ropes, which are magnetic flux tubes containing helical magnetic field lines. In the magnetic flux ropes, the azimuthal magnetic field is superposed on the axial field. The time evolution of a localized magnetic flux rope can then be studied.

Magnetic flux ropes have been measured, and there seems to be a cluster of four ropes spiraled around a central rope. It is interesting that the four ethers cluster around the akasha ether as they "descend" into the atmosphere at the north pole. Guenther Wachsmuth describes this in more detail in his book, *The Etheric Formative Forces*. Portions of his book will be highlighted later to illuminate this phenomenon further in the terms of Steiner's ideas.

The Ethers According to Rudolf Steiner

The greatest prophet of the etheric formative forces is Rudolf Steiner, who speaks about the ethers and the etheric body more comprehensively than any other author. Steiner doesn't leave the ethers with the ancient interpretations of the tattvas, but brings the pertinent wisdom forward into a spiritually scientific perspective that can be applied in modern life to enhance consciousness and utilize the living forces of the etheric.

What Steiner says about the etheric is profound, and an essential part of human development and spiritual evolution. The role of the ethers is as an "alphabet of the spirit." Our task is to take Steiner's indications concerning this elemental alphabet of the spirit and turn them into a Language of the Spirit.

In *Foundations of Esotericism*, Rudolf Steiner describes the ethers as follows:

> "The first element which is finer than the air is the one which causes it to expand, which always increases its spatial content. What expands the air in this way is warmth; it is a fine etheric substance, the first grade of ether, the *warmth ether*. Bodies which

shine send out a form of matter, a second kind of ether, which is described as light ether. The third kind of ether is the bearer of everything which gives form to the finest matter, the formative ether, which is also called the *chemical ether*. The finest of all the ethers is that which constitutes life: prana, or *life ether*. The earth, essentially speaking, developed itself out of these four types of ether. It condensed itself or, in other words, "put on" these ethers. The ether is sensitive to what is called in esoteric language the "Word," the "Cosmic Word."

Starting from this rather Theosophic and Eastern definition of the ethers is comprehensive, but still mystical and not Western enough for the modern reader. We need to scan the entire works of Steiner to gain his comprehensive view of the nature of the workings of these ethers. In this section, we shall gather and paraphrase the ideas of Steiner concerning the ethers in order to gain a more well-rounded view of the ethers.

In his pedagogical course entitled *The Astronomy Course* (GA 323), Rudolf Steiner builds up a powerful picture of the foundational importance of the ethers during the prior incarnations of the Earth. The etheric geneses of minerals, plants, animals, and human beings are described in detail, and their correspondences with the elemental forces of the cosmos are drawn out using a grand perspective that is seldom found in his other works.

The human body is the expression of a subtle, supersensible, or etheric body in which the material or physical body is enclosed, like a denser nucleus, as though in a cloud. It forms the basis of the life of the physical body. The human, as an etheric being, stands in an etheric, or elemental world. There is an etheric human being behind the physical human being, and a supersensible, etheric, or elemental world behind the one that is physically perceptible. That world comes to be recognized as the elemental, supersensible, etheric body of the earth—the life body or body of formative forces. Within the earth's etheric body, an etheric human being feels himself to be a member of a whole. Through spiritual development, we perceive a new world that seems to come out of our own being. We feel as though there is a great organism—a *Being*—within which we live.

When the ethers arise from the environment, their effect runs counter to that of the earth's gravitation; they create levity. They also work (ray) into the world from the surrounding cosmos, and attract earthly matter as they do so. Light works in from the cosmos in this way. You can observe the force of light when a seed germinates into a plant and grows towards the light. The plant grows away from the earth and towards the light. Light gives the plant levity-power to overcome gravity. The etheric force overcomes the weight of material substance.

The etheric realm is where nature-spirits and elemental spirits manifest as dynamic forces intimately connected with biological forces and the rhythms of nature. These formative forces and the beings associated with them create growth and life in the physical world. What is present in the etheric body has been woven into man from the stellar formative forces of the cosmos. The cosmic etheric rhythms resonate inside human organs and bodily systems. This harmonic resonance communicates between the cosmic and human etheric bodies.

The most primary form of etheric substance is from the original "Old Saturn" incarnation of Earth formed from *warmth ether*, a substance that consists of "heat" or "warmth." There are generally four ethers, the first and most primal of which is called warmth ether. The three other ethers evolve sequentially from this one through the "Old Sun," "Old Moon," and "Earth" incarnations of the earth. Warmth transforms into light, sound, and life (word). The "remains" of warmth from the "Old Saturn" incarnation of Earth become denser through its next three incarnations until, in our time, it has condensed into the mineral kingdom.

Warmth from "Old Saturn" has become our minerals; light from "Old Sun" has become our plants; sound from "Old Moon" has become our animals. We live among the donations of the archai, archangels, and angels in the mineral, plant, and animal kingdoms.

Ether	Incarnation of Earth	Direction of Force	Form Tendency	State Induced
Warm	Saturn	Radiating	Spherical	Heat
Light	Sun	Radiating	Triangular	Gas
Sound	Moon	Centripetal	Round	Fluid
Life	Earth	Centripetal	Square	Solid

The forces active in fluid bodies arise not merely from the earth, but from the planetary system. The forces of Mercury, Mars, and the other planets are active in everything that is fluid. But they act in a way that arises from the position of the planets, which shows a kind of resultant in the fluidity. Everything on the earth is related, with the whole solar system raying in through this fashion.

The being of warmth (levity) manifests exactly like the negation of gravity. As we pass through these material states, we come to a zero-point or a zero-sphere, in spatial terms—a non-space.

The spherical form is the synthesis of all polyhedral shapes and of all crystal forms. When substance passes from fluid to gas, the diffusion and dissolution of the spherical form is directed outward. Every polyhydric body goes over into its negative only by passing through the sphere, as through a zero-point or a zero-sphere. Gas, or air, is a negative form. Spatial and non-spatial are pressure and suction, respectively.

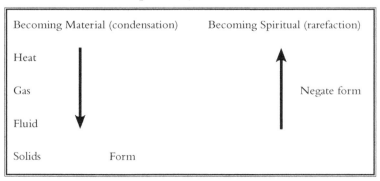

Becoming Material (condensation)   Becoming Spiritual (rarefaction)

Heat

Gas   Negate form

Fluid

Solids   Form

Brightness and luminosity are an enhancement of the condition of rarefaction. Darkening can be thought of as a condensation not yet intense enough to produce matter, but of such an intensity that it is on the verge of becoming material.

Heat has within it a life: a living, weaving activity, manifesting itself everywhere as a tendency to materialization penetrated by a tendency to dematerialization. Heat is intensive motion that continually alternates between the realm of pressure and suction effects.

Thinking is based on the effects of suction, which takes its course outside of space. There is a continual searching for equilibrium between pressure effects of a material sort and suction effects of a spiritual sort. Suction effects emanate from every point of space, while pressure effects manifested material things.

If we wish to comprehend the nature of heat, we must entirely leave the material world and three-dimensional space. The nature of heat works as a vortex. As substance arises, something from the other side that is immaterial enters, slips into the substance, and annihilates it. We experience a physical-spiritual vortex continually manifesting in such a way that what appears physically is annihilated by what appears as the spiritual. We have a continuous interplay between the non-spatial and the spatial—a continual sucking up of what exists in space by the entity that is outside of space. The moment we move out to the sphere where gravity ceases and everything streams outwards, our entire physical view of the world ceases to apply.

Decaying light is electricity. We know electricity is light that is being destroyed in matter. Magnetism is a chemical force that undergoes a transformation in the process of earth evolution. An inward quality must also be ascribed to light; light is itself at every point in space. Warmth will expand in the three dimensions of space. There is a fourth dimension in light that has the quality of inwardness.

The numerical rations in chemistry are an expression of the numerical ratios of the harmony of the spheres, not atomic action. To imaginative consciousness, atoms are revealed as bubbles, and reality is where the empty space exists. Atoms are blown up bubbles. In other words, in contrast to what surrounds them, they are nothing. Where atoms are, the space is hollow; nothing is there. Yet it is possible to push against this hollowness, whereupon an effect is produced.

Human Spiritual Evolution

Rudolf Steiner characterizes the different embodiments of the Earth in stunning descriptions in the le cture series entitled *The Inner Experience of Evolution* (GA 132). This series of lectures has been condensed and paraphrased in the sections below to highlight the four planetary stages necessary to come into our present time.

To describe the nature of ethers, the spiritual scientist needs to examine the seven incarnations of the earth as they manifest over time. The first three incarnations of Saturn, Sun, and Moon created substance that has metamorphosed into the incarnation called Earth—the Earth we experience now. It is very difficult to comprehend these ancient times without Imaginative Thinking, a living thinking that can flexibly hold four different time periods and the activities of countless beings in the mind simultaneously. These ancient embodiments of Earth developed the four ethers into the corresponding elements and helped the hierarchy evolve through their stages of development.

Saturn—Sacrificing—Warmth Ether

Saturn was a spaceless eternity with an ebb and flow of spaceless warmth. Warmth exists and becomes active through the joy of sacrifice. To experience Saturn is to experience trance consciousness, which induces a terrible fear of the abyss, a condition of dread and dizziness that cannot be overcome. Only through understanding Christ can consciousness withstand the experience of the abyss. A person who understands this mystery can take something with him into the abyss that expands as if from a single point and completely fills the void with a feeling of courage and protection. One might then experience the Spirits of Will, the Thrones, swimming in a sea of courage and surging energy. Aspects of space do not apply here; space does not exist. Time ceases to exist.

Beings of other hierarchies penetrate the warmth and become active within the paralysis that is the timelessness of the infinite ocean of courage that comprises the action of the Spirits of Will. Clouds appear, as well as a shimmering radiance filled with wisdom. The Cherubim stream into the ocean of courage. The Thrones sacrifice their own being to the Cherubim. From this sacrifice, time is born. Beings come into existence who are made completely of time; they are called the Archai, or Time Beings. What we call the element of warmth in Saturn is the sacrificial smoke of the Thrones, which generates time. Warmth was generated out of the sacrifice that the Spirits of Will presented to the Cherubim.

The Thrones in this willingness to sacrifice, which is based upon strength and courage, kneel before the Cherubim and offer up their sacrifice to them. The Thrones send the sacrifice forth as effervescent, flaming warmth so that the smoke from the fire of sacrifice blazes upward to the winged Cherubim. And now, arising from this sacrifice, as if we were speaking a word into the air and this word were *time*, but time as being from the totality of these occurrences, the Spirits of Time—the Archai—emerge.

Sun—Bestowing, Giving—Light Ether

During the Sun existence of Earth, the Spirits of Wisdom were added to the spirits already present during the Saturn existence. These spirits have as their defining characteristic the virtue of giving, bestowing, or effecting blessings. They are the mighty Grantors, the great Givers of the Cosmos. Their gift is that with which the cosmos is woven and lives, for they themselves streamed out into the cosmos and first created order.

The Archangels are the ones who receive the Spirits of Wisdom; they do not keep them for themselves. Rather, they reflect them back, just as a mirror reflects the image it receives. The Archangels on the Sun have the task of receiving what was given at an earlier point in time so that it is preserved and reflected again by the Archangels into a later time. Then, an inwardly enclosed globe is created from whose center radiates something to be given away. Something radiates out from the center to the periphery, and from there reflects back to the middle point. A center where the Spirits of Wisdom are immersed in their contemplation of the legacy from ancient Saturn—the deed of sacrifice of the Thrones to the Cherubim.

The Spirits of Wisdom radiate streaming wisdom in the form of the virtue of bestowing. Because this virtue is permeated by time, it is sent forth and then reflected again, so that we have before us a globe illumined from within by virtue reflected to its source and center. Everything is illumined through and through. Their inner most being has been surrendered as a gift to the macrocosm. Now it radiates back; their own being is distributed throughout the cosmos and radiated back as light, as the reflection of their own being.

Inner and outer are the two opposites that now come before us. The earlier and the later transform themselves and become the inner and the outer. Space is born. However, this space is only in two dimensions: only inner and outer.

The Imagination

In the verses below, Rudolf Steiner gives us a poetic imagination to encapsulate the evolutionary process as in inner experience.

- The sacrificing Thrones kneel before the Cherubim
- The choirs of Spirits of Wisdom surrender in devotion to the vision of the sacrifice of the Thrones at the center of the Sun

- Their devotion grows into an image of sacrificial smoke, which spreads out in all directions, streams outward, condenses into clouds at the periphery
- The Archangels are created out of the clouds of smoke
- The gift of the sacrificial smoke radiates back from the periphery in the form of light
- The light illuminates the interior of the Sun
- The gift of the Spirits of Wisdom is given back, thereby creating the sphere of the Sun
- The Sun sphere consists of the outpoured gifts of glowing warmth and sacrificial smoke.
- At the outer periphery sit the Archangels, the creators of light, who reflect what earlier came into being on the Sun
- After some time, sacrificial smoke eventually returns as light
- The Archangels preserve what arose earlier: the gifts of the Spirits of Wisdom that the Archangels received and radiated back
- What previously existed as time they gave back as space, and, by radiating back time as space, the Archangels gave back what they themselves had received from the Archai
- The Archangels thus become the Angels of the Beginning, because they brought what existed earlier into a later time

Moon—Renunciation—Chemical Ether

Following the Saturn and Sun period of development, there was a period when all existing conditions were immersed in a kind of twilight (a cosmic chaos), after which they emerged as Moon. We can see the emergence of sacrifice as warmth. What remains as warmth on the Sun emerges on the Moon as heat. What was previously the virtue of bestowing reappears as gas or air. Resignation—the renunciation of the sacrifice—also continues and is present in everything that occurs on the ancient Moon. What we experienced as resignation on the Sun, we may also think of as an active "force" in all that exists on ancient Moon. What existed as sacrifice appears in maya as warmth, what was the virtue of bestowing appears as gas or air, and what existed as resignation appears as liquid appears as water. During the Sun development, the gathering mass of clouds became water as the clouds pressed together. It emerged as the Moon's ocean during the Moon period.

The Spirits of Movement now come forward with movement that is related to the process of thinking. They lead the beings who would otherwise have had to depend upon themselves to develop relationships with all the other beings. They bring about movement and bring forth relationships between beings. They bring forth picture consciousness. Suffering and pain as manifestations of the soul came into our nature at that time and into other beings bound up with our evolution. Thereafter, the otherwise empty inner self that suffers from longing was filled with a healing balm in the form of picture consciousness. This longing aspires ceaselessly to carry out the sacrifice to the universal being who can satisfy it—not just appease it with an infinite sequence of pictures, but fulfill it once and for all.

Earth—Death—Life Ether

The true nature of earth or solid element is death—the separation of a substance from its cosmic purpose. When this state of separation was initiated, death itself entered as a reality into the world of maya or illusion. The gods themselves could never know death unless they descended in some way into the physical world, in order to understand death in its true nature in the physical world—the world of maya.

Some beings remained behind in the course of development. It is due to these "luciferic" beings that we have desires, drives, and passions in our astral body that continually drive us from a certain height and pull us toward the lower regions of our being. Were it not for our capacity to become evil and stray from the good through the power of the luciferic beings in our astral body, we could not act freely or have free will or freedom of choice. We owe our freedom to the luciferic beings. The one-sided perspective that luciferic beings exist only to lead humanity astray is insufficient. Rather, we must regard the withholding of the luciferic beings as something good, and as something without which we would not be able to achieve our evolution as human beings in the true sense of the word.

The presence of beings who stayed behind is a consequence of the Cherubim's act of renunciation; the Cherubim produced the beings who stayed behind. Thus, the Cherubim created the possibility of "remaining behind." Wise cosmic guidance orders things so that the gods themselves called their opponents into being. The gods recognized that for free beings to be created, the possibility had to be given for opponents to arise against them so that they could meet resistance in whatever was subject to time. We must not look for the origin of evil in so-called evil beings, but in so-called good beings, who by their renunciation first made it possible for evil to arise through beings capable of bringing evil into the world.

Essential Nature of the Etheric Body

Rudolf Steiner gives us a comprehensive picture of the etheric body in a description found in his lecture, *The Etheric Body Brings Life* (GA 167). We will summarize the content of that lecture in the descriptions of the etheric body below.

The etheric body permeates the physical body from conception to death and organizes in it all its characteristic processes of life, such as nourishment, growth, reproduction, etc. An examination of the "life organization" active in these processes also provides insight into the structure of the etheric body. There are "seven life processes" in which the etheric body unfolds its activity with respect to the physical body. These seven processes originated in the etheric body.

The ether body is held together through the elastic force of the physical body as long as we are on Earth. Our ether body is the outspread animal kingdom, which is held together through the elasticity of our physical body. All the possible forms of the animal kingdom are inside us in our ether body. We have all the instincts and all the different drives of the animals already in us. If you remove the elasticity of the physical and etheric bodies, the astral body would fall apart and would represent something very similar to the entire plant kingdom. Through the fact that we have an astral body, the different forms of the plant kingdom exist in us as they are spread out in the world in their manifoldness.

We have received our physical configuration during our earth existence from the Spirits of Form (Elohim). These Spirits of Form work less upon the ether body than do the archai, archangels, and angels. These Beings work upon the ether body and have something to do with the directing of this manifoldness in the ether body. The main factors of the movement of speaking and singing occur within that manifoldness in the ether body.

In our etheric body lives the forces that come from the Folk Soul (Archangel) that exist in our deep unconsciousness. In the etheric, there is deeper wisdom that has been imparted to mankind through living pictures.

Imagination	Inspiration	Intuition	
Light Ether	Sound Ether	Life Ether	
Archai	Archangels	Angels	Human
Warmth Ether	Gas	Fluid	Solid
Saturn	Sun	Moon	Earth
Electricity	Magnetism	Third Force	
Lucifer	Ahriman	Asuras	

We are surrounded by *five ether streams* in the world around us. They are called earth, water, fire, air, and thought (akasha) ether streams. These etheric streams are also active in the human body. An ether stream can be found to proceed from the head as follows: earth ether flows to the right foot, water ether to the left hand, fire ether to the right hand, air ether to the left foot, and then thought ether returns to the head. The spirit streams to man from the heights in similar ether streams.

The cross-sections of the five etheric streams and their connections with color, taste, and body regions are as follows:

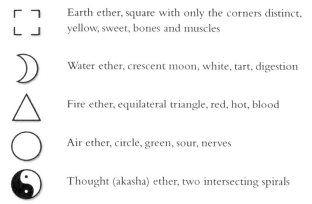

Earth ether, square with only the corners distinct, yellow, sweet, bones and muscles

Water ether, crescent moon, white, tart, digestion

Fire ether, equilateral triangle, red, hot, blood

Air ether, circle, green, sour, nerves

Thought (akasha) ether, two intersecting spirals

As far up as the warmth ether and life ether, we kill that which penetrates us; we slay it unceasingly so that we may have our Earth-consciousness. Light ether and chemical ether are the two kinds of ether that we cannot kill. If we could kill the chemical ether, the waves of the Harmony of the Spheres would sound perpetually into our physical body, and we would destroy these waves with our physical life. If we could kill the life ether, we would destroy and continuously kill within ourselves the cosmic life that streams down to Earth.

Of the Tree of Life, man shall not eat, and the Spirit of Matter he shall not hear! These are the regions which are closed to humans—just as the Garden of Eden is now closed to humans. Only through a certain procedure in the old mysteries were the tones of the Music of the Spheres and the cosmic life, pulsating through the universe, revealed to those who were to be initiated. Then, the initiate's soul could belong to the region of the Music

of the Spheres and to the region of the Word: the living Cosmic
Ether.

Etheric Body During Initiation

In *Initiation and Its Results* (GA 10), Rudolf Steiner tells us
that the etheric body is a highly refined life-body that, to the eyes
of the clairvoyant, appears as a kind of specter of the physical
body. It is, to some extent, a medium between the physical and
astral bodies.

The etheric body has approximately the size and form of the
physical body, so that it practically fills the same space. It is an
extremely delicate and finely-organized vehicle. Its principal
color is peach-blossom. The particles of this etheric body are
in continual motion. Countless currents pass through it in
every direction. By those currents, life itself is supported and
regulated. Everything that has life, including the animals and
plants, possesses an etheric double. There are even traces of these
particles in minerals. These currents and movements are almost
entirely independent of the human will and consciousness.

The spiritual scientist is given certain directions that lead
to the evocation of particular currents and movements within
his etheric body. The object of these directions is to fashion in
the region of the physical heart a kind of center from which
these out-rayings and movements, with their manifold forms
and colors, may go forth. The center is not merely a given point,
but a most complicated structure, a wonderful organ. It glows
and shimmers with all kinds of color and displays forms of the
greatest symmetry—forms that are capable of transformation
with astonishing speed. Other forms and out-rayings of color
proceed from this organ to the other parts of the body, and also to
those of the astral body, which they entirely pervade and illumine.
The most important of these rays move, however, toward the
lotus-flowers in the chakras. They pervade each petal and
regulate its revolutions; then, streaming out at the points of the

petals, they lose themselves in the surrounding space. The more evolved a person is, the greater the circumference to which these rays extend becomes.

The aspirant introduces into his etheric body out-rayings and vibrations that are in harmony with the laws and the evolution of the world to which he belongs. He starts quite simply, with what is necessary above all things: a deepening and an internalization of reasonable and sensible thought. This thought is made free and independent of all sense-impressions or experiences. The center in the head, when it has become duly settled, is then transferred further down, to the region of the larynx. This change is again induced by a particular exercise of concentration. Then the characteristic vibrations of the etheric body stream forth from this point and illuminate the astral space that surrounds the individual.

A further exercise enables the aspirant to determine for himself the position of his etheric body. By means of such development, the individual can direct the etheric body to all sides. This faculty is effected by out-rayings that move approximately along both hands and are centered in the two-petalled lotus that is situated in the region of the eyes. As a result of all this, the rays that flow forth from the larynx are shaped into round forms of which a quantity proceed to the two-petalled lotus, and from there take their way as undulating currents along the hands.

One finds as a further development that these currents branch out, ramify in a delicate manner, and become, in a certain sense, like wicker-work, so that the entire etheric body is enmeshed in a network. The etheric body has had no closure to externals, so that the life-currents of the great ocean of life flowed freely in and out; it now becomes necessary that forces from outside should pass through this "etheric skin." The individual becomes sensitive to these external streams, which become perceptible to him. The time has now come to give the complete system of rays and vibrations a center in the heart. Again, this is accomplished by means of a meditative and concentrative exercise, and simultaneously the aspirant attains the point at which he can hear the "inner word."

All things now acquire a new significance for him. They become audible, as it were, in their innermost nature; they speak to him from their true being. The currents place him in touch with the interior of the world to which they appertain. He begins to mingle his life with the life of his environment, and can let it reverberate in the vibrations of his lotus-flowers. The individual enters the spiritual world, which flows into him from the inmost being of all things.

The repetitions in the sayings of the Buddha are like something upon which he may let his inner senses rest, for they correspond to certain rhythmic movements in the etheric body. Devotional musing on these, with complete inward peace, creates a harmony with these movements, and because they themselves are echoes of certain universal rhythms which also, at points, repeat themselves and make regular returns to their former modes, the individual, listening to the wisdom of the Buddha, puts himself into harmony with the secrets of the universe.

The first of the sayings of the Buddha focuses on the faculty for discriminating between the eternal and the temporal, the true and the false, the truth and mere opinion. The second is a correct estimate of the eternal and true as opposed to the perishable and illusory. The third faculty is that of practicing six qualities: thought control, control of action, perseverance, tolerance, good faith, and equanimity. The fourth necessary attribute is the longing for freedom. They must become so incorporated into the soul that they endure as inner habits in the etheric body.

Under the influence of these four spiritual habits, the etheric body transforms itself. By the first—the discrimination between the true and the false—the center is formed in the head, and that in the larynx is prepared. If the center in the larynx has been prepared, the free control of the etheric body, as explained above, will follow, and its separation—its network covering—will be produced by the correct estimating of the eternal as opposed to the impermanent. If the student acquires this power of estimation, the facts of the higher worlds will gradually become perceptible.

The twelve-petalled lotus in the region of the heart is associated with the life-current of the etheric body. The fourth attribute, which is the longing for freedom, serves to bring the etheric organ situated in the heart to fruition. If these attributes have become real spiritual habits, the individual frees himself from everything that only depends upon the capacities of his personal nature. He ceases to contemplate things from his own separate standpoint. The limits of his narrow self, which fetter him to this outlook, disappear. The secrets of the spiritual world reveal themselves to his inner self. This is liberation.

If an aspirant has evolved her etheric body in the manner just described, an entirely new life is opened before her, and at the proper period during her training, she receives that enlightenment which adapts her to this new existence.

This is the moment when the two-petalled lotus in the region of the eyes is required. If this now begins to stir, the individual attains the power of setting her higher ego in connection with spiritual, superhuman entities. Just as the light makes physical objects visible to the eyes, these currents reveal the spiritual things of the higher worlds. She now has a direct realization of her higher self, and she learns how this higher self is connected with spiritual entities of a loftier nature and how it forms a union with them. She sees how the lower self descends from a higher world, and it is revealed to her how her higher nature outlasts the lower.

She can distinguish between what is permanent in herself and what is perishable, and this is nothing less than the power to understand, from her own observation, the teachings concerning the incarnation of the higher self in the lower.

It has been shown how the student, by arriving at this stage, veritably becomes a new person. Little by little, he can now mature by means of the currents that come from the etheric body, until he can control the still higher vital element called "the fire of Kundalini," and by so doing can attain a complete liberty from the bondage of his physical body.

What happens here on a small scale within man happens also on a large scale in the world at large. World secrets were carried out in the mysteries, in initiation; thereby something was done that, for most human beings, would only happen in a distant future. Already, in the Egyptian mysteries, one could only be initiated if one had worked one's way through one's entire astral body, so that the astral body could be completely managed by the ego. Such a person would stand before the initiating priest. He had no influence on his physical body, nor yet on his etheric body, but his astral body was of his own making. Now it was indicated to him how he could act on his etheric body and on his physical body.

The physical body was brought into a lethargic condition—it had to remain in this state for three nights and three days—and during this time, the etheric body was raised out of it. Since the initiate had become powerful with respect to the astral body, he could now, therefore, gain the power to act on the etheric body. He could learn to let what he had in the astral work on the etheric body. Those were the three days of the entombment and the resurrection in an etheric body that was completely permeated by what one calls the Holy Spirit. Such an initiate was called a man endowed with the Logos, or with the Word. This Word is the Wisdom, Spirit Self, which has been worked into the astral body. This wisdom can never enter the etheric body unless the astral body has first been permeated by it.

At death, man's physical body dissolves, and the etheric body does, too; the physical body dissolves in the physical world, and the etheric body in the general cosmic ether, but this etheric body has been very elaborately created for man by the wisdom that first implanted it from out of the Astral Globe. This etheric body disperses after death. Only the etheric body that has been built up from within is a living body that stays eternally.

Etheric Birth of the First Teeth

In the lecture cycle *The Etheric Body and the Change of Teeth* (GA 298), Steiner tells us about the connection between the change of teeth at age seven and the associated elements of the developing etheric body.

At about the seventh year, the child undergoes the change of teeth and gets her second teeth. The force that produces the first and second teeth has been present in the whole organism of the child, but it shows itself in the strongest form in the head. The second teeth only come once. The forces that drive the second teeth out from the organism of the child do not work again as physical forces during the rest of life. They become powers of the soul, or powers of the spirit; they vivify the inner being of the human soul. Thus, when we observe the child between the seventh and fourteenth years of life, with particular regard to her characteristic qualities of soul, we find that what now appears between the seventh and fourteenth years as qualities of soul, namely in the child's thinking, worked upon the organs up to the seventh year. It worked in the physical organism, forced out the teeth, reached its culmination as physical force with the change of teeth, and then changed itself into an activity of soul.

This super-sensible body is called the etheric body, which strives away from the earth and out into cosmic spaces. It contains forces that are opposed to gravity, and it strives perpetually against gravity. Just as ordinary physical knowledge teaches us of the physical body of man, so does Imaginative Knowledge—the first stage of exact clairvoyance—teach us of the etheric body that is always striving to get away from earthly gravity. Just as we gradually learn to relate the physical body to its environment, so do we learn to relate the etheric body to its environment.

Through Imaginative Knowledge, we obtain a conception of the relationship of the individual etheric body or body of formative forces in man to the surrounding world. That which in Spring drives the plants out of the soil against gravity in all directions towards the Cosmos and that which organizes the plants, bringing them into relation with the upward-flowing stream of light—in short, the part of the chemistry of the plant that works upwards—must be related to the etheric body of man. Thus, in the first stage of exact clairvoyance, this rich, comprehensive, unified thought is able to approach the etheric body or body of formative forces of man—the "second Man," as it were.

Up to the change of teeth, this body of formative forces is most intimately bound up with the physical body. There, from within, it organizes the physical body; it is the force that drives out the teeth. When the human being gets his second teeth, the part of the etheric body that drives the teeth out has no more to do for the physical body. Its activity is emancipated, as it were, from the physical body. With the change of teeth, the inner etheric forces that have pressed the teeth out are freed, and with these etheric forces, we carry on the free thought that begins to assert itself in the child from the seventh year onwards.

The force of the teeth is no longer a physical force, as it was in the child during the time when the teeth were the organs of thought; it is now an etheric force. The same force that produced the teeth is now working in the etheric body as thought. When we perceive ourselves as thinking human beings and feel that thinking seems to proceed from the head, a true knowledge shows us that the force with which we think from out of the head is the same as the force that was once contained in the teeth.

When we look at the human being, we see his head. In the head, the growth-forces of the teeth free themselves and become the force of thinking. It is then pressed down, as it were, into speech. We have all the processes for which the teeth are no longer directly responsible, because the etheric body now takes over the responsibility. The teeth become the helpers of speech. In this, their relationship with thought is still apparent.

Human Heart and the Ethers

Rudolf Steiner shares a profound view of human development in the lecture entitled *The Human Heart* (GA 212). This lecture is a central pillar of the Waldorf perspective of education. In this lecture, Steiner points out that the human etheric body lives in intimate union with the physical body until the change of teeth begins. The change of teeth marks the essential birth of the etheric body. Likewise, we can see the birth of the astral body at the time of puberty.

The etheric body, as it forms and develops itself in the human being, is a universe in itself—a universe in picture form. At its circumference, it manifests something in the nature of stars, and in its lower portion, something that appears more or less as an image of the earth. It even contains a kind of image of the sun nature and the moon nature.

On our descent into the earthly world, when we draw the forces of the universal ether to ourselves, we actually take with us in our etheric body a kind of image of the cosmos. If we could extract the etheric body of a man at the moment when he is uniting with the physical, we would have a sphere complete with stars, zodiac, sun, and moon.

These configurations of the etheric body remain during the embryonic time, while the human being coalesces more and more with his physical body. They begin to fade away a little, but they remain. Indeed, they remain into the seventh year—that is, until the change of teeth. In the etheric body of the little child, this cosmic sphere is still quite recognizable. But with the seventh year—with the change of teeth—these forms that we behold in the etheric body begin to ray out, in a manner of speaking. Previously, they were more star-like; now they begin to be like rays. The stars dissolve away in the human ether body, but as they do so, they become rays with a tendency to come together inwardly.

All this goes on gradually throughout the period of life between the change of teeth and puberty. At puberty, the process is so far advanced that these rays, having grown together here in the center, form, as it were, a distinct structure—a distinct etheric structure of their own. The stars have faded out, while the structure that has gathered in the center becomes especially living. In the midst of this central etheric structure, at the time of puberty, the physical heart, with its blood vessels, is suspended.

So, we have this strange phenomenon of the star-ether-body drawing inwards. As an etheric body, it is undifferentiated at the periphery of the organism—very little can be distinguished in there. On the other hand, during the time from the change of teeth until puberty, it is intensely radiant, raying from without inwards. Then it gathers itself together, and there, clearly suspended within it, is the physical heart.

You must not suppose that until then, man has no etheric heart. He certainly has one, but he obtains it differently from the way in which he acquires the etheric heart that will now be his. The gathered radiance that arises at the time of puberty becomes the true etheric heart of man. The etheric heart he has before this time is one he received as a heritage through the inherent forces of the embryo. When a man gets his etheric body, and with it makes his way into the physical organism—a kind of etheric heart, or a substitute etheric heart—it is drawn together by the forces of the physical body. He keeps this etheric heart during his childhood years, but it gradually decays. The first etheric heart slowly decays, and in its stead, constantly replacing that which falls out in the etheric process of decay, comes the new, the real, etheric heart. This etheric heart is a concentration of the whole cosmic sphere we brought with us as an ether form—a faithful image of the cosmos—when we proceeded through conception and birth into this earthly life.

Thus we can trace, throughout the time from birth or conception until puberty, a distinct change in the whole etheric form that the human being bears within him. One may describe it by saying: not until puberty does the human being possess his own etheric heart—that is, the etheric heart formed out of his own etheric body, and not supplied provisionally by external forces. All the etheric forces that are working in man until puberty tend to endow him with this fresh etheric heart.

When we observe a very young child, we find a multitude of single organs that are distinguishable in his astral body. Very much can be seen in this astral body of a little child; great secrets are inscribed there of what the human being has experienced between his last death and his present birth. Thus we see the whole astral body, which man brings with him through birth and into this physical existence. We see it gradually diving down into the organs. It slides into the organs.

We must know, in the first place, that every single organ bears within it an astral inheritance, even as the etheric heart is, to begin with, an inheritance. Moreover, we must know that this inherited astral becomes permeated gradually, through and through, with that which man brings with him as his own astral body, which dives down bit by bit into the physical and etheric organs.

The heart is an exception, in a certain sense. Here, too, an astral part dives down. In the heart, not only the astral process, but the etheric, too, is concentrated. Therefore, the heart is the uniquely important organ that it is for man.

The astral body becomes more and more indefinite, for it sends into the physical organs the concrete forms that it brings from another life. It sends them down into the physical organs, so that they are imprisoned there, and thereby the astral body itself becomes like a cloud of mist. From this side, the astral body turns into a cloud of mist, while new differentiations come into it from another side—first slowly, and then with full regularity, and then increasingly from the age of puberty onwards.

Untold things can be inscribed in this astral body. The astral body can absorb all that has taken place since you learned to speak and think. Into this undifferentiated entity, all that we do now is inscribed—the movements of our arms and legs, and not only these, but all that we accomplish through our arms and legs. In short, the whole of man's activity that finds expression in the outer world is written into the astral body; thus, the astral body becomes configured in manifold ways and through all our human actions.

This process begins when the child learns to speak—to embody thoughts in speech. It does not apply to ideas the child receives but cannot remember afterwards. It begins from the time he can remember, with ordinary consciousness, in later life.

From puberty onwards, man's whole activity becomes inserted, via the astral body, in his etheric heart, and in that which has grown out of the pictures of the stars—the images of the cosmos. This is a phenomenon of untold importance. Here, we have a joining together with the cosmos of what man does in this world. In the heart, as far as the etheric universe is concerned, you have a cosmos gathered up into a center; at the same time, as far as the astral is concerned, you have a gathering together of all that man does in the world. This is the point where the cosmos—the cosmic process—is joined to the karma of man.

Through this constant coming together—this mutual permeation—the opportunity is given throughout human life for human actions to be instilled into the essence of the images of the cosmos. Then, when man passes through the gate of death, this ethereal-astral structure—wherein the heart is floating, so to speak—contains all that man takes with him into his further life of soul and spirit, when he has laid aside the physical and the etheric forms. Now, as he expands ever more widely in the spirit, he can hand over his entire karma to the cosmos, for the substance of the whole cosmos is contained within him; it is drawn together in his heart, in the etheric body of his heart. It came from the cosmos and changed into this etheric entity. Then it was gathered up as an essence in the heart, and now it tends to return to the cosmos once more.

This ego lives in a certain connection of sympathy with all the complex forms that are present in the astral body. Then, when these astral forms slide into the organs of the physical, the ego retains this sympathy and extends the same inner sympathy to the organs themselves. The ego spreads out increasingly into the organs and takes possession of them. From earliest childhood, indeed, the ego is in a certain relation to the organs.

By way of the forces that run along the courses of the blood, the ego enters into that which has been formed from the union of the etheric and the astral heart, wherein an etheric from the cosmos grows together with an astral from ourselves.

The real fact is that all that happens in the moral life, and all that happens physically in the world, are brought together precisely in the human heart. These two—the moral and the physical—which run so independently and yet side by side are, for modern consciousness, found in their real union when we learn to understand all the configurations of the human heart.

With each heartbeat, a certain amount of material substance is absorbed, taken away from physical pressure, and added to etheric substance. This etheric substance begins to radiate outward. Etheric rays stream out from the center of his heart. As etheric sunrays, they stream far into the cosmos. We too can take these rays into ourselves so that, out of a small etheric Sun in our new etheric heart organ, streams can likewise flow far into the cosmos. We harbor in our ether heart a creatively active inner sun that radiates warmth and light into the surroundings— into the far reaches of the cosmos. It is the warmth ether that is predominantly active in the etheric heart.

When we look into the inner heart, we find that there are forces collecting from the metabolic and limb systems. We know that that which is connected to the etheric heart-forces has been spiritualized; it follows that that which has to do with our outer life and our actions is also spiritualized and woven into it. What is being prepared in the heart as forces turns into karmic predispositions and karmic tendencies. The next life is being prepared today in all karmic detail, but one can point to the "little box" in the heart in which karma rests, awaiting the future.

The very first beginning of the new etheric heart is near the back of the head. It arises as a mighty net of etherized blood that creates a thin skin that separates it from the cosmic ether. This new etheric heart organ becomes a sense organ or Sun-eye. When we look into ourselves, we can experience our etheric eye as a cognitive eye. It can become the organ for going into one's own depth. Here we experience the flaming, scorching, and burning emotions, desires, passions, and drives on the one hand, and on the other, that which does not connect with them, because it is our eternal being. It lives alongside it. Therefore, we can say that the new etheric organ becomes cognitive for our eternal being in the depth of the metabolism and will organization. While our head holds our soul as if buried within, we comprehend ourselves—our eternal being—in the dark depth of will purified from emotions and drives.

In the head or brain, man is physical. That which is soul-like has been buried there; it is like a corpse. But, in reality, the soul is true to itself and connected to the spirit below the heart. The new and wonderful sense organ, which is as large as the blood organism, finds the eternal being of man next to all that which arises from the depth of will as drives and emotions.

When the aspirant rises to imaginative and inspired cognition, that which arises as lower drives and instincts may not speak. A sum of thoughts in mighty pictures arises; these pictures reveal what man was before birth. The pupil is transported into the time before birth.

That which we see as a vision through our heart, which has become a sense organ, is our own eternal being. We experience our own self in our eternal being. When we continue to press forward into our own being, the Sun-like quality changes. We come to a definite point where we meet inspired knowledge and where we weave with inspired cognition in a real picture-world. Now, in complete consciousness through a sudden inner jolt in our spirit-soul, it feels as if we fuse with the Sun itself. But at the same moment when we come to inspired cognition, when our heart-sense becomes a cognitive organ, we suddenly feel as if our very heart is being transplanted into the Sun; we feel as if we go with the Sun, and the Sun is in us, belonging to us. The Sun becomes our eye and our ear, as well as our warmth organ. We are jolted into the Sun-like. We stand within the light, and we touch spirit-beings with our light-organs.

Here, supersensible knowledge reaches another stage, goes a little step further. Then we not only feel ourselves within the Sun; we perceive ourselves "on the other side of the Sun" as well. We have now moved fully into the Sun. We feel part of the Sun with our innermost being, and we experience the world within our being. Previously, it was outside of ourselves—around us. It is an experience we go through unconsciously, during sleep.

Now we need to reach beyond the Sun-sphere, but this only happens through inspiration, and later, intuition. Here the physical Sun separates us from the place in which we live between death and a new birth. The physical Sun hinders us from seeing the spiritual. Through the added step, however, we now consciously experience the spirit of the Sun, and we feel as if we were within the Sun, wandering along world paths. We reach outside that which is Sun-like as "the Sun as a Spirit Being"—a kind of Super-Sun. Just as the moon has a powerful influence on the physical aspect of man, so the Sun has a strong influence on his soul. The Super-sun is rather a world-soul, the Great Sun-Being. This is the crowning of that which can one day be perceived and spiritually known by the new etheric heart organ as a Sun-eye, when the Sun, as spiritual Super-Sun, becomes the cognitive eye of the etheric heart.

In this way, the secret of the Grail lives in the magnificent occult soul and spiritual unfolding of the etheric heart. The new etheric heart as cognitive spirit-eye of man's eternal being is the place where, in the Grail-Cup, the etheric organ lights up as the real force: the blood of the Redeemer. Then you may lift your etheric heart to Christ as a vessel of the Grail, to receive the gifts of the angelic hosts.

Christ and the Etheric Realm

Rudolf Steiner describes the nature of Christ and the etheric realm where Christ now lives in the lecture series entitled *Christ and the Etheric* (GA 155). The extracts below give a good picture of what the future evolution of humanity might look like when the etheric world becomes more accessible to human spiritual perception.

It had to be possible that Christ should permeate the nature of man, but the nature of man is filled with what is slain by human nature in Earth-existence, from the light ether downwards—the light ether that dies in the human eye. The nature of man is filled with death, but the life-element in the two highest kinds of ether was withdrawn so that human nature might not also be laden with their death.

Many other things are hidden behind sense-existence. Man turns his gaze upon the plant-world; he sees how the light of the Sun conjures the plants out of the soil. Anyone who looks at the plants with clairvoyant sight sees living spiritual elements rising out of them. The light dips down into the plants and rises out of them as a living spiritual element.

In the animals, it is the chemical ether that enters, and this chemical ether is not perceptible to man; if he could be aware of it, it would sound forth spiritually. The animals transform chemical ether into water-spirits. The plants transform light ether into air-spirits. Finally, he transforms the cosmic ether, or life-ether—which man is prevented from killing and without which he could not live at all—into Earth-spirits.

Clairvoyant sight perceives how man sends out his moral, intellectual, and aesthetic aura into the world, and how this aura continues to live as earthly spirit in the spirituality of the Earth. As a comet draws its tail through the cosmos, so does man draw the spiritual aura he projects through the whole of earthly life. This spiritual aura is held together, phantom-like, during a man's life, but at the same time, it sends his moral and intellectual properties of soul out into the world.

If the Mystery of Golgotha had not come about, man would not have been able to permeate the radiations he gives out with the essences of the Music of the Spheres and the Cosmic Life. These essences would not have been there. They would not have flowed into the human radiations, but Christ brought them back through the Mystery of Golgotha. When there is a fulfillment of the words, "Not I, but Christ in me,"—when we bring about a relationship to Christ within ourselves—that which rays out from us and would otherwise be dead is made to live.

So long as we have to live out our earthly existence as humans, we cannot hear the Music of the Spheres directly or have direct experience of the Cosmic Life. However, we can experience the incoming of the Christ, and so we can receive that which would otherwise come to us from the Music of the Spheres and the Cosmic Life.

The development of mankind moves forward in such a way that the emergence of the etheric body will occur quite naturally. Since the appearance of Christ, the etheric body begins to free itself again. It becomes more independent and will, in the future, be outside the physical body, as it was in earlier times. The freeing of the etheric body must take place, and has already begun. Now, however, human beings must take with them in their etheric bodies what they have experienced in their physical bodies—in particular, the physical event of Golgotha. This they must experience in a physical way, while living on the Earth. Otherwise, something will be irrevocably lost. The etheric body would move out without taking along something of the greatest importance, and people would remain empty in their etheric bodies. However, those who have lived through a spiritual Christianity will have in abundance what they have experienced in their physical bodies.

How the Etheric Body Effects Health

In *The Etheric Body and Health* (GA 313), Rudolf Steiner describes the working of the etheric body to create good health in relationship to the four human bodies: physical, etheric, astral, and ego.

In the watery part of the human head, we find the imprint of the etheric. It is due to its watery organization that the human head is, in its entirety, permeable to the etheric, because it is an imprint from out of the ether. Thus, only the warmth ether and the light ether can work on the human head from outside. The human being on earth is inwardly filled with life and chemical ether. The effect of the warmth and light ethers radiates in from all sides. The effect of the chemical and life ethers radiates up through the metabolic-limb system toward the instreaming warmth and light ethers. Just as man's head is organized so that as far as possible, only traces of the chemical and life ethers are allowed to enter, so the metabolic-limb organism sucks in the life and chemical ethers from the earth element.

These two kinds of ethers meet in the human being, and he is organized in such a way that his organization is a regulated process of keeping them apart: on the one hand, the life and chemical ethers stream upward from below, and on the other hand, the warmth and light ethers stream downward from above.

It is an aspect of the human organism that light and warmth ethers may not enter organically into the lower organization except by streaming in from above. Thus, the light and warmth ethers must stream in from outside, and the life and chemical ethers from below. These two streams are brought into cooperation in the human being by means of his organization, and their cooperation must be absolutely maintained if he is to remain in a normal condition.

It is a continual occurrence, a continual interplay between light and warmth ethers on the one hand, pressing centripetally from above downward, and life and chemical ethers on the other hand, pressing centrifugally from below upward. By this means, the etheric configuration of the human being is formed. It is actually a transformation of the vortex formed by the mutual impact of these two kinds of ether. The shape that you encounter must be understood, then, as a cooperation between these two kinds of ether.

What has to do with the processes of illness is located in the astral body. What the astral body commits is impressed into the etheric body. Hence, illness appears in its imprint in the etheric body. When the etheric body is perceived more closely, one is led to the astral body. Next, we have that which works against disease as its polar opposite—namely, health.

Ego = Death
Astral body = Illness
Etheric body = Health
Physical body = Nutrition

Health is related to the etheric body as illness is to the astral body, and death to the ego. To heal—to restore health—means to be able to create in the etheric body counter-reactions to the processes that produce illness and that proceed from the astral body. One must work from the etheric body in order to paralyze the forces of the astral body, which are the processes producing illness.

Death from old age is actually the inability of the organism to absorb substance. It is really a failure of nutrition. Thus, the polar opposite of death is nutrition, and we can relate the nutrition in the human being to the physical body. The process of nutrition taking place in the physical body works on the etheric body, and as a result, also has something to do with the healing processes. This action on the etheric body then works on what proceeds from the astral body as a reaction.

The separation in sleep of the ego and astral body from the physical and etheric bodies is only complete for the head and breathing organizations. The ego and astral body remain in the metabolic and circulatory man. It is not quite accurate to say that the ego and astral body depart. It is expressed correctly only if one says that in sleep the ego and astral body leave the physical and etheric bodies of the head organization, but penetrate them even more in the metabolic and circulatory organizations. It is, in fact, a transposition. In the waking state, the physical and etheric bodies of the head and respiratory organism are intimately bound to the ego and astral body, and in sleep, the physical and etheric bodies of the metabolic and circulatory organizations are much more intimately bound to the ego and the astral body than in waking. This is a transposition—a rhythmic process that takes place in sleeping and waking.

When we rise to the powers of "Imaginative Cognition" that enable us to experience our own etheric body or the body of formative forces, we enter the etheric world. We have sufficiently developed and strengthened our faculties when we have kindled the inner light and can experience ourselves, as it were, in the Second Man, in the body of formative forces; we then enter the world that, to begin with, reveals itself to us in images: the world of the angeloi, archangeloi, and archai.

Having broken through into the cosmic spheres where the etheric body—the body of formative forces—becomes perceptible to us, we recognise on entering this world of flowing images that these reveal manifestations of the Beings of the third Hierarchy.

Nature of the Etheric Body and the Music of the Spheres

In *The Mission of Folk Souls: The Souls of Nations (GA 121)*, Rudolf Steiner gives a panoramic view of the development of the ethers over great spans of Earth evolution. He also clarifies the nature of the ethers in relationship to the realms of the hierarchy.

There are also the Spirits of Wisdom, who send their impulses to us from without, working in the light and the music of the spheres that weave through space. Their emanation is the cosmic ether that streams towards the earth. Life streams from the cosmos down to earth and is received and assimilated by the beings there. This comes from the Spirits of Wisdom. Thus, we raise our gaze to far distances of the cosmos and initially look towards the Sun, in which we see these powers concentrated. We can recognize how the threefold qualities of the second hierarchy, of streaming life, weaving tone, and configuring light enter the earthly sphere from space. If you depict the whole musical experience correctly, you actually have the human etheric body before you. In the older mystery schools and the remaining mystery traditions, clairvoyant cognition is also called musical cognition—a spiritual-musical cognition. The mysteries refer to the existence of ordinary bodily, intellectual, and spiritual cognition (which is, in fact, a musical cognition—a cognition living in the musical element).

Etheric Radiance While Falling Asleep

In *The Cosmic Word and Individual Man* (GA 224), Rudolf Steiner describes what happens to the human etheric body when a person falls asleep and the colors, sounds, and warmth that fill the human aura.

What a man can still observe while he is going to sleep—a kind of humming and singing, a changing murmur within his organism—continues during sleep as a music that is extraordinarily rich in melody and harmony and fills the whole interior of man during sleep. From falling asleep to awakening, this musical activity continues. The ego and astral body, which are outside the physical and etheric body, receive strong impressions from what they have left behind: the resounding music in the etheric body. While it resounds in music, the etheric body is, at the same time, radiant with light, but the impression made upon the ego and the astral body remains unconscious.

In the same way, etheric streams of warmth flow into the interior of man from the whole surface of the skin. The result—with much else that is more remote from what we perceive in the external world as warmth, light, and sound, and is thus difficult to describe—is an immensely beautiful and impressive living and streaming activity of the human etheric body.

This particular music, radiance, and flooding stream of warmth stand out distinct, like an island, from the general etheric life of the cosmos. They stand out for inner reasons that are rooted in the very existence and being of man himself. They belong to man's individual etheric body. It is this flooding warmth, this phosphorescent glow, this resounding music that, a few days after man's death, detaches as the etheric body from the astral body and ego, and flows out into the general cosmic ether.

You see what complex processes are embraced in the human etheric body. If the attempt is made to penetrate further—using the methods with which penetration into such realms is possible—then it can be observed that in reality this flowing warmth, this gentle phosphorescent glow, and this living music are an outer revelation of cosmic beings. All that I have described is the external clothing, the revelation, the glory of mighty cosmic beings. These beings disclose themselves as those we know, from anthroposophical writings, as the Exusiai. I have often named these *Exusiai Revelations* because they live, in accordance with

their inner nature, in the shining stream that, during earthly
sleep, flows from the human sense-organs towards the interior
of man. In this stream, the weaving life of those beings we name
Exusiai is revealed.

Now, with the same methods with which one observes these
revelations of the human senses, so active in their etheric
substance during sleep, these streams can be followed further
along their course into the interior of man's organism. If one is
looking at some shining object, one can follow the line from the
eye towards this object. It is to be found somewhere on this line
that leads outwards: the visual line. In the same way, you can
follow the streaming, flooding etheric radiance inward from the
senses.

There is not so far to go. Very soon, something different is
reached. The mild phosphorescent glow, proceeding from the
eyes; the living music, which comes from the region of the organs
of hearing; the streaming warmth, which goes inward from
the whole surface of the skin—all these become an organically
coherent etheric system. Now one sees how all that streams and
flows and shines inwards, from the senses and from the whole
skin, is formed into a shell-like copy of man, but within him,
extending to a certain depth. From the eyes, one sees this
phosphorescent glow, inwards, changing into something I will
describe in a moment. The streaming warmth goes inwards from
the skin, attains a certain thickness like a shell, and then forms
a kind of etheric organism that is composed of the living music,
the glowing light, and the streaming warmth, intermingled
with one another. All these, and much else, flow through one
another, influence one another mutually, and form an organism:
the etheric organism of man. If one contemplates this etheric
organism with spiritual vision and begins to understand its
phenomena, one is bound to describe it as consisting simply
of the forms of thoughts: flowing thoughts. What is flowing
everywhere within it is thought.

If one were to follow this inner activity of the etheric body
during sleep, in its continual fluctuation, and then draw it at a

particular moment, one would, of course, draw lines, or colored forms. But to describe the substance of these lines or colored forms, one could only say, "It is as if thoughts were starting to flow." What lives otherwise in the activity of thought becomes an ever-changing flood and flow. It is the thought process of the Universe individualized. This individualized thought process of the Universe reveals itself as individualized Logos. One cannot really say that this forming of thoughts that streams and weaves within man, connected with these movements shining in from the senses, is only thought, for it speaks. It speaks a silent language, but one that can be perceived as belonging to the interior of man. It speaks, as all things through the Logos speak to us, in an individual form, expressing in an inner Word that can be perceived spiritually: the essential being of Man.

Etheric Donations of the Hierarchy

In *The Spiritual Hierarchies* (GA 110), Rudolf Steiner describes the development of the ethers in relationship to the evolution of the Earth through the stages of Saturn, Sun, Moon, and Earth.

Hence, spiritual science sees in everything that is outwardly perceptible something that has proceeded from an original condition of fire or warmth and which has turned into air, smoke, or gas, when the warmth began to condense into gas, gas into liquid, liquid into solid. "Look backwards," says the spiritual scientist, "look at any solid substance. That solidity was once liquid. It is only in the course of evolution that it has become solid, and the liquid was once upon a time gaseous, and the gaseous formed itself as smoke, out of the fire." But a transmutation, a bewitching of spiritual being, is always connected with these processes of condensation and with the formation of gases and solids.

How are those spiritual, divine beings who surround us able to produce solid matter as it is on our planet—to produce liquids and air substances? They send down their elemental spirits: those which live in the fire. They imprison them in air, in water, and in earth. These are the emissaries: the elemental emissaries of the spiritual, creative, building beings. The elemental spirits first enter into fire. In fire, they still feel comfortable (if we care to express it by images), and then they are condemned to a life of bewitchment. We can say, looking around us: "These beings, whom we have to thank for all the things that surround us, had to come down out of the fire-element; they are bewitched in those things."

While you are thus regarding objects, the hosts of these elemental beings—who were and are being continually bewitched through the world-processes of condensation—are continually entering into you from your surroundings. Let us take it that the man staring at the objects has no inclination whatsoever to think about those objects, and no inclination to let the spirit of things live in his soul. He lives comfortably and merely passes through the world, but he does not work on it spiritually, with his ideas or feelings, or in any such way. He remains simply a spectator of the material things he meets in the world. Then these elemental spirits pass into him and remain there, having gained nothing from the world's process but the fact of having passed from the outer world into man.

Let us take another kind of man: one who works spiritually on the impressions he receives from the outer world and who, with his understanding and ideas, forms conceptions regarding the spiritual foundations of the world. He does not simply stare at a metal, but ponders over its nature and feels the beauty, which inspires and spiritualizes his impressions. What does such a man do? Through his own spiritual process, he releases the elemental being that has streamed into him from the outer world. He raises it to what it was before, and he frees the elemental from its state of enchantment.

Thus, through our own spiritual life, we can, without changing them, either imprison the spirits that are bewitched in air, water, and earth within us or, through our own increasing spirituality, free them and lead them back to their own element. During the whole of his earthly life, man lets those elemental spirits stream into him from the outer world. In the same measure in which he only stares at things and in which he simply lets the spirits dwell in him without transforming them, so does he release and redeem those spiritual elemental beings in like measure as he tries, with his ideas, conceptions, and feeling for beauty, to spiritually work out what he sees in the outer world.

Now, what happens to the elemental beings that, having come out of things, enter into man? At first, they remain within him. Also, those that are released remain at first, but they stay only until his death. When the man passes through death, a differentiation takes place between those elemental beings that have simply passed into him and that he had not led back to their higher element, and those that he has, through his own spiritualization, led back to their former condition. Those the man has not changed have not gained anything from their passage from the outer world into him, but others have gained the possibility of returning to their own original world upon the man's death. During his life, man is a place of transition for these elemental beings. When he has passed through the spiritual world and returns to earth in his next incarnation, all the elemental beings he has not released during his former life flock into him again. When he passes through the portals of his new birth, they return with him to the physical world, but he does not bring those he has released back with him, for they have returned into their original element.

Etheric Currents in the Human Body

In *Wisdom of Man, of the Soul, and of the Spirit* (GA 115), Rudolf Steiner tells us that all that we can see of ourselves with our eyes we perceive through the sentient soul; the sentient body would not be able to perceive it. It is the sentient soul that really comprehends the variety of etheric currents running through the physical body.

The portion of the human being that he sees with his eyes and that the sentient soul confronts is nothing but the image of the sentient body—the outer illusion of the sentient body. Perception comes about through other activities of the sentient soul. The latter extends to every point at which outer perception occurs, and what it perceives there is not the sentient soul, but the illusion of the sentient body. If we could perceive this, we would see that, astrally, something endeavors to approach, but it is pushed back.

This image of the sentient body comes about as follows. From back to front, there is co-operation of the sentient soul and the sentient body. When two currents meet, a damming up occurs, and thereby something is revealed. Imagine you see neither current, but only what results from the whirling together of the two. What shows as a result of this impact of the sentient soul thrusting outward and the sentient body pressing inward from without is the portion of our external corporeality that the eye or other outer sense can perceive. We can actually determine the point on the skin where the meeting of the sentient soul and sentient body occurs. We see how the soul works at forming the body.

We can put it this way: In the human being, a cooperation of the current passes from back to front and the reverse results in an impact of sentient soul and sentient body. In addition to these two currents, there are those that come from the right and from the left. From the left comes the one pertaining to the physical body, and from the right, the one pertaining to the etheric body. These currents flow into each other and intermingle to a certain extent, and what comes into being at this point is the sensibly perceptible human being—his sensibly perceptible exterior. A perfect illusion is brought about. From the left comes the current of the physical body and from the right that of the etheric body, and these form what appears to us as the sensibly perceptible human being.

In like manner, we have in us currents running upward and downward. From below, the main current of the astral body streams upward, and the main current of the ego streams downward from above. The characterization given of the sentient body as being bounded in front should be understood as meaning that it operates in a current upward from below, but that it is then seized by the current running forward from the rear so that, in a certain sense, it is thereby bounded.

But the astral body contains not only the one current that runs upward from below as well as forward from the rear, but also the other one running backward from the front, so that the astral body courses in two currents: one upward from below, and the other backward from the front. This gives us four intermingling currents in the human being. Actually, it is due to the intersection and crisscrossing of the currents that the threefold organization of man comes into being.

The lower currents, streaming from all sides, are held down from above, and we can designate this lower part as the sentient body. Below, the impulses proceed largely from without, while above, it is principally the sentient soul that makes itself felt. From above, there streams the ego, and at the point where this current is strongest—where it is least pushed back by the other currents—the intellectual soul forms its organ.

Now, in addition to this ego current, we have one from left to right and one from right to left. Again, the whole activity is intersected. There is, further, a current running through the longitudinal axis of the body, effecting a sort of split up above. At the upper boundary, a portion of the intellectual soul is split off, and this is the form of the consciousness soul. There, the consciousness soul is active, extending its formative work into the innermost man. Among other things, it forms the convolutions in the grey matter of the brain.

That is the way in which the spirit works on the form of the human body. It evokes all the organs plastically, as the artist chisels a figure out of stone. The structure of the brain can be comprehended only with the knowledge of how these separate currents interact in man; what we then see is the joint activity of the various principles of the human being.

We have considered the various currents in the human being and found them to run as follows:

From left to right, the currents of the physical body.
From right to left, those of the etheric body.
From below upward, those of the astral body.
From the front backward, those of the sentient body.
From the rear forward, those of the sentient soul.
From above downward, those of the ego.

When the etheric body withdraws from the physical body, the substances of the physical body group themselves in the manner that is natural to them, and the body becomes a corpse and falls to pieces. The etheric body, therefore, continually combats the destruction of the physical body. Each organ of the physical body has this etheric body behind it. The human being has an etheric heart, an etheric brain, etc. These hold the corresponding physical organs together. The etheric body consists of a number of currents of force. With respect to the form and size of the human etheric body, we may say that in its upper part, it is an exact image of the physical body. The lower parts are different; here, they do not coincide with the physical body. There is a great secret underlying the relationship between the etheric and physical bodies that throws a strong light upon human nature. The etheric body of a man is female, while that of a woman is male. This explains the fact that in each man's nature, there is much that is feminine, and in each woman's nature, there is much that is masculine.

Etheric Body After Death

In *Etheric Body After Death* (GA 159), Steiner tells us about what happens to the etheric body after a human being dies and how the separation of the physical, etheric, astral, and ego take place as a natural process.

When a man dies, the etheric body leaves him, as well as the astral body and ego. These three bodies rise away and remain united for a time. At the moment of death, the connection between the astral body, etheric body, and physical body is broken, particularly in the region of the heart. A sort of light shines forth in the heart, and then the etheric body, the astral body, and the ego can be seen rising up from out of the head. The actual instant of death brings a remarkable experience: for a brief space of time, the man remembers all that has happened to him in the life that just ended. His entire life appears before his soul in a moment, like a great tableau. Something like this can happen during life, in rare moments of great shock or anger, like when a man is drowning, or falling from a great height, and death seems imminent. He may see his whole life before him in this way.

A similar phenomenon is the peculiar tingling feeling we have when a limb "goes to sleep." What happens here is that the etheric body is loosened. If a finger, for example, goes to sleep, a clairvoyant would see a second little finger protruding at the side of the actual finger: this is a part of the etheric body that has gotten loose. Herein also lies the danger of hypnotism, for the brain then has the same experience as the finger has when it goes to sleep. The clairvoyant can see the loosened etheric body hanging like a pair of bags or sacks on either side of the head. If the hypnotism is repeated, the etheric body will develop an inclination to get loose, and this can be very dangerous. The victims become dreamy, have fainting fits, lose their independence, and so on.

A similar loosening of the etheric body occurs when a person is faced with a sudden danger of death. The cause of this similarity is that the etheric body is the bearer of memory; the more strongly developed it is, the stronger a person's faculty of memory will be. While the etheric body is firmly rooted in the physical body, as normally it is, its vibrations cannot act on the brain sufficiently to become conscious, because the physical body, with its coarser rhythms, conceals them. But in moments of deadly danger, the etheric body is loosened, and with its memories, it detaches itself from the brain. Thus, a man's whole life flashes before his soul. At such moments, everything that has been inscribed on the etheric body reappears. Hence, there is also the recollection of the whole past life immediately after death. This lasts for some time, until the etheric body separates from the astral body and the ego.

With most people, the etheric body dissolves gradually into the world-ether. With lowly, uneducated people, it dissolves slowly; with cultivated people, it dissolves quickly; with disciples or pupils, it dissolves slowly again. The higher a man's development, the slower the process becomes, until a stage when the etheric body no longer dissolves is reached.

Death is the "brother" of sleep. The difference between a man who is dead and one who is only sleeping is that at death, the etheric body passes away with the astral body, and the physical body alone is left behind in the physical world. From birth until death, the etheric body never leaves the physical body, except during certain states of initiation.

The period immediately following death is of great importance for the human being. It lasts for many hours—even days—during which the whole of the incarnation that is just over comes before the soul of the dead, as in a great tableau of memories. The tableau widens out and, in an astonishingly brief span of time, man sees all the detailed events of his life.

After the lapse of the time during which the etheric body and the astral body are emerging from the physical body after death, there comes the moment when the astral body, with the higher members, leaves the etheric body. The latter separates, and the memory-tableau fades away, but something of it remains; it is not wholly lost. What may be called ether or life-substance dissipates in the cosmic ether, but a kind of essence remains, and this can never be lost to the human being through his further journeying. He bears this with him into all his future incarnations as a kind of extract from the life-tableau, even though he has no remembrance of it. Out of this extract is formed what is called, with concrete reality, the "Causal Body." After every incarnation, a new page is added to the Book of Life. This augments the life-essence and, if the past lives were fruitful, causes the next life to develop in the proper way. This is what causes a life to be rich or poor in talents, qualities, and the like.

After death, the period of *Kamaloca* is a time of the breaking of material pleasures and impulses. It lasts for approximately one third of the time of the earthly life. The human being begins actually to live backwards through the whole of his past life. Immediately after death, there was a memory-tableau devoid of the elements of joy and suffering; in Kamaloca, the human being lives through all the joy and all the suffering again in such a way that he must experience in himself all the joy and suffering he caused to others.

The journey backwards begins with the last event before death and proceeds at triple speed to birth. When, in this backward passage of remembrance, the human being reaches his birth, the part of the astral body that has been transformed by the ego combines with the causal body, and what has not been so transformed falls away like a shade or phantom; this is the astral corpse of the human being. He has laid aside the physical corpse, the etheric corpse, and now the astral corpse.

When the life has been lived through backwards as far as earliest childhood and the three corpses have been discarded, man reaches the condition mysteriously indicated in the Bible by the words: "Except ye become as little children, ye cannot enter the Kingdom of Heaven."

The constitution of an etheric body must be of such a kind as to enable it to provide the life-forces required by a human being until he reaches an advanced age. Man's external physical body grows older and older, but this is not the case with the etheric body. It may, perhaps, be difficult to understand this, but the etheric body does not grow older in any way; the etheric body grows younger and younger, in the same degree in which the physical body grows older, until it reaches, as it were, a certain childlike stage of etheric existence, when the human being passes through the portal of death after having reached a normal age. We should, therefore, say to ourselves that when we begin our physical life on earth through birth, our etheric body—which has become united with our physical body—is old (comparatively speaking). In the course of our earthly life, it grows younger and younger, until it reaches its childhood stage, when we pass through the portal of death.

Imaginative Pictures of the Etheric Realms

In *The Earth's Etheric Body* (GA 181), Rudolf Steiner describes the ether realms in imaginative pictures that demonstrate that no simple image of an ether is complete. The ethers are of cosmic proportions and must be approached with an open imagination to behold the full scope of their workings.

Human beings think through their brains, and in the same way, the earth thinks through sleeping human bodies. The earth always perceives by day; it perceives through the fact that the sun shines upon it out of the cosmic spaces. That is the earth's perception. During the night, the earth works out all its perceptions. "The Earth thinks," says the clairvoyant seer. This is because it makes use of the sleeping human beings. Every sleeping human being becomes, as it were, a brain-molecule of the earth. Our physical body is organized in such a way that it can be used by the earth for its thinking activity, when we do not use it ourselves.

Just as the earth thinks through the physical body, so it "imagines" all that is not earthly upon the earth itself—all that belongs to the earth from out of the cosmos. The Earth imagines this through the etheric body.

We may discern in the sleeping human body parts of the earth's brain, when the human being is asleep, in his etheric body, the imagination of that part of the universe which belongs, to begin with, to the earth. The etheric body contains, in a play of wonderful pictures, all the forces that must stream into the earth out of the etheric world, so that the earth's life may take place.

As a physical being, man belongs to the earth, just as he belongs to the heavens as an etheric being. We can only use our physical body as an organ of thinking because it is organized for that purpose, and because the earth sets it free for this purpose when we are awake. And we can only use our etheric body in such a way that it provides us with life-forces because the heavens place it at our disposal when we are awake, and because the heavenly forces of *Imagination* are transformed into life-forces within us when we are awake.

Thus, we cannot speak of our etheric body merely as a misty form, but we should rather speak of it as a microcosmic form that reflects the heavens. When we are born, the etheric body is handed over to us as a specifically perfect form. When we are born, our etheric body glistens and shines inwardly because it is so full of *Imaginations* that come towards it from the great universe. It is a magnificent reflection of the universe! All that we acquire during our life as culture, knowledge, and forces of the will and of feeling is all drawn out of our etheric body as we grow old in the course of our existence between birth and death. Heaven's cosmic forces give us what they must give us during our life between birth and death, and so we are once more young as etheric beings, when we have lived through a normal life between birth and death, for then we have drawn everything that could be drawn out of our etheric body.

The etheric body that man receives through the fact that the human soul enters physical existence through birth contains a whole collection of forces pertaining to the spiritual world. These forces are gradually used up during physical life. They do not come from nothing; they exist in the spiritual world, but when an etheric body belonging to a youthful body passes through the portal of death, it still contains a great deal of unused heavenly light. That is why it becomes a mediator of the forces of *Inspiration*.

Appearance of Christ in the Etheric Realm

In *Christ in the Etheric Realm* (GA 112), Rudolf Steiner tells us about the ultimate secret of the etheric realm and Christ's appearance in this realm. To see Christ in the etheric realm is tantamount to witnessing the Second Coming of Christ.

Thus, an impulse had to come to the Earth through which the exhausted treasure of ancient wisdom might be replenished, and through which the etheric body might be endowed with new life, thus enabling the physical element—otherwise destined for decomposition—to acquire a force of incorruptibility and to be filled with an etheric body that makes it not subject to decay. This rescues it from Earth evolution. This life that pervades the etheric body is what Christ has brought. The Christ impulse has infused man's etheric body with new life, after the old has been spent! Hence, ever since the Mystery of Golgotha, there has been something in man's etheric body that is not subject to death, and which does not succumb to the death-forces of the Earth. The force of etheric bodies that have remained intact will form a sphere around the Earth that is in the process of becoming a Sun. A sort of spirit sphere is forming around the Earth out of etheric bodies that have become alive.

The boundary of the World Ether is described as the akasha, which extends beyond the zodiac and up to the seventh region of spirit-land. It is also the bearer of world memory. The world ether is a thought-forming power that is the spiritual substance of the cosmos. There is nothing else in the universe besides consciousness; beings in various states of consciousness are the only reality in the world.

The world ether is a manifold activity of many cosmic beings, whose main task is to create the phenomenal forms of the nature kingdoms. The evolution of the world ether and the kingdoms of nature are inseparable. The hierarchical beings secreted four kinds of ether into the cosmic world as a sacrificial substance.

Ethers and the Dimensions of Space

In *The Fourth Dimension* (GA 324), Rudolf Steiner speaks about the nature of the seven dimensions and their relationship to the ethers as they were initially created and now develop into the higher dimensions.

Space is a self-contained sphere. What appears to human beings as physical space is only an imprint or copy of self-contained space. We can say that a human being's essence is realized in space. Space itself, from the esoteric perspective, must be seen as something produced as a result of creative activity. Its creation precedes the work and activity of the highest hierarchies, so we can presuppose the existence of space. Space is a creation of the Holy Trinity.

Time has had meaning only since the separation of the ancient Moon from the Sun. Everything external exists in space, and everything internal runs its course in time.

Electricity is light in the sub-material state, compressed to the greatest possible extent. We must also attribute inwardness to light; light is itself at every point. Warmth can expand into space in three directions, but in the case of light, we must speak of a fourth dimension. It expands in four directions, with inwardness as the fourth direction.

In reality, the Sun moves forward while the Earth and the other planets follow it. We have a line like the thread of a screw, with the Sun at one point and the Earth at the other end. Our dual focus on the Earth and Sun and on their progressive, screw-like movement creates the illusion that the Earth is revolving around the Sun. That is, as soon as we move into the etheric realm, we need to apply an axial coordinate system that is the opposite—also qualitatively speaking—of the ordinary coordinate system. Ordinary theories about the ether of physics err in not taking this difference into account, making it difficult to define the ether. It is sometimes seen as a fluid, and sometimes as a gas. It is wrong to apply a coordinate system that radiates from a central point to the ether. As soon as we enter the ether, we must take a sphere and construct the whole system from the outside in, instead of the other way around.

The temporal element in humans runs its course as an independent entity, and the spatial element is governed by the temporal or dynamic element.

The transition to the fourth dimension simply eliminates or cancels out the third dimension. This type of synthetic geometry plays into the perception that develops in the imaginative world.

The first dimension is inherent in your own upright posture, the second in your left-right dimension, and the third in the focusing of your eyes. You do not dwell in these three dimensions when you are in the *Imaginative* world. There, you dwell only in two dimensions. Two dimensions are a reality in the *Imaginative* world, and a single dimension is a reality in the *Inspired* world. All *Inspirations* move vertically. *Intuition* is point-like.

Elemental Beings and the Ethers

In the lecture *The Etheric Formative Forces* (GA 38), Rudolf Steiner gives one of his best descriptions of the elemental beings that are associated with the etheric formative forces.

As soon as we ascend into the ether, we encounter warmth ether, light ether, chemical ether, and life ether. If we look at these kinds of ether with the spiritual vision that sees elemental beings, we find the elemental beings of the etheric spheres: light beings, number beings, and beings who carry life streaming through the cosmos. These beings are quite different from the beings in the lower elemental kingdoms. Man's etheric body is connected with the entire sphere of nature spirits in our environment.

The nature spirits—the descendants of the beings of the Third Hierarchy—are little master builders and foremen in the kingdoms of nature. The gnomes carry life ether into the roots; they carry the ether in which they live into the roots. Undines cultivate the chemical ether in plants, sylphs the light ether, and the fire spirits the warmth ether.

We should point to the fact that just as the lower elements— earth, water, air, and warmth—are inhabited by elemental beings, so there are other beings in the etheric elements: light ether, chemical ether, sound ether, and life ether. But the latter elemental beings are very different from the elemental beings in the lower elements.

The countless materializations that elemental beings bring about are called "enchantments," while the corresponding dematerializations are "disenchantments" of these beings. Spiritual beings, which can also be called elemental beings, are enchanted in the air and bewitched into a lower form of existence when air is transformed into the liquid state. An enchantment of spiritual beings is always connected with the condensation and formation of gases and solids. Spiritual beings send down elemental beings and imprison them in air, water, and earth. These are the elemental messengers of the spiritual, creative, formative beings. These beings, to whom we owe everything surrounding us, are enchanted in the things.

Nothing can be solid or liquid unless some warmth is present in it. Warmth has to be active in some way. So, we can say that heat or fire was and is the foundation of all things. The Seraphim work in what we call warmth; they are behind all forms of warmth. The Elohim hold sway in the warmth on our earth. Dynamis work in airy things, Kyriotetes in liquids, and Thrones and Exusiai in earthly solids. Cherubim are active in the transition of water into vapor, and wherever clouds form in the earth's atmosphere.

What the elemental beings have called into the world, as it were, is the last reverberation of the creative, formative, cosmic Word that underlies all activity and existence. Spiritual beings are everywhere in nature.

Gnomes were created by detaching parts of Archai beings. Undines came from Archangels in the same way, and sylphs from Angels. Salamanders were detached from group souls of animals from the Dynamis. Thrones have undines, the Cherubim the sylphs, and the Seraphim the salamanders. The sum of the four groups of elemental beings is the etheric body of the earth. The Sun is active in all of the earthly elements, and after it has penetrated and inoculated all of them, it works upon the human being through them by way of its servants, which we call elemental beings. The living Sun Spirit works into the elements. Matter is built up in the way the Christ has gradually arranged it. One will find the Christ right down to the laws of chemistry and physics.

The elemental beings in solids (gnomes) are related to the human intellect. The elemental beings connected with fluids (undines) are related to human feeling, and the elemental beings of the airy element (sylphs) are related to the human will. The elemental beings that arose from previous realms are very useful in our nature kingdoms. They continually dive down into individual creatures in the nature kingdoms, where they become enchanted, and then they are released again. All four groups of elemental beings are active in the creation of the physical forms of weather.

Elemental beings are not visible to our physical senses and have a body and a soul but do not have a spirit. Anyone who wants to see them must develop clairvoyant consciousness. The elemental world is one which can only be perceived by what we call *Imagination*. One can also call the elemental world the *Imaginative* world.

The elemental beings will not evolve higher or become human beings. After they have completed their work in the nature kingdoms, they will be redeemed as they are breathed in by the beings from whom they were detached.

Various kinds of consciousness exist in our earth, and what modern physicists call laws of nature are the thoughts of beings, who think on the physical plane and have their bodies on the astral plane. The creative nature forces are beings, and natural laws are their thoughts. The fire spirits are the carriers of world thoughts into man's thought life. If one enters this sphere of the fire beings, one not only sees oneself in the thoughts, but one sees the thought content of the world, which is really an *Imaginative* content at the same time. Thus, world thoughts give one the power to rise above oneself.

Salamanders, which we can equate with the elemental world of thoughts, are the instruments or servants of Angels, at whose behest they become enchanted into the thought corpses of human beings. On the other hand, they can be released from enchantment through the spiritual enlivenment of human thinking. Angles receive the thoughts they will give to the fire spirits from the hierarchy of the Dynamis, who in turn get the thought-archetypes for this from the formless plane, where the forces and the consciousness of the Cherubim and Seraphim originate.

The human being is related to the earth regions through the outer part of his physical body. Through his etheric body, he is connected with the spirits of water. Through his astral body, he is related to the spirits of air, and through his ego, he is related to the spirits of fire. The spirits of the Rotation of Time and the group souls of the plants make up the astral body of the earth. Thus, the astral atmosphere or the astrality of the earth lives in the ascending and descending water cycle.

Rudolf Steiner Concerning the Etheric Christ

"Thus, we see how the Christ, once He has descended to the Earth, begins from the condition of a physical, earthly human being and gradually evolves as an etheric, astral and ego-Christ in order, as an ego-Christ, to become the Spirit of Earth who then rises to higher stages with all human beings." *The Mission of Christian Rosenkreutz*, GA 130

"The new Christ event, which is now approaching, not physically but etherically, is connected with the first kindling of the faculty of memory that is imbued by Christ, where Christ approaches man as an angelic being. We must prepare ourselves for this." *The Mystery of Golgotha*, GA 152

"The etheric body must be revitalized, and this is connected with the new revelation of Christ. Through etheric bodies being revitalized, they behold to Christ." *The Occult Movement in the 19th Century*, GA 254

"Thus, at the time when people will be least inclined to believe in documents, the new profession of faith in Christ Jesus will arise through our growing into the sphere in which we shall initially encounter Him, through our growing into the mysterious land of

Shamballa, a spiritual realm in the Earth's aura which is imbued and irradiated with light and abounding in infinite fullness of life. Already in grey antiquity the true initiates of mankind, and also the bodhisattvas again and again, derived the spiritual forces of their higher knowledge from this land. Among the first things that people will behold when Shamballa becomes visible once more will be Christ in His etheric form. Michael can show himself there with an aura of light, with the gesture of a spirit-being, in which all the splendor and glory of the past intelligence of the Gods is revealed." *The Sermon on the Mount*, GA 118

"The human etheric body will provide the basis, at a higher stage, for the immortal man, who will no longer be subject to death. The etheric body at present still dissolves with the death of the human being. But the more man perfects and purifies himself from within, the nearer will he get to permanence, the less will he perish. Every labor undertaken for the etheric body contributes towards man's immortality. In this sense, it is true that man will gain more mastery, the more evolution takes place naturally, the more it is directed towards the forces of life." *The Temple Legend*, GA 93

"For the ether body is at the same time the 'body of love' where life forces are continually arising out of love." *The Mission of Christian Rosenkreutz*, GA 130

"Just as the light of Christ radiates forth from the Earth, so is there also a kind of reflection of it that encircles the Earth. What is reflected here as the light of Christ and has appeared as a consequence of the Christ event is what Christ called the Holy Spirit. Just as the event of Golgotha provided the initial impulse for the Earth to become a sun, it is equally true that from this event onwards the Earth has also begun to be creative, surrounding itself with a spiritual (etheric) ring." *The Gospel of St. John*, GA 112

"Thus, the Gods have before them an image of humanity as a goal, as their highest ideal, as their religion. And as though on the far shore of divine existence there shimmers for the Gods the temple which is their highest artistic achievement, representing a reflection of Divine Being in the image of man." *The Inner Nature of Man*, GA 153

"Christ is a being who had come down from the Sun leaving His *Spirit-Man* on the Sun and His *Life-spirit* in the atmosphere around the Earth, and brought His *Ego* together with His *Spirit Self* down to the Earth." *Karmic Relationships V. 9*, GA 240

"Conscious working into the ether body is, therefore, chelahood; conscious working in the physical body represents mastery." *An Esoteric Cosmology*, GA 94

"What is new and what will now gradually be revealed to human beings is a recollection or repetition of what St. Paul experienced at Damascus. He beheld the etheric body of Christ. The reason why this will now become visible to us derives from the fact that what could be called a new Mystery of Golgotha has taken place in the etheric world. What took place here in the physical world at the Crucifixion, as a result of the hatred of uncomprehending humanity, has now been repeated on the etheric level owing to the hatred of human beings who have entered the etheric world as materialists after death.

Let us visualize once more how, at the Mystery of Golgotha, a cross of dead wood was erected on which the body of Christ Jesus hung. And then let us visualize the wood of that cross in the etheric world as green, sprouting and living wood which has been turned to charcoal by the flames of hatred and on which only seven blossoming roses appear, representing Christ's sevenfold nature. There we have the picture of the second Mystery of Golgotha which has now taken place in the etheric world. And through this dying, this second death of Christ, we have gained the possibility of beholding the etheric body in which the etheric Christ appears to human beings." *Anthroposophy and Cosmology*, GA 265

Etheric Formative Forces of Guenther Wachsmuth

Rudolf Steiner worked closely with Guenther Wachsmuth on the book *The Etheric Formative Forces*. This book constitutes the most comprehensive picture of the nature of the ethers and the etheric formative forces that we have from Steiner. Wachsmuth was Steiner's personal secretary, who was guided and assisted by Steiner in writing the book as the definitive Anthroposophic treatise on the ethers. Below are sections of the book that lay the foundation of what is generally accepted as Steiner's views on the ethers as given to Wachsmuth. The synopsis of Guenther Wachsmuth's book will add to the evolving understanding of the ethers that developed among other Anthroposophists.

There are seven etheric primal or formative forces that are active in the cosmos. However, only four reveal themselves in the space-and-time processes of our present phenomenal world: the warmth ether, the light ether, the chemical ether (or sound ether), and the life ether.

There are seven etheric formative forces, of which four realize themselves in the present phenomenal world:

Unfallen life ether (Tree of Life)
Unfallen chemical ether (Tree of Life)
Akasha ether

Life ether—solid
Chemical ether—fluid
Light ether—gas
Warmth ether—heat

The phenomenal world of ponderable substance is a medium state extending between the force-activities of the etheric on one side and electricity on the other. The state of substance at any time is the result of this conflict between forces over the mutable world of substance.

- Life ether
- Chemical ether
- Light ether
- Warmth ether—heat, warmth, fire
- Light ether—gas, air
- Chemical ether—liquid, fluid, water
- Life ether—solid, earth

Man's organism is a microcosm, a copy of the great world organism, the macrocosm. It is through the action of the etheric that life comes to birth. The living cosmic architecture through which these formative forces have produced the evolution of the macrocosm, the genesis and maintenance of the earth organism, finally reaches a degree of completion in the architecture of the human organism. This not only places and maintains man in a state of harmony with the macrocosmic process, but strives for a higher ascent beyond that he has already reached in the preceding evolution.

The world of spiritual Being streams into the world of substance, bringing to pass involution, evolution, and "creating out of nothing" in an eternal, harmonious circuit. Thus the cosmic formative forces also stream into the living world of being of the earth organism, bringing forth, through the manifold reciprocal action of the etheric formative forces, the variations of the world of colors in the world of extension, of space, and of time.

The cosmos must be grasped as a world-organism—the product of active spiritual entities—as a world of organisms whose vital phenomena are the work of the harmonious metamorphosis of etheric formative forces. Cosmos, earth, and man are built up according to the same will, through the same etheric forces, and of the same substances. The human being who knows himself perceives the being of Nature. Mother Nature has built him. He builds and masters Nature until human knowledge fully embraces cosmos, earth, and man.

The living earth organism has an etheric system of forces in which processes of breathing and circulation take place corresponding to similar life-processes in the human organism. The earth organism consists of a physical body and an "ether body of the earth," which comprises its etheric formative forces. The "ether body" calls the phenomena of life into existence and regulates and metamorphoses them.

The basis for a new method of studying the etheric will be an organic conception of the various cosmic spheres of etheric action belonging to the several planets and heavenly bodies. By including the other attributes of the etheric, we reach a more profound understanding of the "world organism" and its life processes linked with physical motion, etheric currents, and states of consciousness.

The world consists of "states and their transitions one into another," brought about by the etheric formative forces. The world we perceive has been created and is being created by these etheric formative forces. The spatial comes into existence when the being of a thing passes over into the phenomenal world and mediates the transition from being into phenomenon, and from non-spatial into spatial.

Through thought, the human spirit seeks to coalesce into a unity that is sundered into multiplicity in the perceptible world.

Human thought reverses the action of the etheric formative forces that bring about the phenomenal world; it leads backwards from the phenomenal to real being, and from the separate or spatial into the real or non-spatial. Space and time come to be when the being of a thing passes over into the phenomenal world. Juxtaposition and sequence are other ways to refer to space and time. The etheric formative forces are the bridge between being and phenomena, but they are also the bridge between non-spatial and spatial.

The warmth ether is the primal working entity. When this passes over from the state of rest into activity or, in other words, passes imperceptibly from the "latent" state to our organs and into a state of activity that is perceptible to us, it actually enters into the world of space and time. Gradually, the three additional etheric formative forces proceed from it. These additional etheric formative forces, which weave the perceptible world of color and form, proceed from the warmth ether. This is when, through the action of these four etheric formative forces, the space-time processes that constitute our phenomenal and perceptible world begin.

The warmth and light ethers act expansively—that is, in a space-affirming way—and the chemical and life ethers act contractingly—that is, in a space-denying way. The evolution of the world takes its course, therefore, not merely between primal nebula and heat-death, but between space-genesis and space-annihilation—between the affirmation and the denial of space. First, the space-affirming appeared in the phylogenesis of our cosmic system, and later the space-denying forces appeared. The genesis of the etheric formative forces is the genesis of space.

But the cosmic ether, from the Earth toward Saturn, is by no means a constant and uniform quantity. This world ether is subject—not only as regards space, but also as regards time—to a never-ceasing organic change, though this takes place very gradually, over very long stretches of time. We can divide the cosmos into great fields of space (spheres) that are filled with the etheric active forces of the individual planets.

It is by no means only "electrons" that stream in eternal alternation into the human organism and the living beings of the other kingdoms of nature and out again, but that these are entities that, in their totality, can never be grasped within the range of the theories of modern physics. We do not yet possess any adequate knowledge of phenomena of consciousness associated with the manifestations of force and processes of life and motion in the happenings in the rest of the cosmos.

We perceive that the metamorphosis of states does not merely carry through a meaningless transition from one arbitrary state to some other arbitrary state, but that metamorphosis in the phenomenal world, viewed comprehensively, generally brings an ascent of the evolutionary forms and capacities according to spiritual laws to pass.

The four etheric formative forces have also naturally brought about, in their spheres of activity, the states of aggregation and conditions of substance normal to these forces. The inward-drawing forces of the chemical and life ethers, tending to concentrate, have worked in toward the center of the earth, produced the solid and fluid substances, and assembled these toward the middle spheres of the earth organism. The outward-striving, centrifugal forces of the light and warmth ethers have produced the gaseous state of the earth's atmosphere and, in accordance with their tendency to strive outward from the center, have gathered this atmosphere in the outer part of the Earth organism. The etheric formative forces, in their spheres of activity, not only work in the generation of the corresponding states of chemical inter-relationships and states of aggregation of substance, but also in the formation and union of substance.

The unit of substance consists of four globular spheres that surround one another when they are in a static condition. These may be viewed as the spheres of activity of the four etheric forces, and thus the great earth organism—that is, the solid Earth with its atmosphere—is formed so that it consists of four globular concentric spheres, and in each of these four spheres, there is one of the four etheric formative forces.

The suctional, inward-drawing forces of the chemical and life ethers have their principal spheres of activity, corresponding with their tendency, concentrated at the earth, with its component solid and fluid parts. The outward-tending, centrifugal forces of light ether and warmth ether, on the contrary, have their spheres of activity primarily in the gaseous atmosphere surrounding the globe. This gaseous atmosphere is surrounded by a mantle of warmth ether at the outer borders of the atmosphere, towards the cosmos.

Types of Ether

The four kinds of ether may be classified in two groups. The warmth and light Ethers have the tendency to expand and the impulse to radiate out from a given central point. They act centrifugally. The other two—the chemical and life ethers—have the tendency to draw in toward a center, and the impulse to concentrate all in a given central point; their action is sectional or centripetal. This polarity of the two ether groups—the centrifugal, radiating, self-expanding will, and the suctional, centripetal will to draw inward or to concentrate—is an ultimate elemental principle that lies at the bottom of all natural phenomena.

Warmth Ether (Fire)

Warmth ether tends towards the spherical form. **Warmth ether** is the etheric side of warmth: the inner, impulse-creating warmth, or the warmth of enthusiasm that occurs as the intention that underlies actions. Its elemental counterpart is fire, or externally perceivable warmth. Warmth ether and warmth as an element are closely related. Warmth is the most rarefied element, and is more like a quality than a substance. It represents the transition between the elements and the ethers, and shares features with both. Warmth as an element can be perceived as the external heat of objects and as body temperature. This warmth is produced when material substances are burned. Warmth as an ether is the inner, impulse-creating warmth that incites activity and that arises when you become enthusiastic about something. It arises within you and has no material features. This is the warmth you need to proceed to action. Because it incites action, warmth ether points towards the future.

Warmth ether is characterized by **impulse-creation** and **directionality**. It is a very active quality and is represented by fire as the physical element, which can always burn or grow old. This involves time progressing and has the quality of ripening. In humans, this is found in the will. The fire of love is born from the heart.

Warmth appears in time, ripening, and the human will. The warmth of blood, or blood as the physical bearer of the I/Ego, is dimensionless, non-spatial, and intensive movement. Fire begins as a spark, grows to any size, and then shrinks and dies, disappearing from sight. Time progresses like a slow-burning fire. Through an inner glowing or burning, the will of a human is constantly renewing and rising up. Enthusiasm for life is a steady flame that ignites all around it.

Light Ether (Air)

Light ether is invisible. We have learned to recognize other waves that are invisible, like ultra-violet, infra-red, and electric waves, but these have the same characteristics as light waves, differing only in their lengths. Light ether produces triangular forms. It illuminates everything and makes all material things visible. It is also the force that makes plants grow upwards and makes people stand and walk upright. Light ether corresponds to the air element. It makes everything visible by illuminating material things. Light delineates objects and enables you to see their spatial boundaries. You can't see light itself; you can only perceive its presence through the objects and the air it illuminates.

Light radiates from a source. It diminishes with the distance from the source, as it is scattered in space. As the amount of light increases, the illuminated space becomes larger. Light is linear, can be split into two beams by an object placed in its path, and can't turn corners. It cannot fill a void around a corner, unlike air.

Light ether induces growth and elongation (plants grow towards the light, while bones in animals and humans grow and elongate under the influence of vitamin D, the production of which is stimulated by light) and makes space expand. Light draws your gaze outward to objects. This shows you that light ether attracts. As seen from within the object (matter), it is a process of elongation; as seen from the periphery (ether), it is a matter of attraction.

Because there is light, there is also darkness. Light ether works between the poles of light and darkness, with the colors of twilight in between. Between light and darkness, there is an area that, on the one hand, has qualities that are mixtures of the two poles (half-light) and, on the other hand, has qualities of its own (such as colors). Light ether is characterized by **delineation and the creation of space, linearity and attraction, and polarization.** It leads to the periphery and draws the viewer to feel as though he or she is being sucked into that periphery. This also gives the quality of levity, where there is an elongation or uprightness and overcoming of gravity.

Light rays out luminosity, air, growth, and feelings, and it makes things visible and interesting. It stimulates curiosity, admiration, patience, equanimity, and thankfulness. Light is not visible. Imagine a sunrise from darkness to daylight. Slowly, we can distinguish things around us: the objects are seen separated now, space and distances become clear, and space is created through limitation. Light and space belong together. Structure is to see; light divides the inside from the outside and radiates towards the periphery. Light is expanding in space, raying out. The periphery is the constructive principle of light, and the periphery/horizon is sucking our view or consciousness towards the horizon. Light sucks out the sprouts of plants, and in a living organism, it shows as growth. Light brings interest and feelings to the soul that create our relationship to the world around us.

Light ether works through air. Air is not visible. It fills the space between objects and has no boundaries. It connects everything. It has no structure or direction and is like chaos because it has elasticity, causing centripetal tension and pressure towards a center. Light ether helps create thinking. It is in strong contrast to matter.

Tone, Sound, Number, Chemical Ether (Liquid)

Chemical ether is also called tone, number, or sound ether. Its forces cause the chemical processes, differentiations, dissolutions, and unions of substances. Its forces transmit the tones perceptible to the senses to us. Space is interpenetrated by waves produced by the forces of the chemical ether, which dissolve and unite substances through geometric, morphological, and harmonic resonance. Chemical ether has a tone and sound nature of which sensible sound, or tone heard by the physical ear, is only an outward expression—that is, an expression that has passed through air as a medium.

Chemical ether produces half-moon forms and is centripetal. Cold and contraction are ascribed to chemical ether. It is the force that structures the development of phenomena and can be seen in the natural succession of plant communities. It corresponds to the water element.

Tone ether is the type of ether that separates and connects. Music is thus based on a force that separates and, at the same time, recombines what was separated in a harmonious way. Tone ether works through proportions, distances, and measures. It separates and recombines, creating a unified whole.

Chemical substances also show certain fixed ratios between the chemical elements themselves, as well as in compounds like salts, acids, and proteins. That's why this type of ether is also known as chemical ether. This ether plays a role in all processes where things are separated and then recombined in new and harmonious proportions. It is characterized by the concepts of **separating, structuring, creating proportions,** and **harmonizing.**

The number ether divides, and this creates the numbers (frequencies) and numerical proportions (geometry) of the created world. It brings order and harmony to the growth of all

living things through the Harmony of the Spheres and is the basis
for all chemical activity between substances, sometimes causing it
to be called the valence ether.

Chemical ether works through water, which always wants
to become a totality: one drop at a time creating mass and
integrating like the fusion of two cells during fertilization. Water
is the gesture of sympathy; it is thick and heavy; has mass, gravity,
and weight; and can be active or passive.

Life Ether (Solid)

Life ether is the most highly evolved ether, and therefore
is the most varied and complicated in its qualities. It is that
which is rayed out to us, among other things, from the Sun,
and then modified in its action by the atmosphere of the Earth.
Life ether, together with chemical ether, belongs to the group of
suctional forces: those which tend to draw inwards. It is related
to that which is called "gravitation" and to the phenomenon of
magnetism.

Its form-building tendency, when it can exert its effect
unhindered in substance, leads to square shapes that are
expressed, for instance, in crystallizing salt. It is the force
that makes an object and its environment appear as a unified
whole. It is the force that unifies an object's course of life. Life
ether corresponds to the earth element and is the life force of
organisms. It is the force that creates organic units that are more
than the sum of their parts, and in which each component is an
integral part of the whole. It is the ether that causes delineation
as well as integration. It causes the whole to be visible in each
component. It also ensures that each component readjusts to the
whole when an organism changes.

Life ether doesn't reject anything and adjusts everything to the
whole. It ensures that a changing organism remains recognizable
as an individual. It provides the continuity and individuality
in the biography of an organism. It is also the force that allows
an organism to endure and remain itself, thus maintaining the

organism's integrity. Hence, this ether can restore an organism's health by healing wounds and making them disappear completely in due time.

Life ether is the force that ensures that an organism is a spatially defined and indivisible unit, that an organism is and remains itself, even after changes or injury, that an organism is an individual, and that all its components are expressions of the whole and derive their proper place and function from the whole. Life ether affects the individual. It is the principle that creates integration and individuality.

Life ether is the great healer. This allows physical processes that have gone "wild" to reintegrate themselves back into the life processes to create the balance of health again. This develops the quality of integrating and uniting. More than the sum of its parts, the Life ether brings a holistic feeling and flexible thinking.

Life ether is individualizing, planar, square, or cube-forming. It is integrating, healing, flexible, holistic, coherent, and resilient. It coordinates the inside and outside processes of the organs as the parts work together under one idea or a higher aspect. Each organ sends specific forces and frequencies to all the other organs and is balanced by the life ether. We see the harmony of the threefold human being in the nerves, rhythmic system, and metabolism. Life ether creates the harmony of these three in the mutual interaction of the organs.

Etheric Rhythms

Out of the sublime eternal reciprocal play of day and night activities, chaos and order, summer and winter, near and distant Sun, proceed all the atmospheric and meteorological phenomena. Life actually requires chaotic dissolution: the upsetting of the general laws tending to fixity as substance.

Man, when awake and erect, is coursed through, in his full length, in his brain and vertebral column—that is, in those organs of sense and of thought which, indeed, make him a man—by the

Sun current flowing vertically. On the other hand, man, when asleep, has placed himself in such a position that the vertical current from the Sun works only at its minimum upon the brain and vertebral column. Whereas, on the contrary, he is coursed through in his full length when reclining asleep at night by the horizontally acting current from the Moon.

1. The east-west current, a result of the activity of the Sun, exerts its strongest influence in the vertical direction; it stands in reciprocal relation with man, awake, standing erect in waking consciousness, and also to the vital activities of the rest of the kingdoms of Nature during the day.

2. The west-east current—a result of the Moon's activity—exerts its strongest influence in the horizontal direction. It stands in reciprocal relation with the dream-consciousness and deep-sleep consciousness of man, while he is in a reclining position. The animal, on the contrary, on account of the horizontal position of its vertebral column, is exposed, even while awake, to the maximum influence of this current. This current acts at its strongest during the time when the Earth organism, not upset by the Sun, strives to establish its basic structure— therefore, at night.

3/4. The north-south and south-north currents, have an intimate alternating relationship with the soul-life and with the vital activities of the kingdoms of Nature, especially in the course of a year.

Gravity and Magnetism

Gravitation is that which causes substance (bodies) to tend toward the center of the Earth. It is nothing other than the effect of the suctional activity of life ether centralized in the solid earth.

The magnetism operating from the magnetic pole is only a plus in the sectional pull operating from points where the life ether within the Earth is less disturbed—that is, points of greater concentration. The magnetic poles are not fixed spots in the body of the Earth, but points of the least disturbance, and hence of greater concentration and activity in the force-sphere that belongs to the force of life ether. As such, these are shifting points—that is, they are centers of force in the etheric Earth. In our observation of the occurrences within the etheric Earth, we have seen that the etheric Earth—because of rhythmical influences proceeding from the Sun and the Moon—is subject to a constant alternation, expressed in the alternate chaotic upsetting and restoration of the basic structure of Earth. Now, this alternating, disturbing process is naturally at its maximum in the region of the equator, and its minimum in the region of the poles. Accordingly, there must be points within the Earth organism where the constant concentration of life ether and its unmodified action reach their maximum. Such points, then, of the heightened activity of the life ether are the magnetic poles.

Magnetism and gravitation, both on the earth and in the cosmos, are forms of expression of the same cause—namely, of the life ether. The intensity of the inner tendency of bodies to strive toward a life ether center differs according to their own inner kinship to this ether.

The Sun is a cavity not filled with substance: a "minus space" or a "vacuity in space," as contrasted with the rest of world space, with its substantial and insubstantial contents. Just as "heavy" bodies, more perfectly adapted to the state of life ether, show a greater striving toward the center of the Earth than light bodies, so there is a special form of attraction between the life ether center of the Sun and the magnetic North Pole of the Earth that we have come to know as a point of intensified action of the life ether.

The air in the spheres of the Earth organism are filled with innumerable tiny vacuums (after the manner of the Sun) in which there are suctional forces that, when they issue from these vacuums, cause a drawing together or a condensing of the surrounding substance (water vapor). A condensing process can be established with rhythmic repetitions through which the etheric formative forces cause the genesis of substance, its maintenance, and its reduction—that is, its metamorphosis into another state. We shall understand man—as well as the rest of the kingdoms of nature, with all the phenomena of life—when we acknowledge the living and active etheric formative forces, and the phenomena of matter metamorphosed by these forces within cosmic and earth organisms, in all their manifestations.

Atmospheric Ether

Ozone absorbs life ether with a greater intensity than any other terrestrial substance—that is, it reduces the action of life ether to an intensity that is bearable to the eyes and other organs of man living upon the solid Earth in an atmosphere of twofold oxygen. Pure, unmitigated life ether (in sunlight) would destroy the human eye and the entire human body. The earth organism, through the formation of ozone, prevents the streaming in of direct sunlight, which would be too powerful for his present organs of perception and would destroy him.

Thus, the physical human body can bear the free life ether of the Sun's rays only in the diluted form that has passed through threefold oxygen (ozone) as this diluted life ether, which then appears as the phenomenon light in the twofold oxygen of the lower atmosphere. The layer of ozone in the outermost atmosphere protects man—who lives within the earth organism and in the lower atmosphere—from the intense, destructive rays of the sun. This veil of ozone reduces the intensity of the Sun's rays in such a way that man can perceive the reduced light, which penetrates downwards.

Man, by means of his etheric forces, carries out within himself, in his blood currents and in his breathing, the processes of combustion and of that peculiarly labile transformation of oxygen. Something of the nature of the flame coming into existence under certain conditions and then dying out is also active in man. It is something of the polarity of "heat-light" and "pure light." The human being bears within himself the secret being of the "flame" of fire, of which the myth of Prometheus speaks. Light is thus chained to heat in the case of "heat-light," but not in the case of "pure light."

- Pure light requires threefold oxygen.
- Pure light is radiated out of the cosmos and into the earth by the Sun; within the earth organism, it is given off by phosphorus and by substances that are in process of breaking up (radio-activity).
- Pure light shines as a cold flame. Its action is free from heat.
- Pure light dies under the laws required for heat light.
- Heat light dies under the laws required for pure light.
- Heat light requires twofold oxygen.
- Heat light accompanies terrestrial phenomena of combustion.
- The manifestation of light here is not free, but is chained to heat.
- Pure light and heat light constitute an extremely important polarity lying at the foundation of many mysteries within the earth organism that have not yet been unveiled.

Space is interpenetrated by the forces of chemical ether, which differentiate, separate, and unite substance. Chemical ether is a suctional force, drawing inward; it tends to produce a condensation of substance. What takes place when the chemical ether, or sound ether, becomes active in the light-ether sphere of the air; the light ether strives for a rarefaction of substance, the chemical ether for a condensation. The tone phenomenon arises as an entity at the moment and at the point at which the conflict begins between chemical ether and light ether over substance, for its rarefaction or condensation.

We are dealing with a polaric contrast. Gaseous bodies represent a surrender of individuality, of shape, and of form; the solid bodies represent a demand for individuality, a thing's own shape, and a special form. Two groups of forces work in polaric opposition: on one side, warmth ether and light ether, the centrifugal forces that tend outward from the solid earth with the earth's atmosphere; on the other side, chemical ether and life ether, which hold together the earth organism. It is, therefore, the two latter forces that make the earth organism possible.

Warmth ether may thus be easily demonstrated as a formative force, self-existent and coming to manifestation through the dissolution of substance. A gaseous substance always tends to break through the form imposed upon it; it tends to release itself into the world in every direction. Gas opposes the earth's laws of form. It will not submit, like the other states of matter, to the earth relationships, and tends away from the laws of Earth in order to return to cosmic laws. It denies the sundering, individualizing process toward which Earth tends, as opposed to the cosmos; its tendency is anti-individual.

Water, or fluid, always takes the form of a sphere whose center coincides with the center of the earth. The watery or fluid substance is subject to the laws of the Earth only in part, in that it permits itself to be given its level or its form on its upper surface by the earth forces tending towards the center of Earth. This shape is common to all fluids in the Earth organism and is, therefore, not individual. For the rest, the fluid has the same form-denying tendency as the gaseous. It is a medium state between purely cosmic and purely terrestrial laws. Solid bodies, finally, take the same form-shaping forces which are common to all watery things in the earth organism over and into their own interiors; they completely individualize in themselves the "earth state."

The spiral lines described by the several planets in the motions in and with the solar system in the ether ocean of the macrocosm are repeated in the spiral lines that, in different species of plants, the leaf placement describes on the stem as it grows toward the Sun. It is illogical to admit only the action of the Sun and not also that of the planets in the growth phenomena of the plant world. Since the etheric formative forces control the motions of the enormous planetary organisms in the ether ocean of the cosmos just as they control the motions in the micro-organism of the plants, we see in both processes the same rhythms, forms, and motion tendencies.

Etheric Metamorphoses

In the metamorphosis of the ether body lies the cause of change of functions, change of sensitivity to stimuli, change in states of aggregation in cells and tissues, the appearance of new organs and capacities, and the disappearance of others. In the forming of living organisms, we have been able to perceive that the spiritual, the formative, or the substance-creating and form-shaping is the primary creative. This was the case before any beginning, and still is. The living organism represents the secondary, the shaped, that formed by the formative forces, the object of the creating, the created. The world of substance, woven through by spirit, and the spiritual world working through our phenomenal world is going through an evolution, in which we all share.

Just as the Sun cast the planets out from itself in the process of the evolution of the cosmic system and left them behind so that they might follow the encircling the Sun, so are the instinct beings and their creations in the phenomenal world—the animals—thrown out. They remain behind in the evolutionary course of the human being, surrounding him at lower stages.

The human being is more highly evolved, and the instinct beings and their organic creations, the animals, are a hardened residue of lower portions of being that the self-evolving human being cast out from himself and left behind in his environment.

We shall generally find in the human organism, in relation to its internal organs, that the right half of the body is more adapted to the forces of the light and warmth ethers, and the left half to those of the life and chemical ethers. Certain organs, even from the earliest fetal stage, incline more to the right half of the body (liver, gall bladder, etc.), and others more to the left half (heart two-thirds left, one-third right; stomach two-thirds left, one-third right from median line; intestines, esophagus, and pancreas tending toward the left; spleen altogether left, etc.). This relationship is highly differentiated between male and female organisms.

If it is principally the life ether working upon a certain part of the organism (the lymph system, the center of gravity, the life ether sphere), then the so-called colorless (white) blood corpuscles appear. If, however, as in the higher layers of the earth atmosphere (light ether sphere of the earth organism), the light ether is chiefly active, red corpuscles appear. The etheric systematization of the blood corpuscle of a man is a copy of the etheric systematization of the interior of the earth.

The living being, by means of the forces working within him, brings about that labile transformation from twofold to threefold oxygen, and back from threefold to twofold. The blood causes the so-called "slow combustion." This slow combustion is an attribute of all living beings. The blood causes a transitional metamorphosis from the laws of the "warm flame" to those of the "cold flame"; it thus checks the rapid combustion within the organism and renders the slower process of combustion in the living being possible.

Radiactivity exerts a great influence upon life phenomena as ozone and hydrogen peroxide are formed and destroyed. This also happens because of the etheric formative forces active in the process of the circulation of the blood. The organism receives the air—the twofold oxygen—through the lungs and the breathing tissues. It changes this into threefold ("cold flame," retardation of life process, oxyhemoglobin), and only after a part of the organism has been coursed through in this way does the re-formation take place from O_3 to O_2 and hereby become heat which, is characteristic of the heat-processes in organisms.

While light ether, together with life ether, forms the threefold oxygen, it is working according to the laws of the cold flame, or the upper or consciousness pole. On the contrary, when the chemical ether forms the twofold oxygen, it engenders the life element of the warm flame, or the lower or metabolic pole. Arterial blood or venous blood, slow combustion or rapid combustion, retardation or acceleration of the course of the life-processes, protraction of life in the substance world or hastening of the arrival of death—these alternations work themselves out through this eternal conflict.

The conflict between the two etheric formative forces, light ether and chemical ether, which lies at the basis of the life phenomena of the rhythmic system, leads to many and varied goals. It manifests not only in the rhythm of breathing in the corresponding organs, but also in the inner tone-world of man, which leads to speech. It manifests not only in the rhythm of the blood circulation, but also in the substance-structure of this blood in motion—the most vital of all body-building elements.

In the human rhythmic system (breathing, blood circulation, etc.), the light ether works for the upper or consciousness pole, and the chemical ether for the lower, metabolic or substance pole. The one formative force works for the physical basis of the spiritual life, and the other for the physical basis of the corporeal life.

As long as man lives in the substance world, neither of the two conflicting formative forces is victorious, for the living man establishes and maintains an equipoise until the moment of death. The "life" of man manifests as the maintenance of an equipoise between conflicting polarities.

Since all these processes are extremely labile and in constant alternation—gradually passing from one into the other—they can never be completely understood by means of chemical formulae. Distinguished investigators admit that the formulae established for oxyhemoglobin, hemoglobin, etc., do not fit the essence of the reality. By means of chemical formulae, it is possible to signify merely with what substances, approximately, the formative force complexes are working, but the substance structure is in continuous change. This is the distinction between living beings and inanimate things, as we have already seen in connection with the earth organism; the inanimate hardens according to its general laws and according to its structure (rigor mortis, coagulated blood, etc.), but substance permeated by life, on the contrary, is constantly being disorganized, or reduced to chaos, in its combinations and connections. It is modified and prevented from hardening into fixed, dead laws. In that the etheric formative forces prevent this fixing of substance, they maintain the organism in life and set up the great eternal principle of life: without the ether body, the physical bodies of man, of the Earth, and of the cosmos would change into corpses.

It is significant that the human brain is not, like the rest of the organism, subject to the force of gravity directed toward the center of the earth. Since it is subjected to the upward pressure of the cerebral fluid, it is freed from the attraction of the earth to the utmost extent. The laws of the upper pole of man stand in opposition to the laws of the earth organism, as these hold sway at the lower pole in man, where the nutritional material taken from the terrestrial environment is worked up, and where no organ necessary to our waking consciousness is formed. In the head (upward pressure by the cerebral fluid means release from gravitation), according to this point of view, laws which are anti-terrestrial hold sway; in the lower man (digestive system), on the contrary, we find predominantly terrestrial laws.

Many etheric centers coincide with the nerve ganglia in the human nerve-sense system, but there are more etheric centers than physical centers. Since the same forces—only under different conditions—have formed both the nerve system and the blood system, the second is, in its formation, almost a copy of the first. Let us first consider the two most important organs: the brain and the heart.

As the brain divides itself into an upper and a lower part (cerebrum and cerebellum), so too does the heart. The right and left halves of the brain are distinct, so that there are four parts in total, just as the heart is divided into four chambers. If we now trace this organic differentiation further, it becomes evident that the brain runs out into twelve pairs of nerves.

The structure of the physical heart—which is, at present, still behind the organ of consciousness in its development—has four parts corresponding to the major parts of the brain, but not the twelve-fold division corresponding to the further process of differentiation. The etheric heart possesses this twelve-fold structure.

The human organism possesses a third nerve system in the so-called "sympathetic nerve system," which has its most important organ in the solar plexus and develops its chief activity in the organs of digestion. This is the nerve system of the lower pole, of the metabolic system, and therefore of that part of the organism that is chiefly related to the earth organism in the assimilation of the nutritional body-building matter taken from the earth.

Upper pole, head system, Sun influence	Middle system, spinal-cord nerve system, Moon influence	Lower pole, metabolic system, sympathetic nerve system, earth influence
Brain, 12 pairs of nerves (12 signs of the zodiac)	Vertebral column, 31 pairs of nerves (phases of the Moon in a month)	Assimilation of the substances of the Earth
Voluntary movements		Deep-sleep consciousness
Waking consciousness	Involuntary movements	
	Dream consciousness	

Ethers in the Earth Organism

At sunrise, when Earth breathes out the etheric formative forces that produce the phenomena of life in the plant world, the life current begins to course through the human organism. Beginning at the feet, the current of etheric formative forces enters the human organism and flows through the human rhythmic system, vitalizing many lesser rhythms while it ascends to the brain. In the evening, around sunset, the etheric current flows back to the lower end of the ether body, at the feet.

The etheric current of the breathing of the earth organism rises in the course of the day from the interior of the earth and then returns there, daily giving a fresh impulse through its rhythms and formative forces to the phenomena of life in all the kingdoms of Nature. It also courses through man, giving an impulse to the vitalizing circulation of his blood and keeping this in continuous flow. The life current courses upward through the human organism primarily on the right side, and downward primarily on the left. Through this fact, the development of the circulation of the blood can be explained.

During the day, the life current ascends and principally affects the nerve system. During the night, it principally descends into the blood system. This creates the heightened waking consciousness of the day and the suppressed dream and dreamless sleep consciousness of the night.

A man who breathes normally takes 18 breaths in a minute, or (18 x 60) 1,080 in an hour, or (1,080 X 24) 25,920 in a day of 24 hours. This is the same number of years in the great Platonic Year, as the Sun precesses through the twelve signs of the zodiac in reverse until it reaches its original spot.

Ethers in Science, Art, and Religion

To find the well-spring from which science, art, and religion are born, we must try to recognize the common destiny of cosmos, earth, and man, and to establish how man can grow into a free creative being. A sublime decree—a rhythm reigning in space and time, an organic plan—forms the basis of this world of forces, which, once its principles are recognized, gives meaning and order to all single phenomena and reveals a part of the hidden primal plan of those creative forces, whereby the when and where of all evolution were established, and are still maintained, in an enduring world-harmony.

The cosmic genesis, from the point of view of time, presents a process of condensation, whether we follow its evolution materially from the "primal nebula" to the solid mineral earth, or genetically from the purely spiritual to the condensed content of our present sense perception. Similarly, in space, a rhythmic process of condensation is indicated in the plan, or the "rough draft of the cosmos."

We recognize the world-harmony of these formative force waves, surging with their shaping influence, from the outside in, and again from the inside out. Thus, we obtain a deep and satisfying insight into the plan of creation. From an insight into the plan of the world-structure, we can unriddle the purpose, the composition, and the articulation of the links or the "fibers" in the tapestry of the world.

The individual formative forces lead to the following four conditions of substance:

Warmth ether to a warmth condition,
Light ether to a gaseous condition,
Chemical ether to a fluid condition, and
Life ether to a solid condition.

The two forces of the first group operate in an expanding, centrifugal way, while those of the second group have a contracting, centripetal effect. It is a natural consequence of the formative forces that govern there that Mars, Jupiter, and Saturn, which belong to the outer planet-group, are controlled by warmth ether and light ether, and show much less density than Mercury, Venus, and the Moon, which belong to the inner planet-group and are controlled by the centripetal, condensing forces of chemical ether and life ether. Whether we are studying density, light-intensity, color, or any other property of the planets, it will always become explicable by the Ether Theory, and each phenomenon will be evidence for the all-governing principles and harmony imprinted on the universe and its individual spheres by the formative forces.

Four etheric formative forces give rise to and govern our world-organism.

Condition Produced		
Warmth ether	Expanding	Warmth
Light ether	Centrifugal	Gaseous
Chemical ether	Contracting	Fluid
Life ether	Centripetal	Solid

As mighty waves release ever new undulations and rhythms, the creative forces that are surging inward from cosmic space waken the ever-new spheres of force with exalted rhythms. It shows a macrocosmic genesis in space and time, repeating itself rhythmically and increasing toward the center, through ever-new conditions of existence. We see the force-sphere of each planet governed by its special formative force as follows:

Planet	Ether
Saturn	Warmth ether
Jupiter	Light ether
Mars	Chemical ether
Sun	Life ether
Mercury	Warmth ether
Venus	Light ether
Moon	Chemical ether
Earth	Life ether

As the four etheric formative forces have evolved out of one another in a definite series (warmth, light, chemical, and life ether), so do they govern the arrangement of the planetary system in space with similar succession and harmony.

The waves of the four formative forces surge from the region of Saturn to that of the Sun, and then release more waves, which govern the world-spheres between Sun and Earth. The Sun-sphere is the starting point of new force-waves, which is a repetition of the first rhythm.

When the world-rhythms reach Earth, they do not release a rhythm of the same series of force-spheres (warmth, light, chemical, life ether), but a wave tumbling over itself, so that the force-spheres follow one another in exactly the opposite order (life, chemical, light, warmth ether). This process of reversal makes the outside in and the inside out, and is repeated many times within Earth, toward its center. While this third series of reversed waves dies out within the still purely etheric Earth-envelope, the organization of Earth mirrors the harmonies of the rhythmic macrocosm. The law of reversal, of turning upside down, governs this reflection of the microcosmic spheres within the Earth.

When we investigate the effects of these cosmic formative forces on the plant growth of the earth's surface, we must remember that the growth of plants presents a triple rhythm of expansion and contraction. This threefold rhythm of plant-growth is only a continuation of that fourfold rhythm in the alternation of expanding and contracting forces that governs the planetary spheres from Saturn to the earth's surface. When we can see a breathing rhythm of the cosmos in each alternation of expansion and contraction, we recognize that the four breathing rhythms that flow from the outermost spheres of cosmic formative force right in to the earth's surface are partially reflected there. They then release three breathing-rhythms of plant-growth in the opposite direction. Thus, seven breathing-rhythms of the formative forces take part in the cooperation of cosmos and Earth for the creation of a terrestrial plant. By this natural means, the planetary constellations exercise an important influence on the differentiation of plant-growth. We understand now why the ancient Indian wisdom spoke of the "breath of Brahma," and Christian wisdom of the "breath of God."

If we describe the planets Saturn, Jupiter, and Mars as "outer" planets, and, on the other hand, Mercury, Venus, and the Moon as "inner" planets, another distinction is established between the first force-wave that formed the "outer," and the second force-wave that formed the "inner" heavenly bodies. While, in the first rhythm, the older group of formative forces (warmth and light ether) predominates, in the second rhythm, which is dying out within the world-organism, the latter group (chemical and life ether) generally dominates. Each individual force-sphere of the "outer" planets is modified in its influence by the first group of forces, while every individual of the "inner" spheres is modified— that is, strengthened or weakened in its peculiar properties, by the second group of forces. In the outer planets, taken collectively, warmth and light ether preponderate. In the inner planets, taken collectively, chemical and life ether preponderate.

If we study the formative forces of the separate signs of the Zodiac, four groups, each containing three constellations, appear in such a way that each group is governed by one of the formative forces that, together, give the twelve-fold plan of the Zodiac.

Three sets of constellations are thus allied:

To the Warmth ether	Leo, Sagittarius, Aries
To the Light ether	Libra, Aquarius, Gemini
To the Chemical ether	Scorpio, Pisces, Cancer
To the Life ether	Capricorn, Taurus, Virgo

Professor Emanuel Kayser says in *Textbook of Geology*, "Actually the Moon and the Earth form a double planet which moves round a common center of gravity about the Sun. Originally the two bodies must have formed a coherent mass, from which the Moon only later disengaged itself."

Concerning the Moon's re-approach to the Earth from which it was split off, Professor Joseph Plassmann says in the first volume of his *Astronomy*,

> The movement of our own Moon has experienced in thousands of years a slight acceleration, independent of its many periodic inequalities, and after study of the relationships between the Earth and the Moon. The attraction must increase, and so quicken the movement of revolution; this actual acceleration exists as well as the apparent one; and even though the system moves in so fine a resisting medium, yet the theory shows that the two bodies are getting nearer and nearer to each other, and in the end must crash together.

These statements coincide exactly, then, with the researches of spiritual knowledge, although modern theory generally postpones the re-entrance of the Moon to a distant future reckoned in millions of years, whereas Rudolf Steiner estimated a period no later than 8,000 years hence for the reuniting of the Moon with the Earth. Though the interval of time occupied in the severing and reuniting of the heavenly bodies may still be under discussion, but the Nebula Theory and the view of spiritual science are one in this: the whole of the fixed stars, the wandering stars, and the satellites once belonged to a common, united heavenly body and then separated from this and differentiated themselves, and finally strove toward union again.

The planetary spheres outside the earth are formed, governed, and systematized by a two-fold etheric wave, and each of such waves hears within it—in space—the same rhythm which has led—in time—from the coming into existence of the warmth ether, on to the light ether, to the chemical ether, and to the life ether. This outer two-layered sphere-world is continued inward into the three-layered world of the Earth-spheres. Between the spheres of the outermost Earth-waves, which form the purely etheric Earth-envelope, and the innermost sphere-world, which forms the inside of Earth, there lies, as a rhythmic adjustment, the atmospheric outer covering of Earth. The elastic, atmospheric covering of Earth acts as a separating and softening mediator, bearing within itself something of both polarities, and thus making it possible for man to live in a sphere where the war between cosmic and terrestrial polarities is toned down to the more peaceful skirmishing of atmospheric weather-changes. Mankind of today is exposed to wind and rain, heat and cold, thunder and lightning, hail and snow, the finely powdered dust of former volcanic lavas from the interior of Earth, and the dust of former cosmic meteorite swarms in our atmosphere. These meteorological occurrences are a softening, mitigating adjustment of above and below, outer and inner, through the intermediary spheres of the three-layered Earth, in which the human of today, with his consciousness and his body-building formative forces and substances, can develop his characteristic being.

We can study the configuration of the etheric body of the earth, which is a reflection of our own inner being, and we must realize that the etheric forces molding the body of the earth are the same as those in our blood corpuscles. When a change takes place in the etheric structure of the human blood, this will be reflected in the etheric sphere of Earth, because Earth and the blood corpuscles are formed according to the same laws. We are thus led into a quite different relationship with Earth: a truly Christian knowledge of the spirituality of Earth, or a Gaia-Sophia.

The permeation of warmth and life ether, the luciferic forces into the earth-sphere signified for the human organism acceptance of the forces of the "Tree of Knowledge." This event is shown in the Old Testament as the "temptation," the eating of the fruit of the "Tree of Knowledge." It indicates that man has accepted the forces that were surging in upon him and that he was unable to resist.

Man could not remain as he was after he had taken the luciferic influences into himself; he must be protected from the luciferic influences in his astral body. This was achieved by making the man of that time incapable of using the whole of his etheric body. Part of the etheric body was withdrawn from man's jurisdiction. If this beneficial action had not taken place and he had retained power over the whole of his etheric body, he would never have been able to rightly find his way through earth evolution. That is the inner meaning of the teaching that man had attained the distinction between good and evil. Then, the partaking of the "Tree of Life" was also withdrawn from him. That is to say, man retained absolute power over the forces of Warmth ether and Light ether only; power over the formative forces of Sound ether and Life ether were withdrawn from him.

Further Anthroposophical Ideas on the Ethers

Dr. Ehrenfried Pfeiffer

After the time of Guenther Wachsmuth, the work on the etheric formative forces was taken up by another assistant of Steiner's named Ehrenfried Pfeiffer. Dr. Pfeiffer came to America and developed bio-dynamic farming and gardening throughout the country. He set up a laboratory in Spring Valley, New York, where his work on the ethers expanded the practical aspects of working with the etheric formative forces. His insight into the "etheric heart" adds to what Wachsmuth presented.

In our time, there are certain changes taking place in the heart by which a fifth chamber will develop. In this fifth chamber, man will have a new organ which will allow him to control life forces in a different way than is possible at the moment. The heart is not a pressure pump, but an organ in which etheric space is created so that the blood is sucked to the heart rather than pumped out of the heart. With every pulse of the heart, a certain amount of substance is absorbed and is taken away as physical pressure and added to the etheric substance. This then begins to radiate out-ward. The radiation from this etheric organ of the heart is actually developing into a spiritual sense organ. (Ehrenfried Pfeiffer, *The Heart Lectures*)

Dr. Karl Koenig

Karl Koenig knew Steiner personally and had the advantage of being able to ask Dr. Steiner clarifying questions about the ethers. Koenig's insight as a doctor brought the consideration of the ethers into the realm of health and chemistry and added to the developing picture of the etheric formative forces.

The ether, streaming in through our senses, carries light, sound, and life. It travels down by way of our nerves into our entire organization. Now we must imagine: one stream goes out into the world, and its ash nourishes the brain; the other stream goes down into the body, furnishing us with ether substance. In the sphere of our senses we actually inhale warmth; and in this in-haled warmth, light, sound, and life are contained. We also exhale this warmth, but we do not exhale it into the outer world. The exhaled warmth flows into our body. In our chest-organization, we inhale air, and exhale warmth, but the exhalation goes out not into the world, but down into our body. These two streams, the exhaled warmth which carries light, sound, and life, and the inhaled air, meet and finally settle in what science describes as lymph. This cosmic stream carries light, sound, and life as it descends, and in descending it leaves the light behind in our head where it becomes our inner light. The sound is left behind to change into the inner activity of our rhythmic system. The life goes right down into physical substance, and this is what really fills and nourishes us. The Life ether takes hold of carbon, the sound ether unites with oxygen and nitrogen, and Light ether works together with sulphur and phosphorus. (Karl Koenig, *Earth and Man*)

Dr. Ernst Lehrs

Dr. Ernst Lehrs brought the discussion of the ethers into the realm of science, physics, and philosophy. His books clarify the crucial steps in the development of human consciousness needed to perceive the ethers—a schooling in perception of the etheric body and in the pivotal role of the human being in all considerations of nature. Changing one's perception can be accomplished by observing the observer, who is a participant in nature, from the thinking that is observing nature. The ethers are both inside and outside of the individual, and the relationship between the inner nature of the etheric body and outer world of the ethers is bridged through consciousness found in the etheric formative forces that are manifesting in the world.

Chaoticising (warmth), weaving (light), sounding (chemical), and speaking (life) the form-creative Word into the realm of gravity—these are the four activities through which the dynamic realm, which we first designated comprehensively as Levity, brings forth nature's manifold entities of which we finally become aware through our corporeal senses.

Warmth ether is the "highest" among the four elements, and the "lowest" among the four ethers. Warmth ether creates a border-condition between two worlds, the seen and unseen. It receives the picture-weaving transmitted to it by the higher ethers and brings physical matter into the state where it becomes receptive to the working of the etheric forces. Warmth melts solids and evaporates liquids. The universal function of warmth ether is to divest matter of all form and to lead it over from the realm dominated by gravity into that of levity bringing about at the upper border of physical nature the chaos which the earth needs for the renewal of her life. Warmth also brings about the Earth's seismic activity. It is sometimes referred to as the chaotizing ether. Warmth ether thus acts as a sphere of reflection for the other kinds of ether and the elements respectively.

Light ether teaches us to conceive of electricity and magnetism as polarities of the second order—effects of a polarically differentiated interaction of the primary polarity, levity-gravity, with the difference that on both sides of the electrical polarity the stress lies more on levity, whereas with magnetics it lies more on gravity. What we designate as electricity is light ether thus mastered by gravity, and magnetism is chemical (sound) ether in a corresponding condition. Electricity is an offspring of light. Electricity is disintegrated light. We have come to see that levity itself may be differentiated by the various modifications of ether. What is set free through atomic fission as well as fusion is levity in the form of heat, light, and chemical action which, as a result of having been age-long captives of gravity, has become alienated from their cosmic origin.

Sound (chemical) ether is the form-endowing element in nature. Chemical ether is the "magical" ether. Its effects reach into the watery element which is already bound up with gravity. Besides the external order of matter revealed in space-form, there exists also an inner qualitative order expressed in a body's chemical composition. Upon this inner chemical order is based all that we encounter as color, smell, taste, etc., of a substance, as well as its nourishing, healing or harmful properties. Accordingly, all these parts of an organism, have a certain inner material order, apart from their characteristic space-structure. All that happens through the action of the Chemical ether there belongs the quality of cosmic youth, while everything brought about in a purely physical manner is of necessarily cosmically old.

Life ether has two forms: its original and the form that is captured by gravity. Only when the power of the life ether is added to the three others can etheric action reach as far as the sphere of solid matter. Thus, the life ether is responsible for all solid formation in nature, both in her organic and inorganic fields. It is to the action of the life ether that nature owes the existence in her different realms of multitudes of separate solid forms. Snow formation and crystallization illustrate the life ether's matter-shaping might. It has the power to bind flowing action into solid form. Life ether adds form and shape to solid objects as the consonants add such to human speech. The emergence of the sense-bearing word from the merely ringing sound is an exact counterpart to what takes place in nature when the play of organic liquids, regulated by the chemical ether, is caused by the life ether to solidify into outward-ly perceptible form. Life ether is called the "word ether." (Ernst Lehrs, *Man or Matter*)

Ernst Marti

Ernst Marti shows the polarity of the ethers manifesting in space and time through the scheme of the seven dimensions as taught by Rudolf Steiner. He also creates an overview of the dynamic between the ethers that allows the reader to find their way to the direct soul experience of each one. He tells the story of the manifestation of the ethers that is the same story as the spiritual development of humanity. Marti's insights are unique and go further than perhaps any other Anthroposophist to create a topology of the etheric world.

Modern science does not recognize the four elements of fire, air, water, and earth. The solid, liquid, and gaseous forms of matter are not elements. The Greek concept of nature was based on the recognition of the four elements. Somewhat as a fifth, ether was added. Aristotle said of ether: "It is that which is different from earth, water, air, and fire; it is eternal and eternally revolves in a circle."

The elements have their origin in the center, the ethers in the periphery. The former are central, the latter peripheral; the former are point-like, individual, the latter universal, comprehen-sive. Mathematically speaking, one could say they relate to each other like plus and minus, positive and negative. In the same way that the substances are connected with the forces of the stars, so too are the formative forces. The shape of man's body is formed by the forces of the zodiacal stars. The expression "etheric body" refers more to the substance of the life body, "life body" to the life-giving functions, and "body of formative forces" more to the shape or form-giving forces. With each of these terms the object "etheric body" is considered in a different relationship with the other world phenomena.

Substances and formative forces are born of the stars; substances physically, formative forces etherically. What we thus separate in our thinking meets us united in reality. Nature's beings bear form and substance as a unity: they are formed substance. The etheric formative force has descended into what can be perceived by the senses and there produces the form. What in its own realm is pure force and movement, here becomes form at rest.

The elements only appear clothed by a substance, the ethers only by a formative force. Physics deals with them in thermodynamics, aerodynamics and hydrodynamics, mechanics, etc. Technology, medicine, agriculture, and other disciplines work with the elements. None of the four principles: formative force, form, process, or substance occur isolated in nature. Process and formative force are related as are form and substance in the sensory world.

When one speaks of etheric body or formative forces body, they are two views of the same thing. The foursome of—formative force, form, process, and substance provides the basis for understanding nature and man according to spiritual science. They themselves are again like four elements or sources. They are the four archetypal factors of existence.

Warmth is not spatial, it is zero-dimensional. The Old Saturn consists only of warmth/fire. Warmth is "intensive movement." The opposite is extensive movement which presupposes space, which does not exist until the Old Sun. On Old Saturn, warmth and fire are not separated, they are a single mobile unity; separation also presupposes space. On Old Saturn time originates, as space does on Old Sun. Warmth brings time into appearance. One can nevertheless attempt somewhat to differentiate warmth/fire.

Warmth ether is the birth of time; fire is its dying away. They are like future and past interpenetrating each other. In the present, warmth creates time, makes time. In Saturn's warmth, there is no matter because matter requires space.

Light ether is the expanding force that creates space; warmth ether is the ripening and approaching of time (which works together with fire and the waning warmth). One can characterize these ethers' collaboration as space creation within a span of time.

Tone or *chemical ether* can be characterized as that principle which separates, creates distances, forms nodes, makes buoyant versus heavy, harmonizes, and creates order. Measure, number, and weight have their origins in water and tone.

Life ether is the force of self-permeation in an inward direction, of inner self-assertion, of inner integration. It does not reject, but absorbs, thereby providing the basis for assimilation. Life ether heals; it restores; it creates a whole, a healthiness; it replenishes, restores each part to another whole. Life ether enlivens and individualizes in such a way that complete organisms develop which enclose themselves in a skin, permeate themselves as a unity, and form and structure themselves. Life ether forms living bodies.

Matter and space mutually determine each other. During the evolution of earth, space first appeared on Old Sun. Only from then on can one speak of matter. The first material substances to arise were light and air. Spiritual science points out that all substance is condensed light. Light and air behave towards each other in a negative and positive manner. The ethers relate to the elements as active to passive.

Negative matter is also matter in active form. In this way one arrives at the concepts of process and matter. Therefore, we have to distinguish, for example, silica and the silica process, gold and the gold process. By gathering all characteristics of the elements and ethers and looking at them from the viewpoint of positive and negative matter, insights into the problem of matter and process come about.

The elements represent the physical, the ethers the etheric; the physical is lifeless, the etheric is that which is actually alive. In the living organism, all elements and ethers are working together. Singly, the elements and ethers are active inorganically, physically. In a living being the elements make up the physical body, the ethers make up the etheric body. In the universe, they make up the body of the earth and the body of the universe; both are living organisms. Earth exists through the mutual interpenetration of etheric body and physical body. It ends when they separate. Then, the physical body disintegrates and becomes a part of the whole earth. In the same way, the etheric body dissolves and becomes absorbed by the periphery of the universe.

What is it that appears through the working together of light ether and chemical ether? Light ether creates space; tone ether separates and creates order. The growing plant does not remain only a simple line, a bare stem. It sprouts leaves, twigs, flowers, fruits. Visualize a tomato plant. A finely structured object in space has developed. Light ether and tone or chemical ether allow the structure of space to appear. Segments develop. Segments are separations and arrangements within one unit of space. In music one can also speak of arrangements in segments which have a character relating more to time; they are, however, also structures in space, when they resound.

Also belonging to reality are the forces of electricity, magnetism, and similar forces, which, according to their nature, are opposites of the ethers. They are not peripheral forces, connected with the periphery, but centric forces, exerting their influence out of the earth, as if from the earth's center, from "below," as the ethers exert their influence from "above," from the world's periphery. (Ernst Marti, *The Four Ethers*)

Olive Wicher

Olive Wicher understood the molding forces of the ethers to be the same forces found in the development of architecture and spatial design. In her work, she develops a three-dimensional understanding of the formative forces—which ray inward from surrounding space and into the stream of the ethers— that penetrate the human etheric body and etheric kingdoms of nature. The same formative forces of the etheric realms of nature also formed the internal organs of the human body. The transformation of matter into etheric matter can be found by studying Wicher's books.

In the world of organisms, we learn that the substances of which the forms are created are drawn upward, under the influence of the ethers—the watery ether, the airy ether, the light ether and the warmth ether. These upward-drawing ethereal forces are all related to the Sun and to the universe as a whole. They cannot be fully understood by means of the type of thinking which only sees and calculates the way substance sinks down towards the gravitational center or are hurled outward and upward in an explosion. We must build the bridge from Earth to Sun through understanding the etheric realm.

We can describe these upward drawing forces using the word "suctional"; and the kind of space that accords with such phenomena as "negative." We learn to create thoughts with which to envisage a "negative" or "counterspace," in which also the forces are anti-gravitational. The forces working to create living forms work in a way which is entirely opposite to the all too well-known gravitational and explosive forces. The upward-drawing, living forces of the organic world, are very expressive of a force more akin to the light of the Sun than the darkness and weight of matter.

In the ethereal space, with its "absolute" in the counter-spatial "center" and its planar quality, it is the force of levity which works as a force of "negative gravity." According to its nature, the force of levity works in negative space through the fact that all the planar entities in such a space have an affinity for one another—a force of attraction working between them, which is polar to the gravitational force of attraction, working between two mass-centers. There is an active field of upward movement, which balances out the gravitational forces at work in earth-substance. (Olive Wicher, *The Heart of the Matter*)

Dennis Milner and Edward Smart

Dennis Milner and Edward Smart wrote a wonderful exposition of the ethers that told about their scientific studies trying to make the ethers become "visible" through Kirlian photography and other such cameras. Their exploration into the etheric realms also entailed examining human consciousness and human temperaments in relationship to the ethers. Like many who gain insight through study of the ethers, they created a scheme that displays the social development of humanity throughout history in relationship to the ethers. Their scheme of the historical sequence of developing civilization is much akin to Jean Gebser's stages. Milner and Smart divide history into five groupings: Egyptian/Sumerian/Hebrew, Greek, Roman, Present

Day Western, and Future Western Civilizations. Each of these civilizations has made a contribution to cultural history in terms of the evolution of awareness and consciousness.

Behind the substance world lies the activity of the Spiritual Hierarchy, manifest as etheric forces in the world ether. For man to experience and to acquire the qualities inherent in this etheric world, he too must be a being of etheric forces. Thus, permeating the physical body, is a body of etheric force activity which brings about etheric functioning of the physical body i.e., the physical body "lives" in accord with the etheric activity of the Spiritual Hierarchy.

The etheric structure of the earth now comprises four etheric forces. These are the warmth and light etheric forces which try to expand material and entities outwards to gaseous and warmth states of substance; the condensing, inward-drawing chemical etheric force which creates liquid; and the negative life etheric force which creates solids and a stronger inward contraction.

The Sun, as the center of the solar system, is the primary source of activity of the life etheric force and it causes substance to become incorporated in the individualized living forms of plants, animals, and man. Earth, the planets and the Sun then take up their relative movements. The beings at the periphery of Earth are then alternately subjected to the deadening, mineral-izing action of Earth's negative-life etheric force field, which tries to reduce everything to this state, while during periods of sun-light the Sun force tries to raise substance up into individualized living forms. The alternating action of the Sun's life etheric force produces ebb and flow in the etheric forces. These give rise to life cycles and the rhythms of day and night and of the seasons. Al-though life is due to the combined ebb and flow of all the etheric forces, it is the Sun's life etheric force that calls this ebb and flow into being.

According to the *etheric force viewpoint,* we have to envisage that at the beginning of creation a warmth/energy state of the cosmic ether came into being. Then, as subsequent etheric forces came into operation to develop the warmth spheres into bodies for the higher kingdoms of Nature, they also became incorporated with the left-behind warmth/energy state to give rise eventually to the mineral world. Whereas in the main-stream of evolution the higher etheric forces entered into the warmth entities raising them to a higher level of development, the left-behind warmth/ energy substance was not sufficiently evolved to take into itself these higher forces which instead became incorporated as forces which imposed successively higher levels of external organization on the warmth spheres.

As each etheric force entered into creation (warmth, light, chemical) it further condensed the previously existing state with, finally, the negative life etheric force bringing about the most highly condensed, or compacted, state of organization of the warmth spheres. The first etheric forces to enter into creation had brought about less condensed organizations of the warmth spheres. Under the influence of the negative life etheric force these forces and states of organization became compressed within substance and within the atomic structures of substance. Thus, atoms comprise forces of compression in opposition to forces of expansion. If the more expansive forces of warmth ether and light ether are increased, for example by putting heat, light or electric- ity into the substance then they may bring about a disintegration of the atomic structures and emission of its components, as in thermionic emission, photo-emission, the field emission of elec- trons, and the disintegration of structures.

The negative life etheric force forms a highly compacted atom- ic nucleus and would equate with the strong bonding force that science has found to exist in the nucleus. The chemical ether and light ether forces are the electromagnetic forces that are at work in the atomic structures. According to the latest scientific results, the atomic nucleus can be viewed as rotating strings of particles held in place by centrifugal forces, which is well in accord with the etheric force viewpoint. (Milner and Smart, *The Loom of Creation*)

Sylvia Francke

Sylvia Francke takes the bold step to address the two ethers that become the Tree of Life in the future: the unfallen sound ether and the unfallen life ether. Both the sound and life ethers must go through future stages of evolution before they can manifest to human beings as forces that bring life and not death. Humans must evolve further, through the stages of Future Jupiter and Future Venus, before the two "higher ethers" are available for human development. When these ethers are made available, they become a new form of nourishment for humans who have evolved into angels and archangels. These ethers will become the "food of the gods" in a literal way, and the true forces of the Sun will reveal themselves as the Tree of Life.

> Within the etheric our familiar experience of distance and separation vanish. The concept of kinship replaces the concept of special distance. Those things which are akin are joined in unity in the etheric, irrespective of the distance between their physical manifestations. This explains how if there is a kinship between the blood cell and the earth organism changes in the one will reflect in the other.
>
> The etheric realm streams forth life forces and can be thought of as a vast cosmic ocean which stretches to the zodiac and controls and qualifies the planetary movements while also imbuing the tiniest living creatures with life and motion.
>
> In the act of forming mental pictures, voluntary as well as involuntary, the etheric body loosens itself slightly from its physical attachment. In imaginative activity man's thinking organization adapts itself to the rhythm of the circulation of the blood—an inner breathing takes place.
>
> As humans evolve and perfect their moral and cognitive faculties, the realities of the world of life-processes—the etheric realm—are made more directly available to them. This gives access to the "Grail Castle" and then lays firm foundations for what could be described as a "Science of the Grail." (Sylvia Francke *The Tree of Life*)

The Language of Nutrition

"One who understands nutrition correctly

understands the beginning of healing."

Nutrition and Health, GA 354

It is essential to have good nutrition, or the spiritual thoughts of this book would be wasted on souls who were not free enough to hold the sense-free *Imaginations* that arise from its study. Only a vessel that is clear and empty can be filled with the unsullied light of the divine and commune with wisdom. To learn wisdom concerning the proper nutrition necessary to become a worthy vessel for spiritual thinking requires a language of nutrition that brings light to the true nature of the elements and forces at work in digestion. This language is like many of the languages we shared in Volume 2 of the *Gospel of Sophia*: it consists of consonants and vowels that blend together to give form and life to the cosmic forces that are raying into physical substance. We call these cosmic forces "spiritual" because they are the outer effects of spiritual beings from the ranks of hierarchies that permeate the visible and invisible realms.

We will study the spiritual nature of many physical substances and processes in this examination of a Language of Nutrition as we build the alphabet, grammar, semantics, and syntax of this amazing world of beings and forces that seem to go beyond human comprehension, but in the final analysis, we must put things in simple forms, symbols, and parables that shine light on the beings behind the forces and substances.

Essentially, good nutrition is a relationship with the beings who provide us with the food we eat. Our human consciousness is only slightly aware of the processes of digestion and new cell formation that stand behind the concept of "life." New, miraculous discoveries about human physiology abound, and we can hardly incorporate the new information before shocking new discoveries displace the old. Often, the old theories of the ancients are recycled and found to be more applicable than anyone ever imaged. Our approach will start with the ancient view of the four elements.

It may seem too simple to say the living world consists of basically four elements: fire, air, water, and earth. This concept is so simple that it blinds the modern thinker to its ramifications. Let's look at the correspondences that spiritual science lays alongside this simple scaffolding.

Greek Element	Substance	Ether	State of Matter
Fire	Hydrogen	Warmth	Plasma
Air	Nitrogen	Light	Gas
Water	Oxygen	Sound	Liquid
Earth	Carbon	Life	Solid

Not only did the Greek philosopher define the basic parameters of the physical world through this parceling of creation, but he also insinuated the deeper significance of a four-fold worldview that has many "cosmic" correspondences ascending a ladder of ranked hierarchies. Heraclitus believed that all things arose from fire and will return to fire. Thales believed water was the primal element, while Anaximenes championed air. Aristotle added a fifth element that he called *aether*: a quintessence of unchangeable heavenly substance. Each element had their philosophic hero who championed the primacy of each of the four elements, with a complete philosophy based upon the primal significance of one element. Eventually, Empedocles proposed the four elements of earth, water, air, and fire, and he called them the four roots.

It would be easy for a modern thinker to choose Earth as the primal element, since all organic life comes from carbon, which is associated with the element Earth. Carbon's unique bonding ability with oxygen, nitrogen, and hydrogen create all the acids and bases and are the four elements necessary to create amino-acids, the building blocks of starches, carbohydrates, fats, oils, sugars, proteins, and even DNA. These four substances act as two sets of polarities that are always dynamically creating life and death in our cells through their polarity of expansion and contraction. Even the four substances that create the coding for DNA (adenine, cytosine, guanine, and thymine) are directly paired to these four substances (carbon, oxygen, nitrogen, hydrogen).

The real question that arises when examining these four substances is: Why does carbon become so "selfless" as to share its form and substance with the other three elements, thus creating all organic life? Again, the answer is simple, but the ramifications are profound. Carbon is the Holy Grail of life. Carbon creates all form, and thus is the Mother of life, death, and rebirth. In the distant future, we will perfect the carbon in our systems, and the human body will become crystal clear carbon, like a liquid diamond. We will slowly burn carbon until we clarify all other substances from it, and the result will be our shining higher self. This mystery of carbon was discussed in Volume 2 as the Mystery of ONE. The Mystery of THREE refers to the other three of the four primal substances: oxygen, nitrogen, and hydrogen.

In the Language of Nutrition, the four primal substances hold a special place that, in a way, define the direction in which the letters are written (space), the use of verb tense (time), the nature of beginnings and endings of sentences (thought), and the use of punctuation (feeling). These four "states" of the language are necessary to create the envelope of expression. Without them, it would be impossible to communicate this language to others. In fact, the language could not exist without these four forces, directions, or states of being. The *Primal Four Substances* create the substructure of the language.

From the cosmos—the entire sphere of stars, which we will refer to as the zodiac—come formative forces that *ray into* plants the information concerning the shape and design of their specific nature. These formative forces carry the plan or design of each type of plant into its specific characteristics through the amino acids that create a signature protein found in the seed. This seed is a protein derived from combining carbon, oxygen, nitrogen, and hydrogen into amino acids that "remember" the exact forms and growing processes that develop from seed to stem, to leaf, to blossom, and back to seed again. This "living memory" is found in seed DNA and somehow carries a "record" of what the plant is and will become. Perhaps pre-memory or premonition might be better used to describe this amazing process found in plants, animals, and humans. The amazing phenomenon of heredity is seldom considered to be built from four basic substances.

Another question that might arise: How do proteins properly remember the exact way they should create new cells? The DNA of all cells "remember" the complicated form and function of every cell and can direct new cells to the exact place in the body to work effectively. This living memory is also a pre-vison of what the body will become in the future. Our future adaptations and subsequent mutations are already developing in the DNA as our enzymes "listen" and "sense" our environment and respond and adapt to them in real time. The memory of everything our ancestors have ever eaten is written on the mitochondrial DNA. This DNA can trace humans back to our ancestors from Africa. We are also writing new information and memory into our mitochondrial DNA as we eat different foods and attempt to adapt and produce the enzymes that will digest that food properly.

Unfortunately, our ancestors have given us the hereditary enzyme foundation upon which we must digest our food. Often, one generation after the next receives a weakened set of internal enzymes that cripple their ability to adapt to new foods. This then produces a great necessity to understand amino acids, enzymes, proteins, and their components. Through understanding the Language of Nutrition, the wisdom child can become filled with the life and substances necessary to develop higher thinking, feeling, and willing.

Let's take a look at these somewhat magical four primal substances and see if we can form a living picture of their functions in human physiology and consciousness.

The Four Primal Substances

"Earthly substance is the material form of cosmic realities, or incarnated ideas or archetypes."

Nutrition and Health, GA 354

Carbon is the form-giving element throughout organic nature. It combines with hydrogen, oxygen, nitrogen, and itself to create the organic world composed of millions of compounds, while the other 72 elements create only tens of thousands of inorganic compounds. Carbon is the carrier of form, and nature's stabilizer. It creates the scaffolding of plants, animals, and humans. It is the crystallizing agent that brings what is endowed with spirit, soul, and life into physical manifestation. Carbon—along with oxygen, nitrogen, and hydrogen in various combinations and permutations—enables the creative cosmos to become effective for the earth and to continue reproducing miniature likenesses of the universe in earthly matter. This capacity is most apparent in the seed. Its protein provides the material that brings the prototypal image of the plant into physical manifestation.

Oxygen is found abundantly in water because it is 89% oxygen, and this makes oxygen the source of life—life-substance. Oxygen is the element that carries life into physical manifestation. Plants can be called organized water infused with the vital processes of growth. Oxygen is the carrier of this enlivening process or life-force, which presses into material embodiment to catalyze growth in the plant realm. It is the bearer of forces whereby being becomes appearance—blossoming and germinating or expanding and contracting—that underlies the processes of metamorphosis. Oxygen is the carrier of life that even brings movement into the mineral kingdom. It combines with almost all substances and makes them capable of chemical reaction. The rhythmic interaction between hydrogen (fire) and oxygen (water), being and appearance, expansion and contraction is stabilized at every stage in carbohydrates and by carbon (earth).

Nitrogen is the carrier of air, comprising 80% compared to oxygen's 20%. Nitrogen is movement-substance or air-substance. It is the carrier of motion and rhythm that enables oxygen to be inhaled and expelled again. It repeats universal rhythms in the human body. Nitrogen helps provide a feeling of our surroundings through breathing. It is the force that permeates life with feeling and motion. It cannot be bound and brings movement and mobility to everything. Its mobility enables seeds to form through the blossoms that draw the swarms of insects for pollination or the winds to spread pollen. Sensation is a motion of a higher order, soul-movement, provided by nitrogen. For an animal, nitrogen is interiorized as a unified organism capable of free, independent motion. Internalizing the cosmic formative forces builds up a system of internal organs that carries out cosmic movement within the organs. Nitrogen turns the cosmos outside in. It enables earthly processes to repeat cosmic motions and rhythms in independent organisms.

Hydrogen is the Earth's lightest substance, and is the common element in all acids. Hydrogen is a fire-substance. It is a subtle fire-process that dissolves form and etherealizes matter everywhere. It rises to liberate warmth and dissolve metals. It is the last visible remnant of a cosmic fire-force that pervades the universe as a dissolving, de-materializing element—a type of anti-gravity. Hydrogen is the strongest power of ascent from the material to the spiritual. In plants, warmth etherealizes starch into oils, sugars, fragrance, pollen, fruit, and seed. The fragrance and blossoming of the plant ascends into the heights on the wings of hydrogen. Hydrogen imparts buoyancy and warmth to water, making it a dissolving agent for salt, sugar, and other substances.

The Cross of the Four Primal Substances
The Cosmic Source of Protein and Organic Life

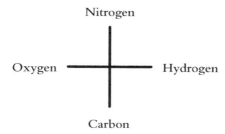

Once we have established an understanding of the four primal substances, we can then look at the formative forces that ray into the physical world from the twelve cosmic directions of the zodiac. We can imagine that the minerals are the result of the twelve cosmic directions raying into physical creation, a sort of "falling into" matter, or a shattering of spirit into matter. Specific formative forces arise from these directions of space and carry with them the "forms," or crystalized archetypes of life that form resonant life processes in the human body as a mirroring or duplication of these living formative forces.

In our Language of Nutrition, we can see minerals as the consonants and metals as the vowels of the alphabet. Minerals constitute a language of formative forces raying in from the zodiac that can be seen as consonants that bring structure and form. Vowels carry movement and give voice, music, and articulation to this language of substance through expressions of feelings—the music of the spheres. Consonants are crystallized, rigidified expressions of a world of form beyond the human;

vowels are carriers of mobile personal feelings that arise from the movement of the planets. Consonants are a skeletal framework, whereas vowels are the soul and heart of a language. Every planet travels the heavens at its own particular speed, which can be expressed mathematically in terms of its angular velocity. These planetary motions are metamorphosed into the properties of earthly metals. The planets move on their rounds in great curves and loops, creating geometric patterns against the stationary background of the fixed stars. Veins of metal run through the body of the earth, and vowels sound through the consonant structure of words and syllables.

The periodic system of chemical elements is an expression of the same laws found in music and the harmony of octaves. Chemistry is music in matter. The ancients could clairaudiently hear the ordered movement of the planets as a musical experience called the Harmony of the Spheres. The relation of the seven planets to the fixed stars, especially the twelve zodiacal constellations, is built upon a rhythmical law that finds reflection in the seven intervals and the twelve semi-tones of the scale. Stellar movements, music, and chemistry thus seem to be varied expressions of the same cosmic ordering force. A higher cosmic order permeates the universe and manifests at different levels, down to ultimate physical expression in earth substances. They clearly show the imprint of their starry origin. Every substance is the materialized expression of a process—of a cosmic essence. These beings dwell in the world of stars, but the world of dense matter bears their imprint everywhere.

Electricity plays a key role in condensing and materializing cosmic forces, whereas light radiates as the opposite pole. Electricity forces the beings and images of the universe into earthly form. Electricity endows condensed warmth, which is the basis of all natural phenomena, with stability. Heat has been captured and condensed by the flowing of electricity as it binds stellar forces to earth substance. This is a type of hieroglyphic writing of the universe impressed into matter. Matter is the last step on the path of divine creation.

Rudolf Steiner tells us in *Inner Reading and Inner Hearing* (GA 156) about a group of nineteen habits that relate to the consonants and vowels of this new Language of Nutrition.

> The entities of the world are reflected sevenfold in the etheric body. It is something like a tablet, upon which esoteric writing is engraved through the processes of the world. The essential lives in the cosmos, and all of it replicates itself, inscribes itself, in the etheric body. And the human astral body constantly reads what the world inscribes in the etheric body. We also inscribe in our etheric body what we ourselves experience in our soul. When we remember something, the astral body reads what has been inscribed in our etheric body, and this is called memory.
>
> Basically, our astral body has been planted through the cosmos with 12 (zodiacal) plus 7 (planetary) habits = 19 habits of movement. Our astral body makes particular movements that are combined from these 19 habits of movement. The movements are inscribed in the etheric body, and then, at a later time, the astral body can re-read what is inscribed there. That is the foundation of memory.

What are these nineteen habits of movement that create a system of writing and reading that is key to the life body of the human being? This movement of the seven planets through the twelve zodiacal areas of space creates the possibility of repeated replication. These habits seem to reflect the cosmos and create the movement of life in the etheric body.

It is easy to see the twelve non-essential amino acids and the seven essential amino acids as a correspondence to these nineteen habits. Amino acids are an alphabet of life that builds enzymes that help cells to replicate at an amazing rate of recognition (reading) and replication (writing). This occurs through a recognition process in an enzyme that catalyzes the substance that reads the enzyme's form. This happens through a system of lock and key recognition, and then is given a boost of energy to transform and replicate. One enzyme can be recognized (read) and become a catalyst of energy (write) to more than a million resonant substances in a single second. The enzyme loses no part of its substance or its energy through this transaction. Enzymes are seemingly immortal if contained in a fluid biological condition. Enzyme production and content is hereditary and cumulative.

> Behind everything material is spirit. Thus, behind all the matter we take in through our nutrition, there is also spirit. By means of nourishing ourselves with this or that, we enter into a relation with something spiritual, with a substrate which is behind the material. (*Inner Reading and Inner Hearing* (GA 156))

Let us examine the nature of enzymes. The force which is active in an enzyme—itself a protein body—is of a higher order than the mere life force of the organism. It is the same force which alone is capable of building up a new protein—specific to the body and based on the pattern of the individual—out of the ruins, the substance which has become dead and physical. It must, therefore, be a force possessed of "Ego character," or Ego-organization, which is a spiritual element in the body. Everything that comes into the realm of the ego-organization dies. This deadening effect is exercised upon protein where trypsine (an enzyme)—a product of the pancreas—is active in the digestive organization. In animal protein, the forces of growth, regeneration, and reproduction do, in fact, largely hold sway. But the human being must push these forces back in developing his spiritual forces—his Ego-consciousness. The human being is capable of creating its own protein from the amino acids by taking them into the formative forces of its etheric body.

We can begin to see that enzymes, made from the consonants and vowels of the amino acids, constitute a language or memory system that can remember how to replicate cells and digest proteins, carbohydrates, sugars, and minerals.

In Volume 2 of the *Gospel of Sophia*, the twelve convolutions of the cerebral cortex of the human being were shown to be a set of twelve forms that correspond to the formative forces of the zodiac. The sphere of the head reflects the dome of the starry sky (twelve zodiacal signs), and the seven chambers of the midbrain were shown to be reflections of the seven planetary spheres and their resonant energies. Thus, amino acids are directly connected to the forming processes of the brain as they ray into the human form and it develops. Consonants and vowels, zodiac and planets work together to find balance between space and time. Memory is the result. Enzymes are forces of memory that seem timeless and spaceless.

Let us take a closer look at enzymes and proteins. They stand as the central question of good nutrition and proper digestion. First, we must see how starches build up from minerals to carbohydrates, and thus to protein.

The Ego-organization of the human has a special relationship to minerals in the human body. The human ego could only incarnate because of the minerals and the crystallization process that raises the mineral into the realm of the plant. Minerals come to us from the World Ego, or the womb of the world. Humans are part of a raging battle fought with the material realm against mineralization. The individual fights against these hardening forces within himself. Understanding this battle between hardening and sclerosis on the one hand and dissolution and inflammation on the other hand is critical for health.

The mineralization process reaches a kind of culmination, as part of the calcium process, in the formation of "brain sand" in the pineal gland. This formation is made up of the same substances as our skeleton—calcium carbonate and phosphate— which is, ultimately, the entire calcium metabolism process in the human being. The proper crystallization and dissolution is closely connected to the development of our intelligence, our Ego-consciousness. We incorporate in ourselves the dense process of becoming earthly by means of calcium carbonate and phosphate. At the same time, we constantly oppose this with the most active process, the warmth process which culminates in the blood and in the entire fluid organism. The warming process is dominant, and our individual soul-activity takes hold of it directly.

Rudolf Steiner speaks further about the warmth process in digestion in the lecture entitled *The Penetration of Substance with Spirit* (GA 230):

Before anything can become part of the human form it must have gone through the completely volatile warmth-ether stage and then have been transformed again into a part of the living form of the human organism.

Solid substance loses its solid form when it is changed in the mouth into a fluid and is then further transformed into the condition of warmth ether. It also gradually loses weight as it passes over into the fluid form and becomes more and more estranged from the earthly. But only when it has ascended to the warmth-ether form is it fully prepared to absorb into itself the spiritual which comes from above, which comes from cosmic widths.

This warmth ether has a strong disposition to absorb into itself what radiates inwards, as forces from cosmic spaces, from the widths of the cosmos. Thus, it takes into itself the forces of the universe. And these forces of the universe now become the spiritual forces which here imbue warmth-etherized earthly matter with spirit. And only then, with the help of this warmth-etherized earthly substance, does there enter into the body what the body needs to take shape and form.

You must know how much force the human organism has to exert in order to bring an external mineral substance to the fleeting condition of warmth ether. If it is unable to do this, the external mineral substance is deposited and becomes heavy earth matter before it has passed over into warmth; it remains foreign inorganic matter and is deposited in the tissues.

When we consume the plant as nourishment we give it the opportunity of carrying further, in the right way, what it began outside in nature, striving back not only to light-filled spaces, but to the spirit-filled spaces of the cosmos. We must take the plant substance within us to the point where it becomes aeriform, or gaseous, so that the plant may follow it's longing for the wide spaces of light and spirit. Plants are not simply ingested but are completely spiritualized through human digestion.

Everything we do happens because will impulses are active in us. Then what is going on in the external world through us, insofar as it is a moral action, is collected by the Seraphim, and this moral activity is the source of warmth for the entire world order. Under the influence of moral action, the Seraphim obtain the forces through which the cosmic world order is preserved, just as the physical world order is preserved through physical warmth. When you act, when you do something, when you unfold your will, then you are the sources of warmth, the source of fire of the Seraphim. When I think, I am the illuminator of the Cherubim; when I act, when I act in willing, I am a heater of the Seraphim. I live inside the entire spiritual structure of the world. Thinking then becomes a religious attitude and action becomes a moral prayer. We must find again in the upward course of our development what we lost in the downward course. (*Inner Reading and Inner Hearing* (GA 156))

Plants build up the Four Primal Substances with amino acids that create starch and carbohydrates in the plant kingdom. Carbohydrates are the product of the interaction of carbon, hydrogen, and oxygen. If carbon were to function without restriction, the rhythmical action between hydrogen and oxygen would cease, and the carbohydrates would take on a rigidity like that of cellulose. If no restrictions were placed upon hydrogen, the carbohydrates would become formless, as in sugar, color, scent, and pollen, and would be etherealized away into the cosmos. Carbohydrates are formed in fire-quickened cosmic life that rhythmically pulses between crystallization in cellulose and dissolution in sugars.

Another dynamic polarity in the mineral realm is between calcium and silica, or the earthly and cosmic forces, respectively. Together with carbon and protein, calcium gives man the earthly forming force. Silica, in combination with carbon, brings forth the cosmic forming force in plants. Calcium and protein, and silica and carbon, can be found as the formative basis in the plant, animal, and human kingdoms. They act as forces of form on both the earthly and cosmic sides. In the human, silica forms the physical basis of the Ego-organization. One can speak of a special silicic acid organism as a member of the entire organism.

Phosphorus has the same capacity as electricity to condense oxygen in the air into ozone. At room temperature, it ignites with a brilliant white flash of spontaneous combustion. It is a primary substance in nerves and gives off a cold light. Phosphorus stands between silica and calcium and provides awareness of our body and the bodily consciousness of the self.

The Mineral Cross
The Earth's Hard Core

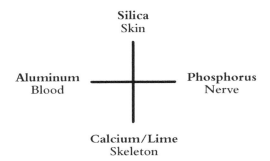

Without minerals, all nutritional proteins become ineffective and lifeless. This is seen dramatically with iron, as the rhythmic infusion of iron brings about cleansing and purification throughout the whole body. The selfless metal forces from iron develop a healing force by creating a radiating force that branches out into all limbs. A congesting action is set against this by protein, which acts to impede this radiating force of iron. This battle between radiating and congesting forces in the body is a continuous cycle. If this interplay between iron and protein does not balance out, illness results.

Whoever brings forth the forces to nourish themselves from plant fat will thereby gain more inner forces. Carbohydrates (sugar) from plants are mediators of form and consciousness. The individual builds up within himself a carbohydrate with carbon that constantly forms and then later dissolves itself. This is the glycogen in the liver, which man breaks down into human sugar, or glucose. He then allows it to circulate in his blood, carrying sugar all around. The human Ego makes use of a physical carrier in this carbon, which moves in the blood. The human Ego lives as the actual spirit in man in carbon and finds its highest expression in the formation of sugar. Where there is sugar, there is Ego-organization.

Constitution of the Human Being	
Physical body	Sense Organs
Etheric body	Glands
Astral body	Nerves
I/Ego	Blood

Plant acids in the developing seed are a vessel in which the scent flowing back from the periphery of the cosmos is gathered up. The fire-forces in this essence warm and permeate the developing seed-organism. Oil is the perfect plant substance produced in this interaction. It began with starch and progressed through sugar and fragrance to the final synthesis in oil. Plant oil is materialized cosmic fire.

Starch is a bewitched rainbow drawn down into matter by the plant's vital force. The creative process travels over the rainbow on its descent into the material world of nature.

Mouth:	Carbohydrate digestion
Stomach:	Protein and Carbohydrate digestion
Small Intestine:	Fat and Protein and Carbohydrate digestion

We can have an image of our diseases spread out in the entire plant world. At the same time, however, these plants carry within them the forces to heal such sicknesses. The forces which work in man's rhythmic organization against becoming plant-like (the extension of the life-formative force as such) are of a higher nature—a soul nature. The human being ensouls these processes of nature in his process of breathing. That which the plant develops upwards, man develops downwards. The plant grows towards the Ego-activity, toward the astral activity of the cosmos, whereas the human uses sugars (carbon) in the blood to carry Ego-activity.

The formative forces are partially lifted out of the nerve and sense organs and appear as soul-spiritual forces. Whenever I think or feel, I think or feel with the same forces that exercise a formative activity in the animal or plant kingdoms. They also work similarly in the human metabolic and reproductive processes. When we carry into our bodies the world of the hierarchies the substances from which moral impulses are born and these penetrate our whole organisms, impulses and actions follow.

A good part of what we call aging lies in the fact that the astral body becomes dull to taste; when an individual human organ loses the fresh capability of taste, this means it is not permeated by its astral body in the corresponding way, and diseases arise.

Protein in Nutrition

"Every single piece of protein is an image of the entire universe."

"From the protein we eat, we keep and use only the carbon. Oxygen, nitrogen, hydrogen, and sulphur we take from the air we breathe. We make our own protein, using only the carbon from protein we have ingested."

Nutrition and Health, GA 354

Protein is the indispensable, formative force of life that has the ability to give up the form that nature gave its material components, when called upon to take a form for the sake of the organism. Protein cannot be stored or conserved like fats or carbohydrates. It is a kind of equilibrium that can appear either as a base or an acid. It is constantly changing, coming and going, and always subjected to an intense process of renewal. It is always on the point either of being taken into the activity of the etheric body or of falling away from it. The protein in the ganglia in the brain is renewed, on average, every nine hours. In the liver, it takes about 10 days; in the muscles, 150 days; and the interstitial tissues, about 160 days. These cycles demonstrate the constant movement of protein throughout the human body.

Proteins in digestion correspond to the production of mental pictures in thought activity. If we burden the metabolic sphere with the consumption of too much protein, the higher activities of thinking will correspondingly suffer. The consumption of protein should be kept within certain limits.

Carbon is the carrier of all formation processes in nature. It is the great sculptor. Oxygen carries the life influences into the earthly world. Nitrogen, on the other hand, becomes the carrier of sensations, soul forces, and the astral body. Hydrogen is the lightest element and is related to warmth. In it, protein has a substance that is as closely related as possible to the physical, and yet is also related to the spiritual as closely as possible. Hydrogen works powerfully through sulfur as the carrier of the spiritual and the bearer of light, similar to phosphorus.

These four primal substances are cosmic forces of formation found in protein, but they take hold in plants at a different point than animals and human beings. In the latter, they are internalized, and therefore organically active. The plant, on the other hand, receives the protein-forming forces from the periphery: the air, light, and warmth of the sun. Nitrogen comes from the periphery, too, and hydrogen is present everywhere. Thus, the plant constructs its protein by using the formative forces of the periphery that ray into it. Animals and human beings internalize these forces, thereby connecting to the hereditary stream and constructing protein from the internalized universe.

The four organs of the liver, kidneys, lungs, and heart are structure-forming centers of force. These organs form the stable protein-formation centers in the organism, an inner world-system that provides the impulse toward protein formation. All growth and regeneration are connected with protein. The essence of protein cannot be understood without spiritual science.

Carbon is the bearer of all formative processes in nature and is especially related to earth forces. Hydrogen dissolves everything and bears everything that is at all formed—all enlivened astrality—back into the expanses of the cosmos. Protein is enlivened by oxygen, and nitrogen acts as the bearer of sensation. In protein, sulfur and phosphorus are the mediators between the spirit spread out over the earth—between the forming forces of spirit and the physical realm.

The formation of the organism is a transformation of protein, which works together with mineral forces. Such forces are found in calcium, which is at work in the metabolism everywhere. It directs the enzyme activities, either promoting or suppressing them. It acts both as a partner and opponent of sodium and potassium, another dynamic polarity, controlling the balance between base and acid.

Alkalines are hospitable to life and are waxing, flowing, expansive, passive, receptive, and support-giving. With alkali, we internalize our being and remain within ourselves; with acids, we externalize our being and become active and aggressive. The human blood is slightly alkaline.

Within the human being, the basic elements predominate in the liver, the small intestines, and the brain, where the foundation is laid for the taking hold of the forces of individuality. The greatest factor determining the pH of the blood is the relationship of carbonic acid to bicarbonate. A deficit of the latter leads to acidosis, while a surplus leads to alkalosis. Acids are dry, contractive, and hostile to growth. They are also positive and active, breaking down substance.

Vitamins are directive functions of the life-processes which are joined to the element of formative forces—the etheric body. The whole complexity of functions of enzymes, hormones, vitamins, and trace elements belongs to one realm of a higher order. They are expressions of higher forces and activities.

The Oceanic Cross
Ocean Salt

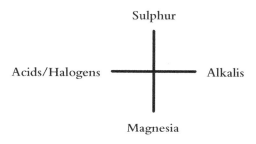

Sulphur

Acids/Halogens ———————— Alkalis

Magnesia

Salts and Kingdoms

Calcium salts	Mineral	Earth	Physical body
Potassium salts	Plant	Water	Life body
Sodium salts	Animal	Air	Soul
Magnesium salts	Human	Fire	Ego

Rudolf Steiner gave an excellent description of the processes of protein in the human body in the lecture *Problems of Nutrition* in Munich, January 8, 1909 (GA 68).

When external light shines on a plant, the plant builds up its living organism by producing proteins, carbohydrates, starches, oil, and sugars. Protein in seeds are engendered as a physical precipitation of the commingling in the blossom of plants and animal worlds. The plant is formed by the universe and extends into the starry cosmos. It is entirely a product of forces outside its organism. Plants are carriers of life endowed with shape by carbon and then etherealized again by hydrogen. The protein animals create is an internal product, formed by cosmic forces which have been turned outside in. The internal organs of animals are really an interiorized reflection of forces and processes of the external universe, dynamic foci of an inner cosmos.

Conversely, the task of inner light is to break things down, and this process of disintegration is part of the activity of the astral body. There is indeed a continuous dissolution and destruction of the proteins and other substances that we consume so that these substances are utilized in a sense to direct counter-effects against what external light has built up. Without this activity of inner dissolution, a person could not be an ego being, and it is only by virtue of his ego nature that he can have inner experiences. So, while the etheric body is concerned with the preservation of the physical body, the astral body takes care that the food human beings consume is constantly built up and again destroyed. Without this process of disintegration within the physical body, the astral body, in which the ego is incorporated, could not live a full life within the material world.

The body, permeated by the ego, performs an action in disintegrating substances, and through this action something is created inwardly. The inner activity of consciousness particularly comes about through the astral body's process of dissolution. Actions, activities are called forth by the process of destruction. First, inner warmth is produced and second, something that is less noticeable than inner body heat, the physical expression of inner light. Just as the internal warmth that permeates the blood is the result of the breakdown of proteins, so the activity of the nervous system is the expression of this inner light. With regard to its inner activity, the nervous system is also a result of a disintegration process—not the nerves themselves but the activity of the nerves, the actions within the nerves, that which makes possible *Imagination* and calls forth thinking. It is this activity that can be called the physical expression of the invisible light and that is brought about through the degeneration and breakdown of substances.

Inner body heat is generated by the breakdown of protein. Inner light is produced within the organism as a result of processes involving fats, carbohydrates, starches and glucose, which are also utilized in the production of warmth and inner movement. All this represents the expression of the activity originating from the astral body. Human beings do not nourish themselves properly simply by ingesting the correct quantity of food, but rather when these inner processes can be carried out in the right way. The inner life is founded on them. Human beings are beings continually occupied inwardly with movement and animation and their inner life consists of these. If this inner life is not produced in the right way, it cannot react properly and a person then becomes ill.

In Plant Carbohydrates			
Cosmic formative forces	Carbon	Cellulose	Rigidity
Cosmic life forces	Oxygen	Starch	Carbohydrate
Cosmic fire forces	Hydrogen	Sugar	Dissolution

In Animal Protein		
Carbon	Form	Physical
Oxygen	Life	Etheric
Nitrogen	Mobility	Astral
Hydrogen	Warmth	Ego

Human Constitution			
Ego	Hydrogen	Fire	Proteins/DNA (sulfur)
Astral	Nitrogen	Air	Fatty Acids
Etheric	Oxygen	Water	Amino Acids
Physical	Carbon	Earth	Minerals

Rudolf Steiner has also described some of the actions of digestion and nutrition as the work of specific beings of the hierarchy in his lecture *The Question of Food* (GA 145).

Therefore we must say that in so far as human beings permeate their organism with the effects of nutrition derived from meat they are deprived of the forces that could free them from the earth. By eating a meat diet, we bind ourselves in the most direct and intimate sense to the planet earth. A vegetarian diet stimulates the forces in the human organism that bring us into a kind of cosmic union with the whole planetary system. In other words, we have the experience that through taking in plant nutrients the soul is assimilating something that does not possess earthy weight but belongs rather to the sun, that is, to the central body of the entire planetary system.

Whereas the cosmic forces of the beings who are the Spirits of Form are concerned with protein, those beings called Spirits of Movement are mainly concerned with the production of the fatty substance. No living being could assimilate either protein or fat without the cooperation of the cosmos—this is, the Spirits of Form and the Spirits of Movement.

Just as the etheric body combats the rotting of proteins, so the astral body combats the going rancid of fats and the I/ego combats the fermentation of sugar and starch. Looking at the etheric body we have to say it is mainly active in the abdomen. The astral body is mainly active in the chest region. There are four substances necessary for human nutrition—minerals, carbohydrates, fats, and protein—that effect the different organs of the human being.

States of Matter and the Human Constitution

Solid	Physical body	Minerals	Physical body
Fluid	Etheric body	Protein	Etheric body, abdomen
Gaseous	Astral body	Fats	Astral body, chest
Warmth	I/Ego	Starch/sugar	I/Ego

Functions of the Three Bodies

The Etheric body combats rotting

The Astral body combats going rancid

The I/ego combats fermentation

Substances Related to Human Organs	
Protein	Abdominal organs
Fats	Heart and blood vessels
Carbohydrates	Lungs, throat, palate
Minerals	Head

Dr. Otto Wolff tells us in *The Anthroposophical Approach to Medicine* (Anthroposophic Press, New York, 1982) that the quality of food rests on its content of formative forces. When a person eats a food, he reverses the formation of these substances. In a differentiated process of catabolism, the proteins, fats, and carbohydrates are broken down in their outer and inner structures. In this way, the formative forces that initially formed the food from inorganic substances are released from it, becoming free again. Only when they are not in bound form can they have a stimulating effect on the human etheric body. In animal foods, there are also astral processes. The foreign astrality must likewise be overcome by the human organism in the catabolic processes of digestion.

It is the etheric body that continuously fights against putrefaction, the astral body that prevents the decomposition of fats leading to the rancidness or steatorrhea, and the ego organization that suppresses fermentation of the carbohydrates, leading to fermentative dyspepsia.

In the healthy organism, the astral body is so strong that no foreign astrality can survive within its domain. While the etheric forces primarily act in water and protein, the astral forces are active in air and fat. The astral body stands between the etheric body and ego just as fat stands between protein and sugar. The bile acids are substances through which the astral body works in the chemical ether. Sodium is the substance through which the astral body engages in the water organism. Nitrogen is the principal component of air, and the astral body lives in the airy element, just as the etheric body lives in the watery element. An ensouled being requires a "living nitrogen" as body substance; this is protein. Protein is the universal vehicle of life, and is infinitely malleable and accessible to the action of the formative forces. That is why protein is the real vehicle of life.

This living protein—as yet, it is "only" living—is then molded species-specifically by the particular animal. The "laws" of the animal's existence and its essential quality can then unfold in this protein.

In the human being, an individual stamp is added to the etheric and astral qualities of the protein. Each human being constructs his own individual protein as the specific forming substance of his bodily nature; this expresses his ego. Herein lies the essential difference between protein and the other bodily substances. All human beings have the same sugar in their blood: glucose. Only such a super-individual substance as glucose can serve as the vehicle for the organization of the ego, which every human being possesses. Human protein, however, is the expression of the etheric body, astral body, and ego.

The etheric body wages a constant battle against putrefaction. The production of enzymes and hormones in the glands takes place through the etheric body. Protein, as the vehicle of life, is governed directly by impulses of the etheric body, but all the higher members of man's being are active in protein. Fat metabolism is governed by the astral body. It is through insulin that the ego organization engages in the metabolism.

The Twelve Substances

If we combine the three crosses of substances that have been presented, we have a group of twelve substances that are associated with particular zodiacal signs that correspond to their inherent natures. The Primal Four Substances, the Mineral Crosses, and the Oceanic Crosses display the polarities that are often found in the dynamic, rhythmical interactions of the etheric formative forces. Always, a balance point or homeostasis is the goal of health that arises from knowing our place among the elements. Each set of polarities creates a spectrum of manifestation that pulses between extremes. It is the goal of the Language of Nutrition to know and understand these elements so that consciousness can be the directing influence that strives for balance and equanimity in the surging forces that bring the formative elements into digestion.

Zodiacal Associations of Substances	
Aries	Silicon
Pisces	Chlorine
Aquarius	Oxygen
Capricorn	Aluminum
Sagittarius	Magnesium
Scorpio	Carbon
Libra	Calcium
Virgo	Sodium
Leo	Hydrogen
Cancer	Phosphorus
Gemini	Sulfur
Taurus	Nitrogen

These substances, or "habits," as Steiner calls them, are indeed processes that are like habits, or rituals. They are dynamic substances that go through changes that are regular and predictable, but always somewhat new. They build substances up and then dissolve them. Rhythmical pulsing between extremes on a spectrum of processes that expand and contract regularly drives these polar substances into different shapes and forms. Each paired polarity follows a dynamic habit, like the human heart as it contracts and expands as a sense organ perceiving the needs of circulation and respiration throughout the body. The form of the heart changes depending upon the stage of the process. So, too, the twelve substances of life change and metamorphose as rhythmic habits of polarities' give and take.

Once the normal expressions of the habits of substances are understood, good nutrition can follow. Each person is unique and has an individualized relationship to these substances and their dynamic processes. No two people react in quite the same way to food and sense perception. It is consciousness that must mitigate the circumstances and design a "habit" of digestion that balances all twelve substances with the individualized conditions in each human body. "What is one man's meat is another's poison"—so the saying goes. It is the individual's metabolic, rhythmic, and nerve/sense systems that must be brought into harmonious interaction with the twelve substances. One or another substance might play a larger role in an individual's diet based upon personal characteristics and temperament.

These twelve substances, or elements, are the building blocks of the etheric formative forces that create the human etheric body. These are the forces that generally "build up" the life systems in the body. The physical body is comprised of these substances, but it is the etheric body that brings in the cosmic forces to raise these elements into human life.

The Seven Metals

The sevenfold forces of the planets raying into the earth and the human body donate the harmonic music of the spheres as the formative forces that build the ethers into cohesive life. This Sounding ether is a cosmic mathematics that continually streams living sound into life. Steiner speaks of this in the following words:

> The mathematical proportions of chemistry are really expressions of the mathematical proportions of the music of the spheres, which has become mute by condensing into matter. (*The Mission of Christian Rosenkreutz*, GA 130)

The music of the spheres creates the balanced proportions between the planets, and also manifests in the organs of the human body and the structure and form of DNA and other such mechanisms. Through morphic resonance, the organs receive and broadcast the same music—or vibrations—that keep the organs in alignment with the healthy formative forces that are streaming into them from the planetary spheres. This communication between the heavenly and earthly "spheres" is the source of cohesive life on earth. The combined forces of the seven planets, the seven intervals, the seven organs, the seven levels of atomic weights, and the many other complete cycles of seven found in the human environment are all linked together in a grand symphony of music played on a heavenly harp with seven strings. The human constitution is a symphony of beings, sounds, and life that make it an instrument for the gods to play. In *Art in the Light of Mystery Wisdom* (GA 220), Steiner tells us much the same thing:

> If I were to describe everything to you, I would describe a wonderful music within the human body; music that is not heard, but is nonetheless experienced inwardly. What we experience musically is essentially nothing other than outer music meeting with the inner singing of the human organism. This human organism is a reflection of the macrocosm, which we carry within us as Apollo's lyre, in the form of concrete laws that are much stronger than natural laws. In us, the cosmos is playing Apollo's lyre. The human body is more than simply the aspect that biology recognizes; it is also a most wonderful musical instrument.

Thus, music is the gift of the planetary spheres to humans to draw us into heavenly harmonies that bring health and higher consciousness. We don't need to travel to the planets because they are here in our organs, sounding the music of the spheres as the metamorphic life pattern of the harmony and resonance that designs and creates the morphological development of humanity and cosmos.

Planet	Metal	Organ	System
Moon	Silver	Brain	Reproduction
Venus	Copper	Kidneys	Elimination
Mercury	Mercury	Lungs	Respiration
Sun	Gold	Heart	Circulation
Mars	Iron	Gall Bladder	Reproduction
Jupiter	Tin	Liver	Nourishment
Saturn	Lead	Spleen	Preservation

Amino Acids as the Building Blocks of Enzymes

"Enzymes are the bridge between the physical and the spiritual world."

Nutrition and Health, GA 354

Just as letters of the alphabet form every word in the dictionary, amino acids congregate in an endless array of patterns to form protein molecules that influence and define every cell in our body. Amino acids are the alphabet, and enzymes are the language of life. There are nineteen (to twenty-two) amino acids, just like the nineteen or so letters in many early phonetic alphabets. These amino acids, just like DNA and enzymes, are based upon four substances comprising both our outer and inner worlds: oxygen, hydrogen (sulfur), nitrogen, and carbon. Amino acids build upon the fourfold structure of these elements to create protein bundles that are so long and complex that the human DNA genome, when unfolded, is about six feet long, and the total DNA in the human body can stretch from Earth to Sun and back five times.

Four primary elements become the building blocks that can then create the over 50,000 proteins and 15,000 enzymes found in the human body. These four elements, much like the Greek elements, are the basis of our living natural world and the keystones around which life grows, dies, and grows again.

Amino acids are the building blocks of the body that construct cells, repair tissue, form antibodies, build the enzyme and hormonal systems, create nucleoproteins (RNA and DNA), carry oxygen through the body, and are required for muscle activity. At least seven or eight of the amino acids can't be manufactured by the human body (and thus are termed as "essential"). The rest of the amino acids, with proper nutrition and cellular functioning, can be manufactured by the human body (thus termed "non-essential," for supplementation purposes).

All amino acids are essential to life, health, and longevity. Wisdom indicates the importance of paying close attention to amino acids and enzymes. A person can receive adequate amino acids by consuming proper amounts of complete proteins and multi-purpose digestive enzymes. Complete protein foods contain all of the essential amino acids that cannot be produced by the human body.

All enzymes, including digestive enzymes, are made from amino acids, often with vitamins acting as coenzymes, and sometimes with mineral activators. When protein is consumed, the body first breaks the protein down into individual amino acids before the cells can use them in specific metabolic pathways, or for building enzymes or proteins. But to break down protein, it is first necessary to have enough of the right kind of enzymes. The symbiotic relationship of all life energies begins to come into clear appreciation by studying amino acids.

The body needs amino acids in order to get amino acids from the food consumed. A lack of free amino acids can be followed by an inability to produce the digestive enzymes necessary to break protein down into its component amino acids. Amino acids play a key role in normalizing moods, attention, concentration, aggression, sex drive, and sleep.

A complete protein is a source of protein that contains an adequate proportion of all of the amino acids necessary for the dietary needs of humans. This is the optimal profile of the essential amino acids which comprises a complete protein:

- Tryptophan
- Threonine
- Isoleucine
- Leucine
- Lysine
- Methionine (+Cysteine)
- Phenylalanine (+Tyrosine)
- Valine
- Histidine

All foods contain amino acids in some quantity, and nearly all animal foods contain the essential amino acids in sufficient quantity. Proportions vary, however, and most plant foods are deficient in one or more of the essential amino acids. Some sources of complete protein are:

- Animal foods: meats, fish, poultry, milk, eggs
- Plant foods: legumes, seeds, grains, vegetables, chickpeas, black beans, pumpkin seeds, cashews, cauliflower, quinoa, pistachios, turnip greens, black-eyed peas

Miracle of Enzymes

Enzymes are the spark of life that runs through your entire body. You can't digest or absorb food without enzymes, and they regulate tens of thousands of other biochemical functions that take place in the body every second, in every cell. Enzymes cause seeds to sprout, fruit to ripen, and leaves to change color—even thinking needs enzymatic action to occur. Enzymes create catalytic actions that are the source of life. They help maintain the life-body, or etheric body of formative forces, that builds and sustains the physical body. Enzymes combine with co-enzymes to form nearly 100,000 various chemicals that help us see, hear, feel, move, digest food, and talk.

Every organ and tissue, and all the one hundred trillion cells in your body, depend upon the reactions of enzymes and their energy transformation, which can cause catalytic reactions that increase metabolic processes unimaginably. A single enzyme can cause one trillion reactions in one second and still not use up its individual substance. Bio-energetic reactions in every cell can only be described through the vital role played by enzymes.

Vitamins and minerals are co-enzymes that require enzymes to work, underscoring the primal necessity of enzymes in life functions. Enzymes are the vital workers and key communicators responsible for the breakdown and absorption of all nutrients, and thus the bioenergy of the human body.

Enzymes are macromolecular biological catalysts, or biocatalysts. Enzymes accelerate, or catalyze, chemical reactions. Almost all metabolic processes in the cell need enzymes in order to occur at rates fast enough to sustain life. Enzymes are known to catalyze more than 5,000 biochemical reaction types. Most enzymes are proteins, and their specificity comes from their unique three-dimensional structures.

Like all proteins, enzymes are linear chains of amino acids that fold to produce a three-dimensional structure. The sequence of the amino acids specifies the structure which, in turn, determines the catalytic activity of the enzyme. Enzyme structures unfold (denature) when heated or exposed to chemical denaturants, and this disruption to the structure typically causes a loss of activity.

Like all other proteins, enzymes are made of amino acids. Each enzyme is made of between a hundred and upwards of a million amino acids placed like pearls on a string and bonded to the next by chemical valence. The vast majority of enzymes are made of only nineteen different kinds of amino acids. The structure and function of the enzyme is determined by the order of the amino acids. No two enzymes are alike. Each enzyme has its own unique sequence of amino acids, which is determined by the genes in the cells. In most enzymes, the string is coiled and folded thousands of times to form a highly complex three-dimensional structure. It is the chemical interactions between the amino acids that force the enzymes into their three-dimensional structure, which is held together by the many different links between the different amino acids.

Enzymes are protein molecules that carry vital energy catalysts needed for every chemical action and reaction that occurs in our body. Approximately 2,700 different enzymes help digest and catabolize small molecules or break down larger molecules, including fats, proteins, and carbohydrates. This process takes place in your stomach and intestines during digestion, allowing for normal nutrient absorption. Enzymes also help your body release larger, broken-down molecules for use as energy.

Enzymes do all the work inside any cell. A human cell has about 20,000 different types of enzymes floating around in the cytoplasm. Enzymes are chemical-reaction agents that work extremely fast. Enzymes do everything from breaking glucose down for energy to building cell walls, constructing new enzymes, and allowing the cell to reproduce.

One of the most important things our body does is to continue the process of building our enzymes. Enzymes play an important role in every function in the human body, including eating, digestion, breathing, kidney and liver function, reproduction, elimination, and more. Several places in your digestive system secrete enzymes, including the mouth, stomach, pancreas, and cells of the small intestine—even your gut bacteria secrete digestive enzymes. Enzymes help with nutrient absorption and break down foods in the digestive tract by breaking apart the bonds that hold nutrients together—nutrients that will be absorbed so the body can use them for energy and other critical functions. Proteins, fats, and carbohydrates are the most basic foods the body breaks down and absorbs; the enzymes protease, lipase, and amylase are made by the body for this purpose.

Humans used to get a lot more enzymes from their diet. In the past, humans consumed plenty of raw foods to help re-supply the digestive tract with beneficial enzymes, but today most of the foods we eat are cooked, irradiated, or heavily processed—all of which deplete natural enzymes. Even the raw foods we eat are typically transported and refrigerated, so their natural enzyme content is reduced. As we age, our bodies produce less protease, lipase, and amylase, which means the digestion of protein, fats, and carbohydrates can be impaired as we get older.

Enzymes are not living organisms; they are simply biological molecules. Therefore, they do not live or die. Given the right conditions to function, an enzyme can go on and on for as long as needed. Wherever one substance needs to be transformed into another, nature uses enzymes to speed up the process. Enzymes catalyse all processes in the body, enabling organisms to build up chemical substances such as other proteins, carbohydrates, or fats that are necessary for life.

Overwhelming evidence shows that food enzymes play an important role by pre-digesting food in the upper stomach.

Supplementation of food enzymes is necessary today because so much of the food is processed or cooked. Most food enzymes are destroyed at the temperatures used to cook and process food. Food enzymes are extremely sensitive to temperatures above 118 °F. When raw foods are processed or heated in any way, they may lose 100% of their enzyme activity and up to 85% of their vitamin content. Unfortunately, even raw food might be enzyme-deficient if it was grown in nutrient-lacking soil.

To function properly, food enzymes must also work in tandem with the coenzymes of vitamins and minerals. Unlike the enzymes in raw plant foods, coenzymes are not completely destroyed by cooking. Unless the enzymes from raw food are present, the coenzymes in the food cannot be utilized to their full potential. For all these reasons, supplementing with enzymes is crucial to achieving a more efficient digestive process and better absorption of food's nutrients.

DNA Enzymes

There are an estimated 20,000 to 25,000 genes that carry three billion bits of genetic information and instruct our DNA in how to make our proteins (enzymes) for life. DNA guides the cell in its production of new enzymes and is a carrier of genetic information. DNA is a self-replicating pattern that tells the cell how to make its proteins. It carries the instructions for how to form an enzyme.

Since the tight control of enzyme activity is essential for homeostasis, any malfunction (mutation, overproduction, underproduction, or deletion) of a single critical enzyme can lead to a genetic disease. Germline mutations in gene coding for DNA repair enzymes cause cancer because cells are less able to repair mutations in their genomes. This causes a slow accumulation of mutations and results in the development of cancers.

Reading the Language of Nutrition

We have heard about the alphabet of the Language of Nutrition from a variety of vantage points. Zodiacal consonants have been described as twelve formative forces that join with planetary vowels to create nineteen habits or letters in this alphabet. We have also heard about nineteen amino acids that have seven essential amino acids that "ensoul" our digestion with the materials necessary to dissolve food into its constituent parts and then use those substances to create new cells—new life. Both languages use the same Four Primal Substances to create amino acids that develop into highly complex proteins, like human DNA. Substances all arise from these four primal elements and are ensouled by the astral body and I/ego of the individual. While we are awake, the physical and etheric bodies build these substances up, and the astral and ego destroy these same substances.

From life to death, these substances give and take with their polar opposite substance in a pulsing dynamic of life—a cosmically harmonic dance. To see the life in substance is to see etheric formative forces raying into life from the twelve directions of space and calling forth movement, growth, and life. Truly, this Language of Nutrition is a mystery language that can help define the manifestation of the divine in the material world.

Without proper nutrition, the substances of calcium and phosphorus would never reach the pineal gland to make brain sand, and thus the human being would be dull and unaware. It is the refined mineral substance of the earth that is needed to feed the divine with our warmth, light, and love. Without good nutrition, the mineral substance of the earth cannot be redeemed and raised up to the mineral substance the brain needs to spark higher consciousness. Nutrition is directly connected to consciousness and awareness, and wisdom children need both good nutrition and the understanding of the Language of Nutrition to fully refine food and sense perception into "consumable" food for the hierarchy.

We need to "taste good" to the angels and the other hierarchy, or else we are of little service to the spiritual world. Our higher thoughts, feelings, and deeds feed the gods, and then, in turn, the gods feed us. Wisdom, insight, love, inspiration, intuition, and all the higher virtues are the menu the gods offer to us if we can, in like kind, offer a tasty menu to them each night in our dreams.

All the details of what the world goes through to create us and our environment are incomprehensible to the human mind. We have seen that even the actions of enzymes are truly beyond our capacity to hold in our thoughts. Enzymes, like stem cells, seem eternal and are almost omnipresent and omnipotent in the chemical world. We cannot imagine the speed at which enzymes work, nor the many tasks they can accomplish quite independently of our conscious mind. It is therefore important to study their spectrum of manifestation as a dynamic picture (*Imagination*) of their processes and functions that might reveal the "beingness" or the "beings" behind matter. There is an invisible world that creates our visible world, and through study, we can arrive at a sense of the miraculous found in every cell of our body. Study of these substances and forces reveals that much is known but little is understood about these wondrous processes of Mother Nature.

A Theory of Everything–
The Etheric Formative Forces

As we have been presented with many ideas about the ethers, from ancient Hindu sources to modern ether theories, we have seen that each new thinker has a different vantage point from which to describe these wondrous forces, or "entities," as numerous authors refer to them. At the beginning of our presentation, we stated that it is impossible to speak of the ethers without also speaking of the genesis of space and time and the beings, forces, elementals, and elements that are associated with the etheric formative forces and their rhythmic cycles. To address the first ether that was created demands an understanding of a cosmology that can "hold" the metamorphosing nature of that ether from the most ancient times to the present, and far into the future. Ethers evolve alongside of human and hierarchical evolution. Ethers are not only the building blocks of space and time, but also of consciousness and the beings and forces that work together to create the confluence of Earthly and cosmic forces that are found in and around each human.

Both the world within and the world without are populated by invisible beings whose growth and activity create elements and elementals as a "shadow" of those spirits. Spirits "fall" into matter, and we can witness the forces, effects, and outer manifestation of these beings as the substance of our environment, and likewise our consciousness. Spirit and matter are hyper-connected to the cosmos and the hierarchy through the ethers. Truly, ethers are magical in their nature and effect.

It is hard to find a place to begin describing the etheric body of a human being. According to many theorists, the ethers pervade all space and all living aspects of the human being. Every atom, molecule, and cell is filled with the dynamic, rhythmic exchange of the four ethers. This pulsing of cosmic and human life is linked, and we can find the duality of the physical plane explicated through the opposing sets of two ethers that alternately give and take in a dynamic field of forces involving electricity, magnetism, levity, and gravity.

Beyond these moving and undulating forces, beings, and substances is the mysterious Cosmic ether, or the Akasha ether. In ancient texts, this primal entity is clearly a being who is the director of the four basic ethers, like a Mother with four rowdy boys who like to wrestle as they express themselves. This Akasha ether is called Fohat by H. P. Blavatsky and others. It assumes the role of the prime creator and prime mover. Akasha weaves between the other four ethers, creating a space for them to play. After hearing all the different theorists, it might be fair to assume that Akasha is primal space that is beyond the hierarchy and is a donation directly from the Divine Trinity.

New theories of the Akasha ether align with the most ancient ones. Akasha is the void of space that all manifestation comes to exist within. It is an ocean of ether, not unlike the mysterious "substance" ether that the ancients referred to with awe. Even Einstein believed in the "hypothetical ether" that was the foundation of his theory of General Relativity, which was his best version of a Theory of Everything. Einstein only referred to this Luminiferous ether quite obliquely, but his concepts of the propagation of light are based upon this ether.

Most Theories of Everything have a mysterious force, fluid, substance, vacuum, vortex, or medium in which the forces of the universe act. Many new theories place the ether or ethers at the core of the cosmos. In the Appendix of this book, you will find numerous other ether theories that point in the direction of what we have come to see is a complex but understandable system of seven ethers that have different effects on the Earth compared to the cosmos.

The key factor in understanding the ethers is to know how many there are and how they came into being as a process of metamorphoses that evolves over the seven incarnations of the Earth. Not only can the ethers tell us about the past and the creation of the world, but the three "extra" ethers that are added onto the standard four ethers can inform us about the nature of the future. The ethers are a window into viewing the entire plan of human and world evolution. Each ether is connected to a soul or spiritual capacity of the human being. The future spiritual capacities that the human being will develop are also written into the Akasha ether, the Unfallen Sound ether, and the Unfallen Life ether. These three ethers will become more and more available to human use, and this will lead to the future capacities of *Imagination* in the Spirit Self, *Inspiration* in the Life Spirit, and *Intuition* in the Spirit Human. These steps of evolution will take long periods of time to unfold but are available for the initiate at this time. The future can bring to us our future capacities of spirit through the workings of the etheric formative forces.

The human etheric body is an image of the entire cosmos, from ego birth to ego ascension. Thus, the etheric body is virtually immortal and has the past, present, and future inscribed into it as the key to human spiritual metamorphosis. The ethers are the ladder to the spiritual world, and at the first stage of ascension, the initiate gains "Etheric Vision" as an outward sign of development. New, supersensible, spiritual organs of perception develop through the interaction with etheric vision as it is unfolding. Christ is perceived in the etheric realm with this new etheric vision, and He teaches the initiate directly through offering His perfected etheric body as a model to emulate and embody. The higher ego of the individual is the perfected etheric body that exists in the realm where Christ is found: the etheric realm of the Life Spirit.

The Earthly ego weds the higher ego, and the human being takes the Akasha ether and consciously weds it to the unfallen sound ether. This brings the active world of *Imaginations* (Akasha ether) into the world of *Inspiration* (Unfallen Sound ether—the Harmony of the Spheres). Unfallen sound ether is the Water of Life and the redeemed Tree of Knowledge of Good and Evil. When the unfallen life ether is attained, the initiate merges with the Cosmic Ego of Christ and becomes a co-creator through *Intuition. Intuition* brings us to the Tree of Life and the cosmic Word made manifest.

The evolution of taking on warmth ether (minerals), light ether (plants), and fallen sound or chemical ether (animals) created the kingdoms of nature that we exist within. These ethers also provide the substance and processes of the realms of consciousness we call dreamless sleep, dreaming, and waking. Thus, the outer world of the kingdoms of nature and the three states of consciousness generally found in the human being are connected and work from the same principles and with the same ethers.

Working with the fallen life ether develops the capacities to recognize eternal truths in ourselves and the world. Gleaning these objective realities leads us over to communion with the spiritual beings who stand behind the outer world of senses. Fallen life ether is the place where the eternal "I" (or ego identity) of the individual is born. Fallen life ether builds up the human constitution at this time in evolution, but in the future, humans will be able to access unfallen sound and unfallen life ethers. As long as humans are "on the earth" and in the "atmosphere" we experience now, the higher ethers are as yet unavailable, generally speaking. Again, an initiate can rise up to these ethers and pull down the forces and processes of the higher ethers from the future.

While an "earthman," the human being must evolve slowly and with great effort. Suffering time and space is the current fate of human beings unless awareness of the three higher ethers takes place. The gifts of the past are offered through awareness of the evolution of the ethers, and these lessons of humanity are written into the ether body of each individual. The past is summarized in the present etheric body, and the future is insinuated through the evolution of the ethers.

The etheric body is the memory body of humanity and the schemata of the future human being. We need to study this magical etheric body and unlock its secrets so that we can share this universal process of metamorphosis as it is found in the world ethers and the human etheric body. We need to link our consciousness to the forces of natural law that we perceive to be manifesting the forces of the ethers. As we do this, we train ourselves to listen to the etheric body's lessons of the past and begin to imagine the nature and characteristics of future humanity.

As we work with *The Eternal Ethers: A Theory of Everything* as spiritually aware individuals, we can take the ethers, past and future, as the guideposts for human physical and spiritual evolution, both individually and collectively. We can examine the etheric body while it is the focus of human development, from ages seven to fourteen, when the etheric body is most active and building the connectivity to the world and cosmos. It is these years that create a "sensitive period" for an educator to observe the growing child, and thus observe the developing etheric body. It is a necessity of our times to understand this development and feed this etheric process the appropriate living images that can help build the individual child's etheric body in a healthy way.

It is through images, symbols, and literature that we can "paint" pictures for the growing child to identify with at the particular stage of collective human development that matches their own personal stage of development. The seven-year old child is like a freshly awakened ancient soul that is trying to come into the modern age over the course of seven years. Each sensitive period or stage of development can be met with cultural offerings that meet the longings of the young child (ancient soul). Each grade, from first to seventh, can be structured to offer an experience of what it meant to be a person in ancient India, ancient Persia, or other cultures that created steps of critical intellectual development that led towards modern-day thinking. In this way, the development of the child replicates the development of the natural human intellect and its spiritual capacities.

We have previously pointed at an archetypal system of seven stages that replicate this "memory picture" that we can find in the human etheric body. This scheme is true in the large and the small. The entire cosmos grows through the same stages as a butterfly does, or as a child does from ages seven to fourteen. Part of the process recapitulates the past, while part indicates the future. A teacher's job is to offer soul nourishment for the child's developmental stage through appropriate literature and activities that feed the soul's need to remember and re-embody the wisdom of the past.

Ultimately, understanding the seven ethers constitutes a Theory of Everything. Of course, the best part is yet to come. We can teach the child the past through age-appropriate education up to the seventh grade. In eighth grade, we can help the child become a "citizen of their own time" through summarizing the content of grades one through seven in an objective way. This prepares the child to come into the modern age with a strong association to the stages of human development that have happened over millennia. This is the proper way to welcome and educate the child's etheric body and to build it out of the ethers that have accompanied this evolution. Educating the etheric body is the intent of the Waldorf curriculum. Rudolf Steiner was very conscious of this fact and has provided us with the insight to provide every wisdom child with the content of the etheric body: *The Eternal Curriculum*. There are other curricula that can also point at these ideas, but the Waldorf curriculum is the most comprehensive and effective means of linking child development with human development.

Appendix

New Theories Concerning the Ethers
Adapted from John McGuire's Aether 101

Model G Kinetic Ether by **Paul LaViolette:** The Kinetic Ether is the fundamental component of the overall theory known as *Subquantum Kinetics:* a general systems approach to microphysics/cosmology. Within the Model G framework, the Ether behaves similarly to a transmuting/kinetic gradient field composed of postulated *Etherons*. Ether can be imagined as a feedback-driven, transmuting open system. While there are a number of reacting/transmuting etheron species within the ether, only *X-ons* (embodying negative charge), *Y-ons* (embodying positive charge), and *G-ons* (embodying gravity) have a visible impact in our Universe. These etherons are locked into cross-catalytic reaction loops that are self-generative and self-organizing. This not only gives rise to all four fundamental forces of nature (when sufficient etheron concentrations are achieved), but also provides a logical/consistent theory to explain how matter continuously creates itself in the Universe.

Liquid Crystal Aether by **Harold Aspden:** Aspden characterized the Aether as a "Liquid-Crystal" because it appeared similar to a dynamic, fluid-like continuum, while at the same time exhibiting certain behaviors reminiscent of a rigid, crystalline structure. Aspden saw the Aether as an electrically charged entity, but neutral overall.

Cosmic Neutrino Background by **Wallace Thornhill:** Neutrinos exhibit no discernible charge and little mass, and periodically transform to have their own anti-particle qualities.

> *A vast sea of unreactive neutrinos could be the long debated 'ether' that permeates space. Space is not a void. We then have an electrically responsive medium for the transmission of light in which the characteristic velocity of an electrical disturbance in that medium is the so-called speed of light, in the Electric Universe model.*

Electric Dipole Sea by **Tombe** acknowledges that the Aether is dynamic, stretchable, and compressible. He postulates that the all-pervasive fluid continuum becomes rendered into tiny dipolar vortices that press against each other with centrifugal force while striving to dilate. These dipolar vortices constitute rotating electron-positron dipoles. Hence the sea of aether vortices is equivalent to a dense *Electric Sea* of electron-positron dipoles. Tombe views electrons as aether sinks, and positrons as aether fonts. They rotate around one another to form vortexes that entrain aether fluid further around and within themselves. These dipolar vortices also settle themselves into double-helix patterns that then constitute *Magnetic Lines-of-Force.*

Space Vortex Theory by **P. Tewari:** This theory falls into the fluid-dynamic family of Aether models. It proposes aether velocity as the fundamental process underwriting all fields, forces, and matter.

Subquantum Kinetics: The Alchemy of Creation by **Paul A. LaViolette:** SQK explains in detail how subatomic particles arise from subquantum fluctuations in the ether. SQK derives from general systems principles, admits the possibility of an unseen realm, and harmonizes with mystical teachings.

Light is the Ghost of Mass by **Chuck Bennett:** The quantization of the aether can be explained by the view that the aether consists of a sea of particles that are on the order of a million times lighter than the electron. The mass range of the particles is in the range for the spectrum of all light photons. Therefore, the aether simply consists of a medium of "condensed photons." Light can be viewed as evaporated mass, and mass as condensed light, and light can be considered a "hole" in the quantized aether.

Rotating Wave Theory of the Electron by **William H. F. Christie** uses the classical concepts of ether, space, and time to develop a pure wave theory of the electron (or fermion) as a simple rotating wave. The essential postulate is that an electromagnetic wave is brought into classical rotation by a local binding energy. The spin model then yields the required phenomena of charge, relativity, mass, gravity, and quantum mechanics.

Aethro-Kinematics: Physics of the Third Millennium by **Steven Rado:** Aethro-Kinematics renders an alternate mechanical solution for the polarization of light. Thus, it reinstates Faraday and Maxwell's gaseous model of the aether and resumes the original task of exploring all "action at a distance" forces as fluid dynamical behavior of the all-pervading aether. In Aethro-Kinematics, aether is taken as an all-pervading gas at an ultra-microscopic order of magnitude. The constituents of this medium, the "aethrons," are in constant random motion, with perfectly elastic collisions.

Derivation of Newtonian Gravitation from LeSage's Attenuation Concept by **Barry Mings and Paul Stowe:** Once fully rendered, gravitation is a connective process between matter and the ZPE (Zero Point Energy or aether) field. It not only produces the obvious result we call gravity, but also is the productive agent of elemental charge, inertia, and the deBroglie wave phenomena. This same model rears up again in modern physics in the form of the mathematical topology of string/super string theory, as well as in superconductivity and superfluidity.

An Aether Model of the Universe by **Dr. Allen Rothwarf:** An aether model based upon a degenerate Fermion fluid—composed primarily of electrons and positrons in a negative energy state relative to the null state or true vacuum—is proposed, and its consequences for physics and cosmology are explored. The model provides both insight and quantitative results for a large number of phenomena for which conventional theory provides no answers, or unsatisfactory answers.

EVE A model of the AETHER, by **Carlos Laborde:** The "Eve" model of aether leans on Euclidean space, absolute time, and the Galileo transformation. The simplest aether is postulated: it is made of point particles called aetherinos that do not interact with themselves, only with matter. Reference frames in which all the aetherinos move in straight lines are postulated to exist.

A Theory of the Etherial Space of Newton and Einstein by **Henry H. Lindner:** Gravity is due to the acceleration and velocity of a physical space that flows into all mass. The equations of the ether's flow imply compression of the ether near mass. This simple and objective theory specifies the motion of space, and thus of mass and light everywhere in the Cosmos.

A Framework Hypothesis for the ZPE Field by **Paul Stowe:** A framework hypothesis for a definition of the ZPE field is aetheric in nature. This discussion suggests a common foundation for all physical phenomena and derives the known physical constants. It also provides for the manifestation of the four known forces, as well as a simple explanation of their existence.

Aether Theory by **Frank Meno:** In this model, the known extent of the physical universe is filled with the aether, which is a highly compressed, very hot gas. The particles that make up this gas are called gyrons because the necessary physical properties of the aether emerge from the gyroscopic behavior of these fundamental particles, which have a special, identical oblong form. Due to the special shape of the gyrons, the aether, as a fluid, has very complicated properties that account for all such phenomena as charge, magnetism, spin, gravitation, and neutrinos.

The Theory of Harmonic by **Ray Tomes:** The theory of harmonics is based upon a study of cycles that are manifest across a diverse range of phenomena and disciplines. From cosmological and astronomical scales, to the subatomic, the theory of harmonics postulates the existence of an aether. A black hole would be an aether vacuum.

Neoetherics by **Jerry Shifman:** The underlying premise is that mass is an action of ether, and that the "gravitation" effects observed near a mass can be understood by understanding this etheric action. This model brings the identity between gravity and acceleration into vivid clarity.

Ether as a Disclosing Model by **M. C. Duffy:** The modern ether concept is compatible with relativity, quantum mechanics, and non-classical geometrization. Misuse of the term "ether" in anti-Relativity polemics in former times causes many physicists to avoid the word, and equivalent terms are used instead. The modern concept results from three development programs. First, there was the evolution of Relativity. Relativistic Cosmology and Geometrodynamics which discarded the early twentieth-century passive, rigid ether in favor of geometrized space-time. In his later years, Einstein accepted a non-classical ether, defined as field or space-time. This had two main aspects: static (or geometric) and dynamic (or frame-space perspective). Second, there was a Lorentzian program, which provided a quasi-classical exposition of Relativity in terms of moving rod and clock readings. The Einstein-Minkowski and Lorentzian programs can be reconciled. The third development program is associated with Quantum Mechanics and studies of the physical vacuum. A group of analogues based on the vortex sponge promises to unify these programs of interpretation. The modern ether, from the smallest scale point of view, resembles a "sea of information," which demands new techniques for interpreting it, drawn from information science, computer science, and communications theory.

The interpretation of fundamental phenomena in modern physics has given rise to new perspectives on the ether concept, especially in the context of studies of physical vacuums, particle creation and disintegration, and neo-quaternions theory. Because of the modern and progressive spirit in which these interpretations are carried out, colleagues refer to the "new ether" to distinguish it from obsolete and mistaken concepts associated with the "old ether" concept of a century ago. The new ether concept is employed because it is useful—even necessary—and finds expression in non-classical geometries, multidimensional geometries, relativity, and quantum mechanics. Despite its proven usefulness, many colleagues avoid the term "ether" and use an equivalent expression to define physical space-time. Typical equivalents are urfield, cosmic plenum, physical vacuum, ultimate referent, or ultra-referential reality. The vortex-sponge analogue and its laboratory realization in the form of super-cooled Helium II, have been used to interpret General Relativity, Relativistic Cosmology, and Quantum Mechanics.

Charts and Diagrams

Ethers and the Elements

Physical—Carbon   Astral—Nitrogen

Etheric—Oxygen   Ego—Phosphorus/Sulphur

Spirit—Hydrogen

- Life ether works through carbon (senses)
- Sound ether works through oxygen and nitrogen (senses)
- Light ether works through sulphur and phosphorus (senses)
- Warmth ether works through hydrogen (respiration)

Glands	Substance	Control
Pineal	Silica	Aging
Pituitary	Calcium	Giants, dwarfism
Thyroid	Nitrogen	Metabolic rate, fear, anxiety
Parathyroids	Carbon	Cramps
Thymus	Oxygen	Muscle strength
Adrenals	Sulphur and Phosphorus	Energy
Gonads	Hydrogen	Procreation

Elements and Organs

Ego	Hydrogen	Liver, spleen, gall
Astral	Nitrogen	Kidneys, cerebrospinal fluid, nervousness
Etheric	Oxygen	Lung, rhythmic system
Physical	Carbon	Intestines, chyme, lymph, heart

Fallen Ethers

Ego	Life	Meaning	Higher Third Force	Asuras
			(Fallen Devauchan)	
Astral	Sound	Thinking	Electro-magnetism	Ahriman
			(Fallen Lower Devauchan)	
Etheric	Light	Feeling	Electricity	Lucifer
			(Fallen Astral)	
Physical	Warmth	Willing	Motion	Human

States of Consciousness and Ethers

Life Ether	Intuition	Realm of Beings
Sound Ether	Inspiration	Realm of Ideas
Light Ether	Imagination	
Warmth Ether	Waking	
Elementals 1	Sleeping	
Elementals 2	Dreaming	
Elementals 3	Dreamless Sleep	

Hierarchical Beings and Elementals

Saturn	Thrones	Group soul of minerals
Jupiter	Kyriotetes	Group soul of plants
Mars	Dynamis	Group soul of animals
Sun	Exusiai	Fire: salamanders
Mercury	Archai	Solid: gnomes
Venus	Archangels	Liquid: undines
Moon	Angels	Air: sylphs

Human Constitution and Ethers

Warmth	Light	Sound	Life
Blood	Nerve	Muscle	Bone
Ego	Astral	Etheric	Physical

From the Chaldean Oracles

Having mingled the spark of soul with two, in unanimity;
With Mind and Breath Divine,
He added to them a third,
Pure Love, the August Master Binding All.

Joachim and Boaz
by Rudolf Steiner

In pure thinking thou dost find,
The self that can hold itself.
(Warmth Ether: Spark, Ego, Fire, Egoic)

Transmute the thought into picture life,
And thou will know creative wisdom.
(Light Ether: Mind, Astral, Light, Thinking)

Condense thy feelings into light,
Formative powers are revealed through thee.
(Sound Ether: Breathe, Etheric, Air, Feeling)

Forge thy will into deeds to being,
So shalt thou share in world creation.
(Life Ether: Love, Physical, Activity, Willing)

Bibliographical References
and Literature

Blattman, George. *The Sun, the Ancient Mysteries, and a New Physics*. Floris Books, Anthroposophic Press, London, 1972.

Blavatsky, Helena Petrovna. *Isis Unveiled: A Master Key to the Mysteries of Ancient and Modern Science and Theology*, Quest Books, Chicago, 1997.

Blavatsky, Helena Petrovna. *The Key to Theosophy*, Create Space Independent Publishing, 2016.

Blavatsky,Helena Petrovna. *The Secret Doctrine: A Synthesis of Science, Religion and Philosophy*, TarcherPerigee, 2009.

Blavatsky, Helena Petrovna. *The Voice of Silence: Being Extracts from the Book of the Golden Precepts*, Theosophical University Press, 1992.

Bockemuhl, Jochen. *Toward a Phenomenology of the Etheric World: Investigations into the Life of Nature and Man.* Anthroposophic Press, Spring Valley, N. Y., 1977.

Falck-Ytter, Harald. *Aurora: The Northern Lights in Mythology, History, and Science.* Floris Books, Antrhoposophic Press, London, 1983.

Forward, William and Wolpert, Andrew. *The Image of Blood: The Golden Blade No. 48.* Floris Books, Edinburgh, 1995.

Franke, Sylvia. *The Tree of Life and the Holy Grail: Ancient and Modern Spiritual Paths and the Mystery of Rennes-le-Chateau.* Temple Lodge, London, 2007.

Gabriel, Douglas. *The Eternal Curriculum for Wisdom Children: Intuitive Learning and the Etheric Body,* Our Spirit, 2017.

Gabriel, Tyla. *The Gospel of Sophia: A Modern Path of Initiation* (Volume 2), Our Spirit, 2015.

Gabriel, Tyla. *The Gospel of Sophia: The Biographies of the Divine Feminine Trinity* (Volume 1), Our Spirit, 2014.

Gabriel, Tyla and Douglas. *The Gospel of Sophia: Sophia Christos Initiation* (Volume 3), Our Spirit, 2016.

Gebser, Jean. *Anxiety, a Condition of Modern Man,* Paperback, 1962.

Gebser, Jean. *The Ever Present Origin,* Ohio University Press, 1991.

Hall, Manly P. *The Most Holy Trinosophia of the Comte De St. Germain.* The Philosophical Research Society, Inc., Los Angeles, 1983.

Harrison, C. G. *The Transcendental Universe.* Lindesfarne Press, New York, 1993.

Jocelyn, Beredene. *Citizens of the Cosmos: Life's Unfolding from Conception through Death to Rebirth.* Continuum, New York, 1981.

Katzenellenbogen, Adolf. *Allegories of the Virtues and Vices in Medieval Art.* Medieval Academy of America, Canada, 1989.

Konig, Karl. *Earth and Man.* Bio-Dynamic Literature, Wyoming, Rhode Island, 1982.

Landscheidt, Theodor. *Sun-Earth-Man a Mesh of Cosmic Oscillations: How Planets Regulate Solar Eruptions, Geomagnetic Storms, Conitions of Life, and Economic Cycles.* Urania Trust, London, 1989.

Laszlo, Ervin and Kingsley, Dennis L. *Dawn of the Akashic Age: New Consciousness, Quantum Resonance, and the Future of the World.* Inner Traditions, Rochester Vermont, 2013.

Laszlo, Ervin. *Quantum Shift in the Global Brain: How the New Scientific Reality Can Change Us and Our World.* Inner Traditions, Rochester Vermont, 2008.

Laszlo, Ervin. *Science and the Akashic Field: An Integral Theory of Everything.* Inner Traditions, Rochester Vermont, 2004.

Lehrs, Ernst. *Man or Matter.* Rudolf Steiner Press, Forrest Row, 2013.

Loeteman, Kees. *Gaia-Sophia: A Framework for Ecology: A New Approach to Evolution And Working With the Environment.* Floris Books, Edinburgh, 1991.

Milner, Dennis and Smart, Edward. *The Loom of Creation: A Study of the Purpose and the Forces that Weave the Pattern of Existence.* Harper & Row, New York, 1976.

O'Neil, George and Gisela. *The Human Life.* Mercury Press, New York, 1990.

Pfeiffer, Ehrenfried. *The Heart Lectures.* Mercury Presss, Spring Valley, New York. 1997.

Prasad, Rama. *Nature's Finer Forces & The Science of Breath* The Theosophical Publishing Society, London (1890).

Prasad, Rama. *The Science of Breath & the Philosophy of the Tatwas.* The Theosophical Publishing Society, London (1890).

Prokofieff, Sergei O. *And the Earth Becomes a Sun: The Mystery of the Resurrection.* Wynstones Press, Stourbridge, England, 2014.

Prokofieff, Sergei O. *The Appearance of Christ in the Etheric: Spiritual-Scientific Aspects of the Second Coming.* Temple Lodge, London, 2012.

Ragon, Jean Marie. *Esoteric Studies in Masonry.* Daath Gnosis Publications, USA, 2015.

Spengler, Oswald. *The Decline of the West,* Vintage, 2006.

Steiner, Rudolf. *Anthroposophical Spiritual Science and Medical Therapy.* Dornach, April 12, 1921.

Steiner, Rudolf. *Art in the Light of Mystery Wisdom,* Rudolf Steiner Press, New York, 1997.

Steiner, Rudolf. *Course for Young Doctors,* Mercury Press, New York, 1997.

Steiner, Rudolf. The Human Heart. **Dornach, May 26, 1922, GA 212.**

Steiner, Rudolf. *Foundations of Esotericism.* Berlin, September 30, 1905.

Steiner, Rudolf. *From Crystals to Crocodiles.* Rudolf Steiner Press, Forrest Row, 2002.

Steiner, Rudolf. *Inner Experience of Evolution.* Steiner Books, Great Barrington, 2009.

Steiner, Rudolf. *Nature Spirits, Selected Lectures.* Rudolf Steiner Press, Forrest Row, 2007.

Steiner, Rudolf. *Rudolf Steiner on Astronomy*. Translated by Rick Mansell. The Rudolf Steiner Research Foundation, Redondo Beach, California, 1989.

Steiner, Rudolf. *Science: An Introductory Reader*. Sophia Books, Forrest Row, 2003.

Steiner, Rudolf. *Supersensible Knowledge*, Rudolf Steiner Press, New York, 1988.

Steiner, Rudolf. *The Etheric Body as a Reflection of the Universe*. Elberfeld, June 13, 1915.

Steiner, Rudolf. *The Fourth Dimension: Sacred Geometry, Alchemy, and Mathematics*. Anthroposophic Press, New York, 2001.

Steiner, Rudolf. *The Inner Experience of Evolution*, SteinerBooks, New York, 2009.

Steiner, Rudolf. *The Warmth Course*, Mercury Press, New York, 1988.

Steiner, Rudolf. *Occult Science and Occult Development*, Rudolf Steiner Press, New York, 2005.

Steiner, Rudolf. *World Ether, Elemental Beings, Kingdoms of Nature*. Translated by Harold Jurgens. Mercury Press, New York, 1993.

Stoff, Sheldon and Smith Stoff, Barbara. *The Akashic Field: It Makes Every Place in the Universe Part of the Neighborhood*. Balboa Press, Bloomington, IN, 2011.

Thomas, Nick. *The Battle for the Etheric Realm: Moral Technique and Etheric Technology Apocalyptic Symptoms*. Temple Lodge, London, 1995.

Thompson, Willian Irwin. *Beyond Religion: The Culture Evolution of the Sense of the Sacred from Shamanism to Post-Religious Spirituality*, Lindisfarne Books, 2013.

Thompson, Willian Irwin. *Imaginary Landscape: Making Worlds of Myth and Science*, St. Martin's Griffin, 1990.

Thompson, Willian Irwin. *Reimagination of the World: A Critique of the New Age, Science, and Popular Culture*, Doubleday, 1991.

Thompson, Willian Irwin. *The American Replacement of Nature: The Everyday Acts and Outrageous Evolution of Economic Life*, Lindisfarne Books, 1991.

Thompson, Willian Irwin. *The Time it Takes Falling Bodies to Light: Mythology, Sexuality and the Origins of Cultures*, St. Martin's Press, 1981.

Wachsmuth, Guenther. *Etheric Formative Forces in Cosmos, Earth and Man: A Path of Investigation into the World of the Living.* Anthroposophical Publishing, London, 1932, Volume I.

Wood, David W. *Novalis Notes for a Romantic Encyclopaedia.* State University of New York Press, 2007.

Made in United States
North Haven, CT
23 May 2023

36901164R00166